True Canadian Disaster Stories

True Canadian Disaster Stories

ED BUTTS

PROSPERO
B·O·O·K·S

National Library of Canada Cataloguing in Publication

Butts, Ed,—
    True Canadian Disaster Stories / Ed Butts.

Includes bibliographical references.
ISBN 1-55267-706-0

    1. Disasters—Canada—History. I. Title.
FC176.B88 2005   971   C2005-904028-9

This collection produced for Prospero Books.

Key Porter Books Limited
Six Adelaide Street East, Tenth Floor
Toronto, Ontario
Canada M5C 1H6

www.keyporter.com

Electronic formatting: Jean Lightfoot Peters

Printed and bound in Canada

06 07 08 09 10 5 4 3 2 1

For all thoes who have been
victims of disaster,
and the families that have endured.

Contents

Introduction

HOW DOES ONE DEFINE "DISASTER"? By the number of lives lost? Degree of pain suffered? Financial losses? Surely, if we consider wars, epidemics, economic depressions, natural catastrophes and human errors that result in tragedy, all of those things and more are covered by the dark shadow of the word. Disasters can strike individual families: a home destroyed by fire, the sudden death of a loved one. There is no denying the pain and anguish such tragedies inflict upon the hearts and souls of those involved.

But there are other disasters that stun cities, shock nations, send entire populations reeling. Some of these dreadful events snuff out many lives, others just a few, and still others kill no one at all, but nonetheless leave misery in their wake. In 1949 over 20 people died when a bomb was placed on a Canadian airplane. The number of dead hardly seems shocking when compared with the enormous casualty lists of other air disasters. Yet, in 1949 the world was aghast that anyone could commit so barbaric a crime. No one would have dreamed that an innovation of this form of cowardly mass murder would take 100 times that number of lives on September 11, 2001.

Canada has known disasters from the earliest days of her history. They have been spawned by her climate, geography, wars and the folly of some of her people. They have happened on land and water, and in the air. Some have been preventable, others inevitable. They have been the shattering, yet ironically binding calamities that we Canadians share with the rest of the human race.

While this book was in the early stages of compilation, a devastating *tsunami* struck southeast Asia, killing untold thousands and blighting the lives of millions with grief and despair. As the book was nearing completion, four Royal Canadian Mounted Police constables were senselessly slain by a mass murderer. It was the worst disaster to strike the RCMP in over a century. Whether a victim is one of tens of thousands, or one of four, the loss endured by each mourner left behind is the same.

The Frank Slide, Alberta, 1903

MINERS AND RAILROAD MEN ALIKE called it the best steam coal in the world. It burned cleanly and left almost no ash. What's more, great deposits of it were conveniently located in the Crowsnest Pass, the very route through the Rocky Mountains chosen by the Canadian Pacific Railroad. Of course, the steam-driven locomotives of the late 19th and early 20th centuries had an insatiable appetite for coal.

In 1900, near a place called Tenth Siding at the foot of Turtle Mountain, a prospector named Sam W. Gebo discovered a seam of coal 7 feet (2.1 m) deep. The belly of the mountain was evidently full of the stuff. Gebo staked his claim, and then sold the mining rights to a Butte, Montana, banker named H.L. Frank for $30,000. Frank established the Canadian-American Coal & Coke Company, with himself as president and Gebo as general manager. In 1901 he founded a new coal mining town in the shadow of Turtle Mountain, in the part of the Northwest Territories that would soon be the province of Alberta.

With the railroad at its doorstep, a mountain of coal in its backyard, and a steady stream of immigrants pouring into the west, the future of the new town looked very promising indeed. Mr. Frank honoured the new community by giving it his own name. Miners were soon digging a thousand tons of coal a day out of the Frank mine, and even that wasn't enough to keep up with the demand. There was a spur line connecting Frank to the main railroad, making it the envy of other communities, and within two years of its founding the town's population had grown to a thousand.

Frank was a typical frontier boomtown. It drew immigrant labourers who were willing to work long, hard hours underground for low wages. It also attracted merchants and tradesmen, as well as the shadier element who always turned up wherever there were working men with money in their pockets: the saloon keepers, gamblers and prostitutes. The new town became something of a mecca for local cowboys, too. They would ride in from nearby ranches on Saturday nights to get drunk and brawl with the miners. There were even desperadoes from Montana, of whom one Frank resident said, "Those Americans can steal a hot stove from you, and come back for the smoke."

The manager of the town bank must have considered Frank a wild and woolly place, because he kept four loaded pistols in his upstairs living quarters. To keep the peace, there was a small detachment of North West Mounted Police. Local hellraisers contemptuously called the Mounties "Yellow-legs," after the stripes down the legs of their pants. But thanks to the presence of the Mounted Police, Frank did not have the mayhem and gunfights experienced by American mining towns like Tombstone. One constable left a rather understated account of how he disarmed and arrested a character known as Cowboy Jack Monaghan, who had pointed a gun at him. Nonetheless, there were tragic incidents, and in one confrontation a Mountie was killed by a shotgun blast.

Frank was a rugged place, where tough men worked hard and often lived in primitive conditions. One resident said that Frank had "all hell for a cellar." Another grumbled that, "It's cold enough to freeze the hair off a dog's back." But the town also boasted three churches and a schoolhouse. There were rowdies, drifters, and riff-raff, to be sure, but there were also the solid, salt-of-the-earth types who wanted nothing more than a good place to raise their families, or a decent job so they could send money to the folks back home, wherever that might be. They were the ones who agreed with the admonition in the town newspaper, the *Sentinel*, that miners should "raise less hell and more coal."

All the while, as miners sweated in the depths and people went about their business—legitimate and otherwise—in the frame buildings that fronted on Frank's one main street, a dark shadow hung over the town. The shadow was that of Turtle Mountain, the very source of Frank's reason for being. And the horror to come did not simply lie in the fact that "sunset" occurred in Frank no later than three o'clock, when the sun disappeared behind the mountain.

The Natives had called Turtle Mountain "The Mountain That Walks" because sometimes the ground around it shook. It stood 7,200 feet (2194.5 m) above the valley of the Old Man River, and on its northeast face there was a massive outcropping of limestone. This odd feature somewhat resembled a turtle's head, and gave the mountain its name. According to Native lore, a day would come when the turtle would shake its head, and then destruction would fall upon any who were foolish enough to be at its feet. The Indians stayed away from Turtle Mountain.

But white men had no time for what they considered Native superstitions. There was coal in that mountain, and the only way to get at it was to bore right into the heart of The Mountain That Walks. The entrance to the Frank mine was simply a big hole in the mountainside. It led to the stopes—the cavernous rooms in which the miners worked at the coal face. The stopes were connected by a network of walkways and chutes. Ceilings were supported by natural pillars and wooden props.

There were frequent tremors in the mine, which the men found unnerving at first, but eventually they got used to them. The shaking sometimes buckled and split the wooden bracings, but it also shook down a lot of coal, making the miners' work much easier. In the early months of 1903, the rumblings within Turtle Mountain seemed to increase, but nobody took much notice of it.

It's doubtful if on the evening of April 28, the men preparing to head up to the mine for the night shift were thinking at all of the tremors or of that massive outcropping of rock. They were involved in a labour dispute with management, and things had become violent. It was an era when profits mattered most to the barons of industry. Working men, their families and their safety counted for next to nothing. Even though Frank had an electric power plant, there were no lines running to the mine. The miners worked by the light of little oil lamps in their helmets—always a hazard in coal mines, where gas lurked as an invisible killer.

There had been a warm spell earlier that month, with heavy rains. Then the weather had turned cold again. That evening of the 28th, a blizzard swept through the Crowsnest, delaying the passenger train from Lethbridge by an hour and a half. It was one of the many quirks of fate that would determine who would or would not live to see another day.

That night a settler named Ned Morgan was at the home of James Graham, concluding a livestock deal. It was late by the time the two men had business wrapped up, so Mrs. Graham invited Morgan to stay the night. She said he could bunk with their sons Joe and John, who had just returned from the Boer War in South Africa. Morgan reluctantly declined. His horses were outside, hitched to a sleigh, and he wanted to get them back to his barn.

John Thorley, owner of a shoe shop, had his sister visiting him. He decided that it would be nice to take her to the Frank Hotel for the night, rather than stay in his rather spartan cabin. However, another man turned down an opportunity to spend the night in the comfort of a hotel. Robert Watt's pal Les Ferguson had asked him to stay the night with him at the Imperial, but Watt chose instead to bunk down at the CPR livery stable with another friend, Francis Rochette.

Teenager Lillian Clark, the eldest of six children, had been kept late at the boarding house where she worked. She decided to spend the night there rather than walk home. It was the first time in her life that Lillian had been away from home overnight.

In another household well blessed with children, Bill Warrington's wife put their brood of seven to bed while he got ready to go to work at the mine. Mrs. Warrington had done the laundry that day. The diapers hanging on the clothesline outside were frozen stiff.

Jack Dawe and two other Welsh miners were supposed to have been on a train bound for a port where they could board a ship for Wales. But a mix-up in scheduling had delayed them for a week, so that night they were bedded down in a cabin beside the CPR livery stable. With them was Jack's puppy. Had the Welshmen been able to leave when they wanted to, the cabin would have been occupied by Robert and Charles Chestnut. But with the cabin full, the Chestnut brothers slept at the Union Hotel. Fortune smiled on some, but not on others.

On the banks of the Old Man River, a wizened old trapper named Andy Gresack crawled into his tent for the night. Earlier he had been talking to railroad man John McVeigh about the rumbling sounds coming from the mountain. Gresack had joked that the noise was being made by "the old man of Old Man River."

McVeigh, foreman of a railway construction crew, was another man who was supposed to have been elsewhere that night. He'd planned on going to Calgary with his wife and son, but a last-minute problem at work made it necessary for him to postpone his trip. He'd sent his wife and boy ahead, with a promise that he'd join them the next day. He stayed that night in a railroad construction camp with a gang of workmen. Their bunkhouse was directly below the giant head of the turtle. Before turning in for the night, McVeigh sent liveryman Jack Leonard to Picher Creek to pick up a load of hay. That errand saved Leonard's life.

At midnight the 20 men who made up the graveyard shift headed up the mountain to the mine entrance. Most of the people in Frank were asleep. The exceptions were a few boozers tossing back shots of red-eye in the saloons; Thomas Delap, the one man on duty in the electric power plant; and a crew of men shunting coal cars on a spur line.

When the men entered the mine, Evan "Half Pint" Jones told foreman Joe Chapman that he had a bad feeling. He looked at Old Charlie, the pit-pony that hauled the coal car, and said, "I don't like the way the timbers are groaning tonight. You mark my words, when Old Charlie perks his ears like that, you can expect a mine squeeze."

The foreman just laughed at Half Pint's uneasiness. "Scary Indian tales" didn't spook Joe Chapman. In just a few hours he would learn that the Indians had been right all along to fear The Mountain That Walks.

As the clocks in Frank ticked off the wee hours of April 29, 1903, up on the desolate, snowy crags half a mile above the town, the forces of nature were about to unleash a calamity. The geological history of the Earth has been a never-ending process of building mountains up through tectonic pressure, and then tearing them down through the ravages of the elements and gravity. The massive limestone outcropping on Turtle Mountain was about to come down on the unsuspecting town of Frank.

As the miners worked, they heard a series of groans and sharp cracks. The ground beneath their feet trembled more violently than it ever had done before. Then, at 4:10 AM, just as the Natives had said it would, the great turtle walked. With a roar that could be heard 15 miles (24.1 km) away, a piece of mountain 500 feet (152.4 m) thick, 1,400 feet (426.7 m) wide, and 3,000 feet (914.4 m) long tore free of its ancient perch. Ninety million tons of limestone thundered down the mountain toward Frank. In just 100 life-shattering seconds the community would be transferred from a town with a brilliant future to a disaster area.

So enormous was the mass of splintering rock, and so rapid its descent, that it pushed in front of it a wall of compressed air that was as destructive as the concussion from a major explosion. This shrieking blast of air swept away tents, wooden buildings and people like a compact hurricane. Then came the rocks; some as big as a four-storey building, others as small as baseballs, but lethal in their hurtling millions.

Three miners, Fred Farrington, Alex Clark and Alex Tashigan, were sitting at the entrance having their lunch when the mountain fell on them. They didn't even have time to cry out before the avalanche carried them off. The mine entrance and the ventilation shaft were sealed by tons of rock in an instant, leaving 17 men trapped in the bowels of the mountain.

Engineer Ben Murgatroyd and his crew were shunting empty coal cars on the spur line when they heard a sound like thunder. They looked up, and saw hell coming straight at them.

Murgatroyd immediately realized that he had to get his engine to the other side of a bridge if they were to have any chance of escape. He shouted for his brakemen to jump aboard as he rammed the throttle wide open. Sid Choquette and Bill Lowes leaped for the handrails as the engine shot forward with a shriek of steel on steel. The locomotive raced across the bridge only seconds before the first wave of boulders smashed the span to pieces.

The mass of thundering, bouncing, rolling boulders surged down the mountainside, ripped through the Old Man River, and spread across the valley on a two mile front. The momentum carried the avalanche a full 400 feet (121.9 m) up the opposite slope. Anything that had not been flattened by the deadly wall of air was crushed or carried away by the rocks.

The livery stable, adjacent buildings, and the men and horses in them disappeared. So did the Graham house and its occupants. John Thorley's empty cabin was gone. Jack Dawes and his Welsh friends were no more—though amazingly, Dawes' puppy survived. The camp where John McVeigh and an undetermined number of men had been sleeping was buried, as was the electric power plant. Andy Gresack's tent was now his burial shroud. A row of seven houses on Manitoba Avenue—later quite improperly called "Suicide Row"—crumbled in a cataclysm of rocks, dust and fire. Unbelievably, there would be survivors in some of these houses.

In less than two minutes the most disastrous landslide in Canadian history had smashed one quarter of the town of Frank to kindling. The ruins of buildings and the broken bodies of an unknown number of victims lay under 100 feet (34 m) of rock. Two miles (3.2 km) of railway was destroyed: either buried under rubble, or the steel rails twisted like rubber bands. Telephone and telegraph lines were gone. Even after the avalanche had stopped, boulders continued to bound down the mountainside. A grey cloud of choking limestone dust hung over all.

Engineer Murgatroyd had saved his crew, but the men knew that an even greater railroad disaster loomed. The overdue train from Lethbridge, loaded with passengers, would come pounding down the line at any minute, and the engineer would have no warning of the mass of rock on the tracks. Someone had to stop that train! In a genuine act of heroism, the brakemen Choquette and Lowes scrambled across the huge fan of shattered limestone to try to flag the train down. The rocks were sharp and still hot from friction, and the men had to duck and dodge boulders that still came hurtling down the mountain. Lowes dropped from exhaustion and could not continue but Choquette carried on. He finally staggered down from the mountain of rubble, and by good luck was right at the spot where the steel rails emerged from the debris. Choking on lime dust, he ran up the line waving a lantern. The engineer of the approaching flyer saw the signal lantern waving in the darkness, and brought his train to a stop. Sid Choquette undoubtedly saved many lives that morning. A story later arose that he was rewarded for his courageous deed with a gold watch. Actually, the CPR gave Choquette a letter of commendation and $25.

Inside the mine, the 17 trapped men faced a grim situation. They were sealed in, and expected that at any moment the whole mine would collapse and bury them forever. To make matters worse, the rock barrier had dammed the Old Man River. The water was backing up and forming a lake, and seeping into the mine. There was every possibility that even if the mine didn't cave in, the men might drown before they could be rescued.

Outside, as the cloud of lime dust began to settle and the first rays of sunlight tinted the morning sky, those who had escaped the onslaught of the rock-slide rushed to the aid of the victims. Miners attacked the rubble-choked mine entrance with picks, shovels and dynamite in a desperate effort to free those trapped within. There was a dreadful feeling among the would-be rescuers, though, that if they gained entry they would find only bodies. Others tried to blast a channel through the limestone dam to drain the steadily rising lake. But at both work sites, as fast as the rubble was removed, more tumbled in.

Everywhere in the stricken area was evidence of the bizarre nature of fate. People sleeping in one room of a house had been killed, while those sleeping in the next room had been thrown clear and escaped with cuts and bruises. When neighbours started pulling Jim Warrington from the ruins of his sister's house, he told them to be careful because he had a broken hip and he was sure he could feel another person under him. Sure enough, when they lifted Warrington out, they found a next door neighbour, Mrs. Watkins, underneath him. The woman, whose skin was perforated with needle-like shards of stone, had been thrown from her bed and somehow wound up beneath Warrington in the house next door.

Charles Ackroyd and his wife Nancy both died in their house, but Nancy's 16-year-old son, Lester Johnson, survived. The blast of air had lifted the house right off its foundations and Lester blacked out. When he came to, he was lying between two boulders and had been impaled by a board. He managed to break it off and crawl for help. He was not even aware that his pyjamas had been blown off and he was naked. He dragged himself to the home of some neighbours named Williams. Mr. and Mrs.

Williams wrapped Lester in a blanket and put him in a wheelbarrow to take him to a doctor. The doctor found that Lester's chest had been perforated by feathers from his pillow. He had to pluck the boy like a chicken.

In a house on the same street, all of Lillian Clark's family perished, while she slept safely at the boarding house. Their neighbours, the Ennis family, escaped with a few broken bones, but they very nearly lost their baby daughter Gladys. As she lay stunned and injured in the wreckage, Mrs. Ennis heard the child choking. She called to her husband, "Sam, Gladys is choking to death. Help her if you can."

Sam clawed through the debris and found the infant. He used his fingers to scoop a glob of mud out of her mouth. Then he turned her upside down and thumped her on the back until she coughed up more mud. All six members of the family escaped with their lives.

Even luckier were the Ennis' neighbours, the Bansmier family. Their house was torn from its foundations and flipped over twice. The occupants emerged with hardly a scratch. Less fortunate was the family of Alex Leitch. Alex was crushed to death, along with his wife and their four sons. But their three daughters lived. The survival of the youngest Leitch child, four-month-old Marion, bordered on the impossible.

Sleeping between her doomed parents, the baby had been blown out of the house like a paper doll. Her little body was flying straight at a boulder, against which she would have been smashed to a pulp. But by sheer luck, or perhaps through the intervention of some guardian angel, a pile of hay blown out of the CPR stables half a mile away landed on the rock and cushioned the child's fall. Rescuers found the baby in the straw, wailing but

unhurt. This remarkable story would inspire a popular ballad in which the child, christened "Frankie Slide" was the sole survivor of the disaster, much to the annoyance of other survivors and Marion herself.

As soon as news of the disaster reached the outside world, aid was mobilized for the wounded town. Miners from other communities were rushed to Turtle Mountain to help dig out the entrance and breach the dam. Newspaper stories around the world were comparing the Frank disaster to the calamity that had befallen the ancient Roman city of Pompeii. Nobody held out much hope for the 17 miners still entombed in the heart of Turtle Mountain.

But Joe Chapman and his men were still very much alive. They had been digging non-stop at the plugged-up entrance. Like the workers on the outside, they could make no headway. They had even been shaken up by the blasting done on the other side. The concussion from one charge had slammed Chapman into a wall, knocking his wind out but not seriously hurting him. Water continued to seep into the mine. The men saw little hope in continuing their attempt to dig through 300 feet (91.4 m) of debris that was as unstable as a pile of dry sand.

Chapman's men made their living hacking at coal, and they knew this mine well. They were aware that the coal seams they'd been mining were exposed at places on the outside slopes of the mountain. They reasoned that their chances of escaping would be better if they chopped a tunnel through the solid coal. They just had to choose the right place to dig.

They selected a spot, then went to work with their picks, digging upward. They had no way of knowing for sure if they were digging a tunnel to freedom, or a useless shaft to nowhere. Thirty-six feet (10.9 m) later, at 5:00 PM, some 13 hours after the

avalanche had swept their three colleagues to eternity, they broke through to daylight and filled their lungs with clean, fresh air. They shouted down to the workers below, and rescue parties hurried up the mountainside to help the exhausted men out of the hole. Bill Warrington, who had injured his leg, was the first to be lifted out. When he looked down on the town he was overcome with grief. His house was gone, and with it his wife and seven children. All that remained above the pile of rocks was the clothesline, still strung with frozen diapers.

Legend has it that all of Frank was wiped out by the landslide. That is not so. Three quarters of the community was untouched by the rocks. But in the stricken section the devastation was almost complete. Only 23 people who had been in the path of the avalanche lived to tell about it. Only 12 bodies were recovered from the ruins. The rest remained buried under tons of limestone. Just how many people died is not certain. The official count was put at 76, but no one knew for sure how many workmen were in the camps. Many of them were drifters, accountable to no one but themselves. One group of seven men had spoken the day before of going to Lethbridge. No one knew if they had indeed departed for that town, or if they were buried under the rocks. Such things considered, the number of the dead might well have been over 100.

The Frank mine was re-opened not long after the disaster. Good steam coal, after all, was valuable, even if it had blood on it. But the landslide had doomed the operation. The mine closed for good in 1908, and the whole town was relocated to the outskirts of Blairmore, Alberta. But before that happened, the Frank landslide claimed two more victims.

When the miners finally cleared the entrance to the mine on May 30, they found to their amazement that the aged pit-pony,

Old Charlie, was still alive. The horse had survived in the darkness by drinking seepage water and gnawing the bark off support timbers. Sadly, Old Charlie died when his rescuers fed him some brandy and oats. One miner said that the tough little horse died of a broken heart because he thought he was going to be abandoned again.

At the other end of the casualty list was owner H. L. Frank. The Montana capitalist went insane when he learned of the horror of April 29. He was committed to an asylum, and died there in 1908. His dream of an empire in coal was lost in the shadow of The Mountain That Walks.

The Franklin Expedition: Canadian Arctic, 1845–1859

THE EXPEDITION BEGAN WITH POMP, ceremony and cheering crowds. Another glorious chapter was about to be written in the annals of the British Empire. Or so everyone thought! However, the adventure that started out with such optimism led not to glory, but to despair, cannibalism and death.

For 350 years English explorers had been trying to solve one of the greatest geographic challenges in recorded history; the discovery of a Northwest Passage, from the Atlantic to the Pacific, through the maze of ice-bound islands that make up Canada's Far North—the largest archipelago in the world. As the blank spaces on maps of the Arctic were painstakingly filled in over the decades, the men who braved the polar ice and cold left their names on the islands and the waters that surround them: Frobisher, Davis, Baffin, Hudson. Some also left their bones.

By 1845 the British High Admiralty had become obsessed with solving the Arctic riddle. Great Britain was the most powerful nation in the world, ruling an Empire that encircled the globe. But the secret of the Northwest Passage still lay locked in ice. Explorers brought home new information on coastlines, currents and tides, and the cartographers inched their way across the charts, pencilling in the bays, straits, headlands. The Passage was there, *somewhere*, and they believed they were tantalizingly close to finding it. They *had* to find it! They were British! For someone else to make the magnificent discovery was simply unthinkable.

The honour of finding the last piece to the puzzle fell to 58-year-old Sir John Franklin, a veteran seaman who as a mere lad had fought with Nelson at Copenhagen and Trafalgar. Franklin had already probed the Arctic in 1819 and 1825. He was an outstanding officer, well steeped in the traditions of the Royal Navy. If anyone could find a route through the Arctic labyrinth, it was Franklin. As Sir Roderick Impey, president of the Royal Geographic Society (of which Franklin was vice-president) wrote: "The name of Franklin alone is, indeed, a national guarantee; and proud shall we geographers be if our gallant Vice-President shall return after achieving such an exploit..."

What Sir Roderick and the Admiralty overlooked was that on both of Sir John's previous expeditions he had managed to get lost and lose men. He'd been forced to eat rotten animal skins, and boil bones to make a barely life-sustaining soup. Had it not been for the intervention of Native people, who fed the Englishmen and nursed them back to health, Franklin and all of his men would have died.

No one could say that Sir John Franklin did not have courage. A coward would not have ventured into the unknown Canadian Arctic. But he was ill-suited to Arctic exploration, as were many British officers. He was an aristocrat and a product of his time. He believed that as an upper-class Englishman, well equipped, well trained, and with the traditions and discipline that had built the Empire behind him, he could not fail. The raw power of the Arctic, which did not recognize tradition, nor respect social rank, would prove him wrong.

The Franklin Expedition was one of the most well provisioned ever to sail from an English port. Into the holds of two ships, the *Erebus* and the *Terror*, went a three-year supply of preserved fruits and vegetables, dried and canned meat, flour, sugar, tea, wine and liquor, chocolate and tobacco. There were 2,700 pounds (1,224.5 kg) of candles and 3,600 pounds (1,632.6 kg) of soap. Each ship had a library of 1,200 books. The expedition was equipped with the latest geographical and nautical instruments. And of course there were the luxuries that were the trappings of peers of the realm, such as the huge mahogany desk in Franklin's cabin on the *Erebus*.

The 129 men under Franklin's command were the cream of the Royal Navy. Captain F.R.M. Crozier, second-in-command and master of the *Terror* had also served under Nelson and was a seasoned Arctic explorer. The *Erebus* and *Terror* had been strengthened to withstand Arctic ice, and were equipped with steam engines as well as sails. This was the most ambitious Arctic expedition the Admiralty had ever undertaken.

On May 19, 1845, the *Erebus* and *Terror* sailed down the Thames bound for the open sea. Crowds lined the docks to cheer the heroes. Two tugs carrying extra supplies accompanied the ships as far as the Orkneys. From there a transport carrying yet more supplies sailed with Franklin's fleet as far as Disco Bay on the west coast of Greenland. There, in early July, the extra provisions were loaded aboard the *Erebus* and the *Terror*, so Franklin would have the full, three-year supply. The transport ship returned to England, carrying last letters home. Franklin wrote to his wife, Lady Jane Franklin, "Do not worry if the voyage should last longer than anticipated. We can hold our own for five years."

From this point Franklin would put messages written in six languages into sealed copper cylinders and throw them into the sea. Of these "progress reports," only one was ever found. The men of the Franklin Expedition sailed into the Arctic mist and were never again seen alive by their fellow Englishmen.

Three years passed, and there was no word from Franklin. Other Englishmen in the Arctic, whalers and Hudson's Bay Company traders, had heard no rumours from the Inuit. The *Erebus* and *Terror* and all their men had seemingly vanished.

Then began the greatest "missing persons" search in history. It would cost over $4 million, an incredible sum for that time. In searching for the lost expedition the captains would chart more of the Canadian Arctic than had been mapped in the previous three centuries. The search would involve 38 expeditions and would take many years. The searchers would stumble across evidence over a wide expanse of Arctic desolation, and piece by piece they would put together a harrowing story.

The first clue was not discovered until 1850. On little Beechey Island in the Barrow Strait, Captain William Penny came across Franklin's first winter camp. His men found rubbish: empty cans, bits of rope and oilcloth—and three graves. But there was no written message to indicate the direction Franklin had taken. Nothing more was found over the next four years.

Then, in October 1854, Dr. John Rae, who had been leading a Hudson's Bay Company search party, arrived in England with news. On the Boothia Peninsula he had spoken to Inuit who told him that years earlier, Inuit on King William Island, west of Boothia, had encountered 40 white men. The white men's ship had been crushed in the ice, and they were heading south on foot. They were sick with scurvy and starving. Sometime after that meeting, yet another group of Inuit found 30 white bodies 100 miles (160.9 km) to the south, at the mouth of the Back River on the mainland. From the state of the bodies, it was evident that the starving Englishmen had resorted to eating the flesh of their dead. The Inuit who told Dr. Rae the story had in their possession silverware bearing the initials of Franklin and some of his officers.

Months later, Captain Richard Collison arrived in England with additional clues. On Victoria Island, he had found Inuit in possession of iron and brass tools, a part of a steam engine, and a ship's hatchway. Those items could have come from only Franklin's ships.

The evidence showed that the expedition had met with disaster somewhere between Victoria Island and King William Island. The search was narrowing. But ten years had passed since Franklin had sailed away on his great voyage of discovery. The British Admiralty declared Franklin and all of his men dead, and ended their search.

Lady Franklin, a truly remarkable woman, would not give up hope that her husband or some of his men might still be alive. In 1857, at her own expense she fitted out a ship, the *Fox*, and sent Captain Leopold McClintock to continue the search. (She actually wanted to go with him.) McClintock made an astounding discovery.

He learned from some Inuit that years before, two ships had been frozen in the ice north of King William Island. The white men had left the ships and started a trek southward, dragging behind them sledges loaded with equipment. The white men, said the Inuit, were weak from starvation and sickness. Those who fell were left to die. The two ships eventually sank.

McClintock and his men searched the area the Inuit had described, and were baffled by what they found. There was a 750-pound (340.1 kg) boat, mounted on a 650-pound (294.8 kg) sledge. In it were items that would have been of use, like guns and ammunition, but there were also things that, as he noted in his report, were "a mere accumulation of dead weight... very likely to break down the strength of the sledge crews." There were stacks of religious books, soap and toothbrushes, iron barrel hoops, rolls of sheet lead and brass curtain rods—all of it useless.

McClintock also found three skeletons, and the only written document from the expedition ever discovered in the Arctic. In a stone cairn was a paper with a message that said the *Erebus* and *Terror* had wintered at Beechey Island after exploring Wellington Channel and the west side of Cornwallis Island: "All well."

But all had not been well. Another message, scribbled in the margins of the now yellowed paper said that the *Erebus* and the *Terror* had been deserted on April 22, 1848. Of the original company of 130 men, 105 were still alive. "Sir John Franklin died on 11th June, 1847..." The cause of death was not given. The great explorer who had told his wife that she could write to him in Petropovlovsk, on Russia's Pacific coast, had died thousands of miles short of his destination.

Three graves had been found, and three skeletons. The Inuit had reported finding 30 bodies. Where were the rest of Franklin's men? Could any of them still be alive?

An American explorer named Charles Hall lived with the Inuit for nine years, learning their language and their ways of Arctic survival. In 1864 he wrote about meeting Inuit who told him that they had come across three white men on the Boothia Peninsula. Two of the white men appeared to be in good health, but the third man, an officer, was weak and starving. The Inuit learned that the two men had been eating human flesh, but the officer had refused to stoop to cannibalism. The Inuit were amazed that these men, who had guns and ammunition, should have resorted to eating their dead.

The white men lived with the Inuit for several months. Then, with an Inuit hunter as a guide, they had started out south. The Inuit had heard no more about the three men but believed that they were still alive. There is no record that the three ever turned up at any post or settlement.

In 1868, yet another group of Inuit told Hall that four years earlier, two white men had been living in wooden huts on the northern tip of Melville Peninsula. That was some 600 miles (965.4 km) from where it was believed the *Erebus* and *Terror* had sunk. Hall went there and found a cairn that had clearly been made by Europeans but contained no written messages.

Hall went to King William Island in 1869 and found relics left by Franklin's men, as well as more skeletons. Some of the bones had been cut by saws. The British Admiralty had dismissed the Inuit stories of cannibalism as false. Disciplined Englishmen would never sink to such depravity, they said. But on King William Island, Hall had found proof that the Inuit stories were true.

Inuit also told Hall that they had found books. These had to have come from the ships' libraries and may well have included journals and diaries, perhaps even the commanders' logs. But the Inuit had given them to their children to play with, and not a single page had survived.

The search for clues as to what befell one of the most heralded exploratory expeditions in British history continued well into the 20th century. Relics and human remains would be found. Inuit testimony was closely examined. Based on the evidence available, historians have recreated just what might have happened to the men of the Franklin Expedition.

Franklin spent the first winter on Beechey Island, where three men died. In May 1846 he sailed south into Peel Sound and reached Victoria Strait, off King William Island. This would have been new, uncharted territory for the explorer. Franklin didn't know that he had just sailed into one of the worst ship-traps in the Arctic. In September the *Erebus* and the *Terror* became locked in the ice. They would never sail again.

In May 1847 Franklin sent Lieutenant Graham Gore and a party of men to explore King William Island (which he would not have known was an island). It was Gore who left the "All well" message in the cairn. About two weeks after that message was deposited, Franklin died suddenly.

The ice in Victoria Strait did not break up that summer, and the ship remained imprisoned. Another year passed, and 21 men died. The food supply was running low, so Crozier, now in command, decided that they would have to travel south overland. He evidently hoped to reach the Back River, 250 miles (402.2 km) away. Once they reached the river, they could sail up it into the Canadian interior. For that, they would need the ships' boats.

And so 105 men, all of them probably ridden with scurvy, loaded two or three of the 27 by 8 foot (8.2 by 2.1 m) boats with all of the tools and equipment required by Royal Navy regulations, and lashed them to sledges. Had the men travelled light, they might have made it. But in addition to the burdensome equipment they took books, cook stoves, bags of coal, containers of button polish, silverware, and the officers' swords. They even loaded on Franklin's mahogany desk. It has been estimated that the starving, disease-weakened men piled some 10 tons of cargo onto their sledges. Then they embarked on one of the most disastrous journeys the Arctic has ever known.

The men dragged their enormous loads of useless gear across the ice, every step draining what strength they had. British officers did not do menial work, and there were reports from Inuit witnesses that the officers in Crozier's party walked behind the sledges while the men strained at the ropes. As they passed the cairn Gore had erected the previous year, Crozier added the information of Franklin's death to the paper.

For 150 miserable, heartbreaking, incredible miles (241.3 km) the retreat to the south progressed. Men dropped dead in their tracks. At first their companions stopped to bury them. But as the journey deteriorated into a stumbling quest for survival, the dead were left where they fell, to be devoured by foxes and other carrion eaters.

The struggling men, like any army in retreat, began to dispose of useless equipment. Inuit hunters picked up fine British swords and other artifacts. Hall would find the mahogany writing desk.

At some point the men divided into two groups. It is not known if this was by agreement or if there was a mutiny. Forty continued on to the Back River, and 30 of them actually made it. But they went no farther. Their mutilated bodies would be found by the Inuit at a place that has since been known as Starvation Bay.

The other 40 or 50 men probably tried to return to the ships. If they made it, most of them would have died as they waited in vain for the ice to break up. But a few might have left the ships and reached the Canadian mainland. In 1917 some cairns that were evidently made by Europeans were found on the Barren Lands west of Hudson Bay. Others might have been taken in by Inuit. In the 1920s explorer Vihjalmur Stefansson met Inuit with blond hair and European facial features living on Victoria Island.

The Franklin Expedition failed primarily because officers of Franklin's class would not adapt to Arctic conditions. They insisted on travelling in the style of "gentlemen" and maintaining the social gap between themselves and their men. Other explorers, who adopted the ways of the Inuit, were more successful. An aristocrat like Franklin, however, would have been horrified by the idea.

There is evidence, too, that the men may have been going insane. Autopsies that were done in the 1980s on the bodies from the graves on Beechey Island revealed lead poisoning. In the 1840s, lead was used to seal canned food. The neurological damage caused by the very food they were eating could certainly have been a factor in that absolutely mad attempt to drag tons of equipment across the ice. It might also explain their inability to hunt for game.

According to a story told by the Inuit, Franklin's men buried his body in a substance that "after awhile was all same stone" (cement). If there is in fact a concrete vault containing the remains of Sir John Franklin on King William Island, it has not yet been found. But on tiny Beechey Island there is a monument, paid for by Lady Franklin, to the memory of the 130 men of the Franklin Expedition.

The Great Toronto Fire, 1904

IF A PRESENT-DAY FIRE MARSHAL could go back to Toronto of 1904 and make an inspection, he would be appalled. Though some advances in fire prevention had been made since the city was first gutted by fire in 1849, the potential for disaster was still great. Wood was the most commonly used building material, and even in buildings of brick or stone, everything from the polished pine floors to the paper on the walls to the paint on the ceilings was highly flammable. Exteriors were grandly decorated with wooden window trims and cornices. Firewalls were few and far between, and only three buildings had sprinkler systems. Roofs of factories and warehouses were generally flat and coated with a tar-and-gravel mixture that burned nicely. Stairwells, elevator shafts and skylights combined to provide a perfect chimney effect. Stores and warehouses were packed to the rafters with flammable materials. Most heating was still done by coal-burning stoves and furnaces.

Hanging above the streets were innumerable telephone, telegraph, and electrical wires, as well as cables for the trolley cars. These not only obstructed firefighters, but also helped fires to spread because the insulation used in them was combustible. The utility poles themselves, chemically treated with preservatives, tended to go up like Roman candles when they caught fire.

There were not enough fire-alarm boxes or hydrants, and the water mains feeding the hydrants were much too small for effective pressure. Compared to those of other large North American cities, Toronto's Fire Department was understaffed and underequipped. Fire Chief John Thompson warned Toronto Mayor Thomas Urquhart on April 12, 1904, "We are taking more and more risks every year."

Urquhart, typical of the penny-pinching politicians of the day, replied, "Oh, I guess we will have to risk it another year." A week later, his honour the mayor would regret those words.

Toronto had three fire stations in the downtown area; at the corner of Bay and Temperance streets, on Lombard Street, and at the corner of John and Queen Streets. There were also fire stations in the outlying areas of Toronto Junction, East Toronto, Kew Beach and Toronto Island. To protect the booming city of 200,000, Chief Thompson had 204 professional firemen. His principal weapons were five steam engines. (Montreal had 16; Buffalo had 30.) These machines used steam power to operate the pumps, and were an improvement over the old hand-operated pumpers. Because they were heavy, they had to be drawn by three horses, specially trained not to panic during a fire. They were accompanied by an auxiliary wagon full of coal. It was necessary to keep a fire laid in the boiler at all times so that steam pressure would be quickly available. As with all steam-operated equipment of the time, there was always the danger of an explosion. Thompson's department also had five hook-and-ladder wagons, and a 65 foot (19.8 m) "water tower" from which firemen could direct a stream onto a blaze. All vehicles were horse drawn. They were equipped with sirens and bells, and presented a thrilling spectacle when they raced down the street, but on the night of April 19, 1904, it would become painfully obvious that Toronto needed more of them.

That fateful Tuesday was hardly a fresh, spring day in Toronto.

The temperature had dropped to –5°C, and a strong northwest wind was blowing. By 6:00 PM it was snowing. Most businesses and factories closed at that hour, and soon the downtown core was all but deserted.

Less than two hours later, a night watchman named T.H. Johnson, who was employed by several factory and warehouse owners, was following his patrol route down Bay Street south of King Street. When he neared the corner of Wellington Street, he smelled smoke. Johnson hurried west, and saw flames leaping up from the elevator shaft of the E&S Currie Building at 58–60 Wellington Street West. He turned and ran for the nearest fire-alarm box, which was at King and Bay, two blocks away. At the same time an unidentified constable saw the smoke and turned in an alarm from York and Front streets.

Chief Thompson was pouring a cup of tea when the alarm went off in the Lombard Street Fire Hall at 8:04. As quickly as the firemen could leap into action, three steam engines were clanging down the street, followed by a hook and ladder wagon, the water tower, and hose and ariel wagons. They arrived at the Currie Building and found it hopelessly engulfed in flames.

The Currie Building was what firemen, insurance companies, and fire-conscious architects called a "conflagration breeder"—of which Toronto had many. It was a four-storey brick structure, with its interior all of wood. Neckwear was manufactured there, so it was full of flammable materials. The cause of the fire was never determined (possibly an overheated stove), but it evidently had started near the elevator shaft, and so spread through the entire building within minutes.

The first few minutes are crucial in attempting to contain a major urban blaze. Chief Thompson, veteran though he was, made two errors that would prove costly. The Currie Building was already lost, and the strong wind was blowing the fire toward the six-storey Gillespie Fur Company Building next door. Thompson had seven hoses at his disposal. He should have concentrated his water barrage on the Gillespie Building to prevent the fire from spreading. Instead, he had five hoses trained on the fire, and only two on the Gillespie Building.

The low pressure and high winds turned the streams of water to spray that blew right back at the firemen. Thompson took four of his men and broke into the Gillespie Building, trailing three lines of hose. They wanted to get to the top so they could pour water onto the Currie Building from above. Going into the building himself was Thompson's second mistake. It was the equivalent of a general going in to clear a house of enemy snipers instead of sending in his foot soldiers.

Chief Thompson and his men made it only to the third or fourth floor when they were stopped by thick smoke. The Gillespie Building was already burning. The men could not find their way back to the stairway, so they went to the window and called for help. The ladders on the fire wagons would not reach the window, so Thompson's men rigged a fire hose so that they could slide down it to the ground. The four firemen made it down without a hitch. But when Chief Thompson, the last man out, began his descent, he slipped and fell to the ground, breaking his right leg. He was whisked away to the hospital. Right at the time the city needed him most, Chief Thompson was out of the picture. Command fell to Deputy Chief John C. Noble.

The deputy chief turned in a general alarm at 8:51, and firefighting units raced to the scene from all over Toronto. But the opportunity to contain the fire quickly and get it under control had been lost. The Gillespie Building was now totally ablaze. Wind-driven flames leapt southward across Wellington Street and made a giant torch of Brown Brothers' stationary factory. At the same time, the fire was sweeping westward toward Bay Street and creeping northward toward King Street. It was barely an hour old, and already a dozen buildings were burning. Mayor Urquhart arrived and asked Noble if he needed outside help. The Deputy Chief replied, "We need all the help we can get!"

Urquhart rushed to the Bell Telephone office and called Hamilton, Niagara Falls, Buffalo, Brantford, London and Peterborough requesting help. The Grand Trunk Railway cleared its main lines so that special trains carrying firemen and equipment could get through. A railroad fireman on the train from Hamilton recalled later that the sky was dark, but they could see a dull glow over Toronto. He bailed in coal as the engineer kept the throttle wide open. "I've had many a wild ride," he said, "but nothing has ever approached that night." They roared through towns and the countryside at top speed, hoping all the while that the line really was clear.

The Hamilton firemen reached Toronto shortly after midnight. The men from Buffalo and London arrived at about 2:00 AM. Help came from Brantford, Niagara Falls and Peterborough a few hours later, but by that time there was little for the reinforcements to do.

The fire was galloping along like a creature with a mind of its own, and the situation was getting desperate. Officials considered using dynamite to blast a firebreak, and troops were called in from the garrison at Stanley Barracks. However, the city's chief architect advised against using explosives, arguing that it might only spread the flames. The soldiers were helpful, though, in assisting the police with crowd control. Thousands of people were swarming downtown to watch the fire. Some even brought chairs, drinks and sandwiches. As one reporter put it, "Toronto had a ringside seat at its own destruction."

The chief of police would later say that the crowds "were very orderly," but soldiers and constables got tough with anyone who wouldn't get out of the firemens' way or keep clear of dangerous areas. The streets were littered with pieces of burning wood and glass from exploding windows. Brick walls fell as their wooden supports burned or their iron supports buckled. Electric wires dangled in pools of water left by the hoses. Several people who went to gawk at the inferno received minor injuries. The firemen fought desperately to keep it from reaching Yonge Street, the very heart of the city. It was an exhausting, frustrating fight. Water pressure was pitifully low. The freezing wind blew the spray in their faces, where it turned to ice. If the men moved closer to the walls of fire, the water that blew back at them was scalding hot. Overhead wires interfered with ladders and with the streams from hoses. They were soon heavy with ice. Many snapped, so that live wires lay in pools of water. On several occasions firemen were jolted with electric shocks. They had to keep rushing from one danger point to another, as the foe sought to outflank them. Men with wet hands numbed from the cold, and reddened eyes streaming from smoke and heat, would stumble back from the front line to get a hot drink provided by the staff of the King Edward Hotel, and then wade back into the fray.

Some men ran into businesses that were in the fire's path to rescue valuables and important documents. Safety deposit companies opened their doors to men whose arms were full of account books and papers. One enterprising boy borrowed his father's horse and wagon and made $36—the equivalent of three weeks' pay for the average worker—hauling rescued items.

Here and there the flaming monster encountered resistance. On the western reaches of Wellington Street the wind and some lucky firebreaks halted its progress. On the north side of Wellington it was blocked by some blank walls and a 40 foot (12.1 m) gap. The historic Holland House, a Family Compact mansion built in 1831, was protected by its wide open gardens.

Thanks to the direction of the wind, and a few buildings that had firewalls, the embattled firemen were able to stop the northern spread of the fire. The flames threatened the Toronto *Telegram* Building, one of the places equipped with a sprinkler system. As it was, it was not even necessary for the sprinklers to turn on. The *Telegram* employees stayed to battle the fire. With a rooftop supply of water for firehoses in the building, they kept the windows soaked and saved the building. (Windows were the fire's means of entry in the great majority of the buildings that were lost that night.) This was an important victory because it helped stop the spread of the fire eastward in that sector. *Telegram* owner John Ross Robertson rewarded his courageous employees with generous bonuses.

To the north, east and west, the firemen were gradually getting the fire contained, though the ravenous beast consumed many buildings. To the south the fire was rampaging almost at will. Here, the wind was its ally. The flames invaded buildings on the south side of Wellington Street, and while those structures were being gutted, it burst out from their rear windows to ignite the backs of buildings on the north side of Front Street. As it glutted on these edifices and all that was in them, the demon grew to the point where it was creating its own wind—a firestorm!

The red cyclone howled across Front Street and wrapped its flaming coils around buildings on the south side. Front Street was soon ablaze from a line that almost touched Lorne Street on the west to a line that almost touched Yonge Street on the east. All of Bay Street from Melinda Street (a block south of King Street) down to The Esplanade was a hissing, crackling, roaring inferno. The devil stretched its flaming talons still further south to the rail-yards, where it grabbed the railway signalmen's sheds and the Grand Trunk Railway sheds. Boats moored to the docks at the foot of Bay and Yonge streets were moved out into the harbour.

J. William Gerred, a streetcar motorman, was among the crowd that watched in fascinated awe as the city the rest of Canada called "Toronto the Good" was transformed into a suburb of hell.

"The fury of the fire at this time seemed unbelievable. The flames seemed to leap right across streets. The tumult produced by the wailing of sirens summoning more supplies and the streams of high pressure hose which seemed to be tearing loose the boarding; the babble of the curious thousands, plus the efforts of the policemen to keep them at a safe distance, left me with a never-to-be forgotten impression...the spectacle was appalling: entire blocks were on fire...Everything was burning on both sides of Bay, both above and below Wellington, with one exception: a huge stone building on the southeast corner of Bay seemed to resist all the fire could do. It was surrounded by flames, and for what seemed an interminable time it held out...

"Suddenly, as from an explosion, all floors seemed to be a blazing inferno in an instant. This building had been the centre of all eyes, as if that vast thing was willing for it to survive; but when the explosive blast ran through it, the entire mass of people gave a long, drawn expression of 'Ah...!'"

One legend that emerged from the smoke and flames of that night was the saving of the Queen's Hotel, which stood on the site now occupied by the Royal York Hotel. The Queen's was one of Toronto's most elegant inns and was especially popular with MPPs from across Ontario. A 60 foot (18.2 m) wide garden lay between it and the Warwick Bros. & Rutter's Building that was billowing flames, and the blaze had already danced across greater distances.

As soon as the Warwick Bros. & Rutter Building started to burn, the staff at the Queen's—evidently prepared for such an emergency—evacuated women and removed baggage and the hotel's silver to other hotels. Then they fell in to help Toronto and Hamilton firemen to save the building.

Men on the roof poured water on the sparks and embers that rained down. Footing became treacherous as the water froze. The heat from the Warwick Bros. & Rutter building singed their eyebrows, while the backs of their coats became encrusted with ice.

Inside the hotel, staff and guests filled bathtubs with water and soaked blankets. The wet blankets were hung over window sashes, where the paint was already starting to blister. Several MPPs were part of the wet blanket brigade; most notably James Pliny Whitney, leader of the Conservative party and later Premier of Ontario. A newspaper reporter later quipped, "Wet blankets are not usually popular, but they did the business for the Queen's." ("Wet blanket" was slang for a gloomy person who spoils other people's fun.) The Queen's Hotel escaped with no more damage than some blistered paint and superficial scorching.

East of Bay Street, on the south side of Wellington, the fire seemed to be deliberately trying to break through to Yonge. The small yards and narrow alleys behind and between buildings were ineffective as firebreaks, and the inferno advanced from building to building until it was halfway to Yonge. Then it came to the Kilgour Brothers bag and paper box factory.

That structure might have gone up like a flare, but it was equipped with a sprinkler system and was divided into two sections by fire doors. Buildings around the Kilgour were razed, but the Kilgour itself was a bulwark against which the foe could make no headway. It gave the firemen the opportunity to concentrate their dwindling water power elsewhere.

South of the Kilgour Building the flames lanced through a dozen factories and warehouses, and threatened the Yonge Street dock. Eighteen warehouses on Front Street just to the west of Yonge were afire. One of them was used to store gunpowder and cartridges, and the noise of exploding ammunition was deafening. On Yonge Street, store owners were emptying their shops of merchandise. Toronto and Buffalo firemen were hosing down buildings to protect them from the intense heat and put out the sparks that showered down.

With the Kilgour Building holding the north side of the block, the firefighters made a stand at the Minerva Building, a four-storey underwear factory on the north side of Front Street, just to the west of Yonge. Here they would try to stop yet another fiery surge from breaking through to the main downtown artery.

Inside the Minerva Building, which was equipped with fire-hoses and an emergency water supply, the staff had been keeping the flames at bay. Now Toronto and Hamilton firemen took over. Part of the building was destroyed, but in their "grand stand finish" the firemen prevailed. Once more the monster had been denied a foothold on Yonge.

The battle moved east, almost to the southwest corner of Yonge and Front. There the fire tore through the McMahon and

Broadfield warehouse and threatened the Customs House. Toronto firemen, reinforced by men from London, Buffalo and Hamilton, held the line for two hours. Suddenly the McMahon Building collapsed with a great roar, and the firemen had to retreat. But with the fall of that warehouse, the threat to the Customs House and to Yonge Street was removed. Deputy Chief Noble later told the press, "If it had got a hold in Yonge Street, God knows where it would have stopped."

By 4:00 AM the fire was under control, though there would be flare-ups from the smoldering ruins for the next two weeks. Almost 20 acres (8.0 ha) in the middle of Toronto had been reduced to blackened ruin. The flames had laid waste to 98 separate buildings housing 220 businesses. Insurance companies would estimate the financial loss at $13 million (in 1904 funds). Over 5,000 people were temporarily thrown out of work. Many would find employment cleaning up the debris.

Five firemen, including Chief Thompson, were seriously injured, along with a few civilians. About 20 firemen received minor injuries. It was fortunate that the fire occurred after 6:00 PM, when the factories and warehouses were largely deserted, or there could have been a tremendous human cost. The Great Toronto Fire claimed but one life, and that was indirectly. Two weeks after the blaze, a man named John Croft, part of a demolition crew tearing down the burned-out shell of the W.J. Gage Building, was killed when a dynamite charge exploded in his face. The city named a street in his memory.

It did not take Torontonians long to clean up after the worst fire in their city's history, and to rebuild—though some of the burnt-over lots would remain for years. The city finally invested in a high-pressure water system. Fire regulations were improved somewhat, and more equipment purchased. But changes made to building codes were only marginal, and those overhead wires would remain a hindrance to firefighters for many years.

In the aftermath of the fire there were condemnations of Toronto's lack of preparedness for such a conflagration, words of high praise for all of the firemen and optimistic prophecies of the prosperity that Toronto could still look forward to. But perhaps the most poignant statement was that made by T.H. Johnson, the watchman who had first sounded the alarm: "All my buildings that I have been watching for so long are gone."

The Quebec Bridge Disaster, 1907

THROUGHOUT HISTORY THERE HAVE been men of out-standing talent, even genius, whose belief in their own infallibility has led them to disaster. It put Napoleon on the road to Moscow, and it sent Colonel George A. Custer to the Little Bighorn. It takes a Hollywood film director from being an Academy Award winner one year to being the goat for a major flop the next. Men who have had so much success that they are confident they can do no wrong become a danger not only to themselves, but also to those people who put their trust in them. Such was the case with one of the most ambitious construction projects in Canadian history.

No one could say that New York state's Theodore Cooper was not a brilliant engineer. In 1858, at the tender age of 19, he grad-uated from the Rensselaer Institute as a civil engineer. He served in the United States Navy during the Civil War, and after the war he taught at the United States Naval Academy. When he left the Navy he turned his considerable talents to bridge building. He caught the attention of Captain James Eads, who was constructing the magnificent St. Louis Bridge. That span was one of the engi-neering marvels of its time, and Cooper was largely responsible for its completion. He'd even taken a 90 foot (27.4 m) fall from the bridge, coming away wet but unhurt.

Cooper went on to build other impressive bridges in Provi-dence, Pittsburgh and New York. Cooper wrote books on bridge building that became the bibles of American engineers. Among other things, Cooper stressed the importance of investigation and inspection at every step of a project, from the planning stages to the driving of the last rivet. By the 1890s Theodore Cooper was one of the most admired bridge builders in the United States. There was a great demand for his services as a consulting engineer. But he was also getting on in years, and was looking for a project so grand as to make his name remembered. He wanted to finish his already sterling career with a masterpiece. That opportunity came from Canada.

The need for a bridge across the St. Lawrence River at or near Quebec City had existed for decades. For just as long, however, the technology to build one had *not* existed. The river was too wide, too deep, and had powerful currents, as well as the seasonal hazard of ice flows. Moreover, the river was a shipping lane for ocean-going vessels. A bridge would have to be high enough for ships to pass under easily and would require an extraordinarily long span—unsupported from below—so as not to interfere with the channel.

In 1897 a group of Quebec City businessmen formed the Quebec Bridge Company (QBC). Their goal was to build a bridge across the St. Lawrence at a site 6 miles (9.6 km) upstream from the city, where the river was a third of a mile (0.4 km) wide. The QBC's own senior engineer, Edward A. Hoare, had never tackled so large a project before, so the group met with the American Society of Engineers in hope of finding a man of solid reputation to lend his name to their endeavour. They were overjoyed to learn that the great Theodore Cooper himself was willing to be supervising consultant.

Cooper was more than willing; he was eager. The proposed structure would be the longest cantilever bridge in the world—90 feet (27.4 m) longer than the famous Firth of Forth Bridge in Scotland. It would be the jewel in the crown that Cooper had dreamed of.

Such a project, however, would cost more money than the QBC could raise, even with subsidies from Quebec City, and the provincial and federal governments. It was 1900 before they could even begin stonework on the piers. Then Ottawa decided that the bridge was a necessary link in a new transcontinental railway, and agreed to underwrite $6.5 million worth of QBC bonds.

The contract went to the Phoenix Bridge Company of Phoenixville, Pennsylvania, which said that they could build the best and cheapest bridge. One of their senior engineers, Peter L. Szlapka, drew up plans for a bridge to rival any of the engineering marvels of the new century. It would be 2,800 feet (853.4 m) long—not including the approaches. One span—unsupported from below—would stretch 1,600 feet (487.6 m) across the shipping channel 150 feet (45.7 m) below. The bridge's 67 foot (20.4 m) width would accommodate two sets of railway tracks, two sets of streetcar tracks, and two roadways. It was truly a grand design.

But Szlapka was what people in the industry called a "desk engineer." Like Hoare, he had never worked on a project of such magnitude. The company was fortunate indeed to have Theodore Cooper to turn to. Cooper approved of Szlapka's design, though he made a few modifications. He moved a support pier so that the long span increased to 1,800 feet (548.6 m). Nobody questioned any of this. If Cooper approved of a design, it had to be good.

Due to a variety of delays, construction on the steel framework of the bridge did not begin until July 1905. In the meantime, Cooper had broken one of his own cardinal rules. He did not double-check the design for possible flaws. The Canadian government's chief engineer from the Department of Bridges and Canals, Collingwood Schreiber, suggested having a government engineer examine the plans, but that drew Cooper's ire. He said that such an action would put him in the position of a subordinate, and that would be injurious to his reputation. He insisted that if he were to be involved in the project, he must have the final word on everything. Fearful of losing the services of the great man, Ottawa backed down.

Cooper had visited the Quebec site prior to construction, but he never actually saw the bridge as it was being built. He did all of his work in his New York office. He said that poor health prevented him from travelling. He no doubt did have some ailments, but his health probably was not as fragile as he was to plead later.

Szlapka's working drawings of the plans—the step-by-step blueprints of every phase of construction—were ready in the spring of 1905, but they did not reach Cooper's office until seven months after construction had started. These drawings made it possible to calculate the weight of the cantilevers and the arms stretching out across the water from the piers. When Cooper examined the blueprints, he immediately saw that a miscalculation had been made. The weight of each arm was eight million pounds heavier than had originally been estimated.

Now Cooper faced a dilemma. Should he stop construction on the bridge, the design of which he himself had approved? That would certainly be a blot on his perfect record. Moreover, the Canadian government wanted the bridge completed in time for Quebec's tercentenary in 1908. They planned to have the Prince of Wales (later King George V) at the opening ceremony. Having Royalty cut the ribbon on his masterpiece was a touch that appealed to Cooper's ego. If they had to tear down what had already been built and start all over again, the bridge would not be finished in time. Cooper went over his calculations again, and decided that in spite of the error, the support system designed by Szlapka would bear the extra weight.

Work carried on under the supervision of Norman McLure, a young engineer recently graduated from Princeton, who was Cooper's own man at the construction site. McLure was well trained, and was certainly a competent engineer, but he did not have the experience to make decisions without Cooper's authorization. Neither did Hoare in Quebec City, nor Phoenix's chief engineer, John Sterling Deans, in Phoenixville. The project's captains were well spread out, and the general was in New York City.

Months passed, with construction halted only during the winter. The great bridge was taking shape as the south arm reached out across the St. Lawrence. All appeared to be going well.

Then in June 1907, McLure wrote to Cooper that two girders of the anchor arm were out of alignment by a quarter of an inch. The young engineer said that they had found other misalignments that they'd been able to correct with hydraulic jacks, but that these girders were so placed that jacks couldn't be used. He needed Cooper's advice on what to do. The consulting engineer replied, "Make as good a work of it as you can, it is not serious."

As the span stretched farther out over the river, the stress on the chords—the outside, horizontal pieces running the length of the bridge—became intolerable. By early August McLure was writing to Cooper that they showed signs of buckling. Now Cooper was concerned, and asked McLure for further information. He wanted to know what had caused the bending. McLure couldn't explain to Cooper's satisfaction. The work went on. The span now stretched some 600 feet (182.6 m).

On August 27, construction inspector E.R. Kinloch was alarmed to find that the misalignment had increased to 2.5 inches (6.4 cm). He hurried to the construction office to report his finding. McLure didn't think the problem was serious. Nor did his assistant, Henry Birks. But the senior foreman for the Phoenix Bridge Company, B.A. Yenser, said that he was suspending work because he feared for the safety of his men.

Yenser and Kinloch urged McLure to go to New York immediately to consult with Cooper. Letters were too slow, they said. There was a phone in the office, but it was on a party line and they didn't want word of the problem getting out. McLure thought that Cooper might laugh at him for scurrying off to New York for what was probably a trivial problem, but he agreed to go and see Edward Hoare in Quebec City.

Yenser said that he would have his men dismantle the "traveller." That was a huge metal scaffolding that was moved along the bridge as construction progressed. By taking it down, they would lighten the load on the warped girders.

The next day Hoare and McLure met in Quebec City. Hoare told McLure to get on the next train for New York. He himself would go to the worksite the following morning to look things over. Now began a series of bizarre events that would have fatal consequences.

McLure boarded the train for New York, thinking that Yenser had suspended all work, except for the dismantling of the traveller. But when Hoare arrived at the site at 10:30 AM, August 29, he saw that the traveller had been moved farther out, and the men were continuing with construction. He asked Yenser why. Yenser replied that he'd had a dream the night before that he had been foolish to have been so worried about the bent girders. This man, who was a foreman on one of the biggest construction jobs in the world, had decided to be guided by a dream, rather than by what he knew about the properties of steel. Amazingly, Hoare and Birks went along with it.

McLure met Cooper in his office at 11:00 that same morning. Cooper realized that there was a serious problem, and decided that work should be stopped until he could figure out a way to save the bridge. McLure assured him that Yenser had suspended construction. Cooper wanted to be sure of this, but since Yenser was employed by the Phoenix Bridge Company, he thought that the order to stop work would have to be issued from their office. He told McLure to get on the train to Phoenixville. Then at 12:16 he sent a telegram to John Deans: "Add no more load to the bridge till after due consideration of the facts. McLure will be over at five o'clock." The message did not sound urgent, and it did not specifically instruct Deans to contact Quebec and order the men off the bridge.

The wire reached Phoenixville at 1:15. Deans was out of the office and did not return until 3:00. When he read the message, he arranged for Szlapka to meet McLure at the train station. He did not call or telegraph Quebec.

When McLure arrived he told Deans and Szlapka that work on the bridge had been suspended, and that he was expecting a report from Birks by mail. The three men agreed that there was no point in doing anything more until the report arrived. It was 5:30 PM. Two minutes later, many miles away in Quebec, disaster struck.

Throughout that day it had been work as usual for the mixed crew of French Canadians, Americans, and Indians from the Caughnawaga Reserve near Montreal. There had been an unpleasant incident when six of the Native workers got into a dispute with one of the bosses and walked off the job—an action that quite likely saved their lives. Late in the day Ulrich Barthe, secretary of the QBC, arrived with a party of friends to whom he wanted to show off the magnificent, half-finished bridge. They had gone out onto the span to watch the men maneuver the big girders into place and drive rivets, and were on their way back to solid ground, when an engine towing two carloads of steel rolled onto the bridge. It was 5:30, and a workman named Eugene Lajeunesse had just told his brother Delphis that it was almost quitting time. Another steelworker, Ingwall Hall, was on top of the traveller at the end of the span. That put him 300 feet (91.4 m) above the river.

Suddenly, at 5:32, there was a loud groaning noise, and a tremor ran through the structure. The engineer in the locomotive felt it and applied the brakes. Hall felt the traveller tilt forward. Somebody cried, "The bridge is falling!" Workmen started to run for safety, but very few made it. There was an ear-splitting report, like a cannon being fired. Then the traveller and Hall were plummeting down to the river. The whole span collapsed, according to one witness, like "ice pillars whose ends were rapidly melting away."

Thousands of tons of steel plunged into the St. Lawrence River or landed with a tremendous crash on the foreshore—riverbed left exposed due to low tide. The impact shook the ground in the nearby villages of St. Rumuald and New Liverpool—home to many of the French Canadian workers—and was felt in Quebec City 6 miles (9.6 km) away. People ran out of buildings, thinking there was an earthquake. Down with the bridge that had been Theodore Cooper's dream project went 86 men.

The steel dragged many of them down 200 feet (60.9 m) to the bottom of the river. Others were in shallow water or on the foreshore but were trapped in a tangle of twisted girders. Ingwall Hall came to the surface gasping for air and found that he was missing two fingers from his right hand. A man named Charles Davis and another named D.B. Haley both recalled that as they dropped they wondered if the steel was falling faster than they were, but they could remember nothing else. The train engineer, whose name was not reported, survived by some miracle. He could remember nothing from the moment he put on the brakes until he regained consciousness on the riverbank. Six of the men who were in the mass of wreckage on the foreshore were able to crawl out, the two Lajeunesse brothers among them. About a dozen other men were alive but hopelessly trapped.

The steamer *Glenmont* had passed under the span only moments before the collapse, and barely escaped the shower of steel. Now boats from the *Glenmont* and from both shores were launched to look for survivors and pick up bodies. They found Hall, but not much else. Of the 86 men, only 11 escaped being killed instantly or trapped.

Now the few men who had not been on the bridge, and men who'd been working on the north shore and had come across in boats, worked desperately to save the men who were trapped. The tide would start to rise in half an hour, and would flood the foreshore to a depth of 13 feet (3.9 m). They were joined by people from the nearby villages, many of them the families of the trapped men or men who were already dead. But they had only crowbars to work with; no cutting torches or heavy equipment to move girders that weighed tons. When darkness came, they had no searchlights.

The sun went down and the waters rose, and the frantic would-be rescuers struggled by lantern light. But it was useless. A priest who had been summoned waded out into the rising water to administer the last rites to the doomed men. As the tide rose, the moans of injured men were replaced by the choking cries of the drowning. Then there was silence.

The bodies of those men were eventually recovered, as were 16 that came to the surface of the river. For the rest of the 75 men killed: 20 French Canadians, 20 Americans, and 35 Native Canadians, the bottom of the St Lawrence river would be their eternal grave. Young Henry Birks was among the dead. So was Foreman Yenser, whose deceptive dream had been prelude to a nightmare.

An inquiry into the disaster concluded that the fault lay with the design of the bridge, and that errors in judgment had been made by Peter L. Szlapka and Theodore Cooper. This was not to say that they were held criminally responsible, but that, "The ability of the two engineers was tried in one of the most difficult professional problems of the day and proved to be insufficient to the task."

The Quebec Bridge Disaster, one of the worst on record, was, of course, devastating to Theodore Cooper. He never worked on another bridge. His name would be remembered now not for an engineering triumph, but for a tragedy. Remarkably, the press was very sympathetic toward him, and played up his age and his failing health. Much was made of the telegram he had sent to Deans (of which Cooper gave the reporters a somewhat embellished account), and that Deans had failed to act upon. So much so, that when Cooper died in 1919, journalists made something of a tragic hero figure out of him, saying that if his urgent message to stop construction had been obeyed, a hundred lives would have been saved.

The disaster cost the Canadian government $2 million (in 1907 funds), but that did not stop the project—nor the continuation of tragedy. A bridge was still needed.

Construction began on a new bridge in 1913. It went without a hitch until September 11, 1916, when a central span 640 feet (195 m) long and weighing 5,000 tons was being hoisted into place. One end tore away from the supports, and the whole span plunged into the river, killing 13 men. They died within yards of the spot where the 75 men had been hurled to their deaths in 1907. It almost seemed that the Quebec Bridge was cursed.

The engineers corrected their errors, built a new central span, and successfully fastened it in place on September 20, 1917. Two years later the bridge was formally opened by Edward, the Prince of Wales. Royalty did indeed cut the ribbon on the longest cantilever bridge in the world. But the bridge was not Theodore Cooper's. The ruins of that lay at the bottom of the St. Lawrence River, along with the bones of the unrecovered dead.

The Porcupine Forest Fire,
Northern Ontario, 1911

F OREST FIRES ARE VERY MUCH A PART of the natural
cycle of death and renewal. Spawned by either natural forces
or the hand of man, they can sweep across millions of square acres
of woodland with unstoppable fury, consuming every scrap of
flora; choking or searing the life out of every creature not fleet
enough or lucky enough to get out of the way. But they also clear
away generations of dense, sunlight-stealing undergrowth and
layer the soil with enriching ash, thus preparing the ground for
new growth. There are even evergreens whose cones begin to ger-
minate only after exposure to the heat of forest fires. But when the
natural phenomenon of a forest fire comes into contact with the
workings of man, disaster can result.

In the early 20th century the frontier region of Northern
Ontario in many ways resembled the Old West—without the gunfights, though firearms certainly were plentiful. It was a wild,
isolated country that drew rugged individualists; men and women
big in ambition and often in physical size, who would not be contained by the restrictions of the cities to the south. One of the
things that drew these people to the North was the lure of gold.

In 1909 Tom Geddes of St. Thomas, Ontario, and his partner
George Bannerman boarded the Temiskaming & Northern
Ontario Railroad's Muskeg Special, and took it to the end of the
line, about 220 miles (354 km) north of North Bay. Then they
made their way by canoe and portage to Porcupine Lake, a

1.5 mile (2.4 km) long sliver of water about 30 miles (48.2 km) from the railhead. There, on July 13, they struck it rich. Gold! The rush to "Ontario's Klondike" was on.

The bush around The Porcupine, as the region came to be known, was soon swarming with prospectors. A few, like Benny Hollinger, discoverer of the legendary Hollinger Mine, got lucky. Many didn't. As was typical of gold rushes going back to California in 1849, the people who usually profited most from the stampede were the merchants and "vendors of vice" who moved in to cater to the wants and needs of the men who scoured the bush or worked in the mining camps. Little communities popped up around Porcupine Lake. At the north end was Porcupine, better known as Golden City. A little farther down the north shore was Pottsville, named for Ma and Pa Potts, who ran the Shunia Hotel. (*Shunia* is a Native word for gold.) At the south end of the lake was South Porcupine, the rowdiest of the settlements.

Miners came into these "towns" to buy supplies at Billy Gohr's store, eat at Andy Leroux's cafe, have their clothes washed by Rosie the Porcupine Laundress, or do business at the Waweeatan Mining Exchange run by Tom Geddes and South African ex-patriot Jimmy Forsyth. Forsyth was a big man who, with his English wife Edith, was trying to get a new start in life after losing their general store in Cochrane to a fire in 1910. For Jimmy Forsyth, the old saying that lightning doesn't strike twice was to prove false.

Geddes and Forsyth were well aware that one of the greatest privations a gold miner in the bush faced—along with winter cold, summer heat, blackflies, mosquitoes, and all-round rough country—was loneliness. There were very few women in The

Porcupine, and a man needed some sort of diversion, so in the back of their South Porcupine office, Geddes and Forsyth had a "Snake Room." This was a sort of speakeasy where men could listen to banjo music and buy bootleg whiskey.

The law forbade the sale of alcohol within 6 miles (9.6 km) of any mining property, and Constable Charlie Piercy did his best to enforce that rule. However, liquor was smuggled in by every means imaginable. Bars were allowed to sell weak "near beer," but somewhere out of Constable Piercy's view the bartender would have a supply of the hard stuff. Besides the Snake Room, a man could also get a stiff belt at Leroux's cafe, Basil Wilson's Pool Room or Cliff Moore's King George Hotel. Charlie See had a sign on his drugstore that said "Pills and Things." The "Things" meant booze.

Eating contests were another popular form of recreation. Among the men who could wolf down Paul Bunyan-sized platters of food were Sam "Bear Steak" Shovell of Toronto; Jack "The Nevada Kid" Munroe, a former boxer from Elk Lake, Ontario; and Scotsman Pat Sinnott, a lawyer who was now secretary of the American Goldfields Mine near Pottsville. The champion gorger, however, was Robert "Little Eva" Weiss, a former football star from Butte, Montana, who stood six-foot-seven (1.95 m) and tipped the scales at 440 pounds (199.5 kg). Yet, even with such entertainment to break the monotony, the men drank as hard as they worked. Said Jimmy Forsyth in later years, "You almost *had* to drink a quart of booze a day to ward off the blues."

On the morning of July 11, 1911, Jimmy was sleeping off the previous night's overindulgence, when Edith shook him. "Wake up, Jimmy," she said. "It's awful outside. Looks as if the whole bush is burning. Don't you think we should do something?"

Jimmy grumbled, "Let it burn!," and buried his pounding head in the pillow.

The summer of 1911 had been one of the hottest and driest on record. Small fires had been burning all over the north country for months. That was not unusual. On May 18 a fire had even swept across the site of the Hollinger Mine. Then on July 9 a blaze had blown into Pottsville and burned 20 houses to the ground. A bucket brigade (the only form of firefighting available) of 150 men had managed to save the little downtown section. Still, nobody expected a major fire, and everybody *knew* that the long-awaited rain would come any day now.

What Jimmy Forsyth was not considering, as he nursed his hangover, was that there had been almost no rain at all that summer, and the tinder-dry woodlands surrounding The Porcupine were ripe for an inferno. Even the muskeg was drying up. Added to the natural supply of dead wood on the forest floor were great piles of slash; discarded branches and other waste from felled trees. The towns and the mines used a lot of timber—for building, for shoring up mine shafts, for fuel in stoves and generators, and for ties on the new railway line that had reached The Porcupine a fortnight earlier. All of that logging had left tons of slash, just waiting to burn.

The fire that Edith Forsyth saw that morning probably started near Star Lake, 20 miles (32.1 km) to the southwest. People knew about it, and thought that the Mattagami River would act as a natural firebreak. They didn't count on a sudden gale-force wind that carried the flames across the river and through the treetops at astounding speed, and threw a vanguard of burning birchbark and other debris to start fires well in advance of the main blaze. Soon the sky over The Porcupine was black with smoke. People realized too late that the fires were merging and rushing toward them on a front 20 miles (32.1 km) wide. They were, in fact, trapped!

By 10:00 Jimmy Forsyth was up and very worried. At 10:30 he put Edith in a boat with a suitcase and their spaniel, Peter, and sent her across the lake to Golden City where—he hoped—it was safer. Then he and his partner Tom Geddes went to Andy Leroux's for a drink. "It looks like it will get us," Geddes said.

Leroux poured a round on the house. "We may not see each other again," he said prophetically, as it turned out.

Sparks were now raining down on South Porcupine, and the men formed bucket brigades to douse the buildings. Hopefully, the wind would shift and carry the fire away. It didn't.

At midday the men began loading the women and children into boats to send them to Golden City. Constable Piercy and his partner George Murray supervised the evacuation. When a gang of five Italian miners tried to force their way into one of the boats, the policemen knocked one of them into the lake and sent the others cowering back at gunpoint. As the last boat was about to leave, a woman hurried onto the dock with three suitcases, a fur coat, and a canary in a cage. Men gallantly helped her into the boat, but paid no attention to her angry protests when they tossed the suitcases, the coat, and the birdcage into the lake. With the children and most of the town's women safely underway, the men went back to fighting the fire. But it was a futile effort.

Livery owner Jack Dalton got his horses out of the stable and led them into the lake as deep as they would go. In the King George Hotel, Cliff Moore passed out free cigars. "We might as well smoke 'em as burn 'em," he said. At about 1:15 a worker from the Dome mine named Arthur Ward came running into town on the Dome road. The mine had been engulfed in fire, and he had made a seemingly impossible run, leaping over the blazing trunks of fallen trees. He was sure that whatever the Olympic record was for running and jumping hurdles, he had broken it.

Sixty other men at the Dome jumped into a pond that had been made to store water for the boilers. Manager Thomas Meeks, who lived at the Dome, put his wife and two small children into barrels of water that he kept for his garden, and covered them with blankets. All survived except for two men who panicked and tried to run for it.

Out at the West Dome Mine, no one had a chance to run. The foreman, big Robert Weiss, led a group of 19 people down a mine shaft. With them were his wife Jennie and three-year-old daughter Ariel. "Jennie, you're not afraid, are you?" the eating-contest champ asked. His wife replied, "If we're going to die, we'll all die together." She was right. All but one man, who'd changed his mind and climbed back out, suffocated when the flames roaring above sucked all of the air out of the shaft.

In South Porcupine a blast of wind, possibly created by the inferno itself, brought the conflagration roaring into town. Now all was bedlam. Terrified horses burst out of the lake and ran screaming through the town. Billy Gohr was determined to save his store, even though that was now impossible. He and his two employees, Matt Smith and Rosaire Bourbean, kept soaking the walls with buckets of water. But with the flames closing in, the employees decided to run.

"Come down, come down, Billy Gohr!" Bourbean shouted. "It's no use! It's no use! Come down quick!"

But Gohr paid no heed. He said that everything he had was tied up in the store, and if it went, he'd might as well go with it. His fatalistic attitude did not take into account his wife and child.

Smith grabbed some money from the bar, and he and Bourbean made a dash for the lake. Smith fell, and Bourbean kept going. "I had my life to save if I could," he said later. Bourbean ran through a chaos of blazing streets and fear-maddened horses. Because of the smoke he couldn't see where the lake was, but he ran blindly until he found it.

"I throw myself at the lake on my hands and knees and try to wet myself in the water, but it is too shallow. I crawl out into the lake and go for deep water. We find them the next day. Seven dollars and sixty cents of Billy Gohr's bar where Smith is dead. The dollar bills is all burned up."

Gohr's wife had waited at the dock for him, their baby in her arms. Then she had gone into the water to wait for him. But Billy never came.

Jimmy Forsyth and Tom Geddes ran for the lake. Forsyth had his terrier Toddy under one arm. They hadn't gone 30 feet (9.1 m) when, to Forsyth's astonishment, Geddes stopped and said, "I'm going back for my coat."

"Don't be a damned fool!" Forsyth shouted.

"We'll have need of it before the day is out," Geddes replied. "Go ahead. I'll catch up with you."

Perhaps Geddes believed that the good fortune that had led him to the gold still smiled upon him. If he did, he was dead wrong. He never did catch up with Jimmy.

Forsyth almost didn't make it himself. He ran for the lake as exploding trees shot streaks of flame all around him. The back of his shirt, his shoelaces, and his hair were on fire. The hairs in his nose were singed. There were already bodies on the ground; friends of his who'd been overcome by the heat and the smoke. Animals plunged wildly past him: horses, rabbits, even a bear. Forsyth had to crawl the last 300 yards (274.3 m) on his hands and knees, his mouth close to the ground as he tried to suck in a breath of air. He could not swim, so he grabbed a sidewalk plank and then splashed into the water. He was still clutching Toddy.

Rosie the Porcupine Laundress waded neck deep into the water. She screamed when she began sinking into the oozy muck on the lake bottom. Nearby were two Scottish miners in a canoe. They hopped out of their boat, took hold of Rosie, and held her up. All three survived the nightmare.

Captain Thomas Dunbar, a 65-year-old former skipper of the Lake Temiskaming boats, was heaving on a pump handle for all he was worth. Someone yelled to him, "For God's sake, Cap, run!"

"Sorry, matey," the old man replied, "I got to put out this fire." The captain had more guts than sense, and he did not live out that terrible day.

Lindsay Morton, an English mining agent, was in the water with his wife and baby. "The whole thing resolved itself into a question of dying decently," he said later. "We lay in the mud, sometimes crawling into the water, and then out again to gasp a breath of air. But it wasn't air we got to breathe. Just smoke, so bitter that it made the baby cry out, 'Mama, O Mama, give me air!' At last I became so exhausted, I buried the family books and papers close beside me, so as to make sure I would leave a trace of identity behind me."

Hotel owner Cliff Moore, who had so cheerfully handed out his cigars, waded neck deep into the water. He still had the stub of a cigar clenched in his teeth. It was the last anyone saw of him.

A young prospector named Billy Moore (no relation) got into a canoe with local magistrate Tommy Torrance, lawyer Jack McMurrich, and a gambler known as Sam the Chinaman. They had no paddles; only a board. As they were about to push off, a group of men tried to rush the canoe. Level-headed Billy calmly explained to them that the canoe was already overloaded and in danger of sinking. The men withdrew, but then the local barber, Merv Strain, waded into the water as the canoe again prepared to push off.

"My God, I can't swim. Please take me along," he begged. "If you can't let me in, let me at least hang on to the back. But for God's sake, don't leave me behind or I'm done for."

The men were silent. Then Billy Moore said, "Get in, Merv." The now dangerously overloaded canoe moved out onto the lake. The high winds were whipping up waves to an incredible 7 feet (2.1 m).

Within 20 minutes of reaching South Porcupine, the fire had engulfed the whole town and was racing toward Pottsville. Some boats that had taken people to Golden City returned to pick up more refugees, but a few boat owners were later accused of sabotaging their own watercraft so they wouldn't have to go back. Then, at 1:40, the very waters the fleeing people relied upon for escape became an avenue of death.

The lake was already a boiling fury, when suddenly a carload of dynamite on a railway siding near South Porcupine exploded. The blast made a hole 20 feet (6 m) deep and hurled rocks into the sky. Then gravity brought them back down upon the people like a lethal hail. A piece of railway track sliced through the air like a scythe and cut off a man's arm. The concussion turned the lake into a cauldron. Boats capsized and screaming people were thrown into the water. A survivor later recalled, "The explosion was like the end of the world."

Billy Moore's canoe was one of those that overturned. Billy still had the board he'd been using for a paddle, but when he saw Jack McMurrich struggling in the water, he called, "Here, Jack. Use this," and tossed him the board. McMurrich survived, as did the judge and the gambler who had been in the canoe. Billy Moore drowned. So did Merv Strain, the barber.

Flames were devouring South Porcupine and Pottsville, and surging toward Golden City. Survivors up to their necks in lake water found themselves sharing the puddle in the middle of hell with horses, deer and moose. The parts of the horses' backs that were not submerged were scorched. The people's bodies were numb in the ice cold, spring-fed lake. Above the water, the air was lung-searing hot. The sky, one witness said, was "as black as Egypt's night."

In Golden City, Constable Piercy rounded up every available man to join the bucket brigades. A rumour later circulated that he had to march them out of the bars at gunpoint before they would help, but the story seems to have no basis in fact. Piercy did close the bars, but it did not require armed intimidation to bring out the volunteers.

Golden City had some defences the other communities hadn't. It sat at the end of the lake, and so was not in the path of a direct assault. One flank was protected by a vast swamp, and the other by the burned-out part of Pottsville. The bucket brigades kept throwing water on walls, and when wind-borne firebrands landed within the town, they attacked them immediately. The defenders were stretched thin and the battle was exhausting, but in the end they saved two-thirds of the town.

By next morning the great blaze had burned itself out. Two towns and 11 mining camps were gone, and 864 square miles (2237 km²) of woodland reduced to ashes and charred stumps. Three thousand people were homeless. Damage was estimated at $2 million (in 1911 dollars). The survivors returned to the charred ground that had been South Porcupine and Pottsville, and went out to where the camps had been. They found Captain Dunbar, burned to death by his pump. Some of Tom Geddes' bones were found in the ashes of his office beside the charred remnants of his coat. There wasn't enough left of him to fill a shirt box.

At the bottom of the West Dome mineshaft they found the bodies of Robert Weiss and his party. Tiny Ariel was cradled in her father's huge arms. The men needed a block and tackle to lift Weiss's 440 pound (199.5 kg) corpse out of the hole. It required 14 pallbearers to carry his giant coffin. Andy Leroux was dead, too. The official death count would reach 73, but the actual number of dead was likely much higher. The woods had been full of prospectors, loners and drifters with no family or friends in the towns. Their ashes would be as lost in the burnt wasteland as sailors' bones at the bottom of the sea.

Still, there were many incidents of heroism and unbelievable escapes. Pat Sinnott single-handedly rescued a mother and two children. Hawley Clayton, the Pottsville bank manager, had a house built on posts 4 feet (1.2 m) off the ground, on a point just south of town. Inside were 34 refugees, including Ma and Pa Potts. Determined to save his tiny domain—and no doubt assisted by some of the others—Clayton kept the water flowing on and under his cottage until the flaming monster had passed. His was the only building in Pottsville to escape destruction.

An unidentified young worker from one of the mining camps was running for his life toward South Porcupine when he sprained his ankle and fell. He thought his hour had come. But when the holocaust had roared past, he found himself sitting alive and well in an untouched island of green in the midst of blackened desolation.

Sam "Bear Steak" Shovell and his wife Nellie were sitting down to lunch at the Philadelphia Mine when they saw the wall of fire roaring down on them. Shovell yelled at his men to run for their lives. Then the 6-foot (1.8 m) Sam grabbed his petite wife and carried her through the bush in what seemed to be a hopeless dash for Porcupine Lake, 3 miles (4.8 km) away. They emerged from the bush at a section of railway track, just as a handcar manned by four Italian miners came rattling along. The Italians picked them up, and then put their backs to it as they pumped the little car through a gauntlet of fire and smoke. At a spot where the rail line skirted a little beach, they all jumped off and ran into the lake. For three hours Big Sam held Nellie's head above the water. But when they were finally able to drag themselves back onto land, it was Nellie who had grubstaked their future. Before their dash for safety, she'd tucked a ten-dollar bill into her stocking. Now, as she peeled off the wet stocking, the bill popped out. "Look Sam," she said. "We're not broke!"

Some of the bodies were claimed by families and taken to hometowns for burial. The sad remains of the rest were placed in 17 rough pine boxes and buried at a place between Pottsville and South Porcupine called Edward's Point. It was known thereafter as Deadman's Point. Many of the survivors, like Jimmy Forsyth and his wife, left The Porcupine for good. For Jimmy, being burned out twice was enough. But others stayed and rebuilt, and new pioneers came. There would be further trials by fire for Northern Ontario; a blaze in 1916 that killed 223, and yet another in 1922 that took 44 more lives. But like the evergreens that rose phoenix-like from the ashes, the tough Northern Ontarians always came back.

The Regina Tornado, 1912

JUNE 30, THE EVE OF DOMINION DAY, 1912, and the prairie town of Regina, Saskatchewan, had reason to celebrate. The little frontier city of 31,000 was booming—at least as far as the bankers and the real estate companies were concerned. Regina was the biggest community between Winnipeg and Calgary, and it had started out as just another shanty town along the Canadian Pacific Railway, with nothing to distinguish it from similar hamlets that sprang up beside the ribbon of steel. But Regina's short history had been as remarkable as it was colourful.

The site was originally called Pile o' Bones, due to an enterprising trader who, when there were no more buffalo to be slaughtered for their hides, gathered up their bones to be sent east for the manufacture of fertilizer. Then Edward Dewdney, lieutenant governor of the Northwest Territories, and a dabbler in land speculation, became interested in a large tract of prime land there. Using his political pull, Dewdney talked the CPR into locating a station no more than a mile from the collection of shacks. Then he chose the "town" as the capital of the Northwest Territories and bestowed upon it the grand name of Regina, in honour of Queen Victoria. The unlikely little settlement went on to become the headquarters of the North West Mounted Police (later the Royal Canadian Mounted Police) and finally the capital of the new province of Saskatchewan.

Free enterprise was in its glory as bankers and real estate agents—mostly canny Scots and slick Americans—grew rich from the influx of Ukrainian, Norwegian and German settlers who came, at first in a trickle, and then a flood. Over in Europe, agents charged with the task of "selling Canada" to the teeming masses painted a rosy picture of fields of golden grain ripening under a summer sun. They didn't say anything about the real weather. Nor did they say anything about the outrageous rents the prosperous entrepreneurs of Regina's fashionable West End charged immigrants for disgracefully poor housing in the East End slums.

Making money was what it was all about, and everybody wanted a piece of the action. When the Metis rebel leader Louis Riel was hanged in Regina for treason in 1885, the executioner sold foot (.3 m)-long pieces of "the rope that hung Riel" to morbid souvenir hunters. That was actually a common practice among hangmen who wanted to make a few extra dollars, but this man sold enough rope to hang Riel's whole army!

Late 19th and early 20th century Regina was a city of contrasts. It sent Mounties out to police the entire Canadian West, but to handle the drunks and rowdies in its own streets there was but one town constable—and he was allowed only one uniform. The town was graced by stately brick homes and a beautiful limestone legislative building with a copper dome that could be seen from miles around. Yet most Reginians were crowded into poorly constructed frame buildings. Its leading citizens drove the latest automobiles—on dirt roads flanked by wooden sidewalks. The town council promised that the city would be "illuminated," then installed only ten street lights—which were not used except on Saturday nights.

The stiff-necked Methodists and Presbyterians of the Social and Moral Reform League denounced the vices of the prairie metropolis: Chinese opium dens in the East End's Germantown; bordellos, gambling halls and saloons; theatres that staged risque plays, and the town's annual bonspeil (curling tournament). But poet and performing artist Pauline Johnson, the "Mohawk Princess," bypassed Regina on her tour because it was, she claimed, "a dead town." Eventually most of the saloon keepers and ladies of the night departed Regina for nearby Moose Jaw, a rip-roaring, wide-open town that became Regina's unofficial "red light district."

The Social and Moral Reform League were pleased to have a Carnegie Library bestowed upon their city but objected to some of the "naughty" books on its shelves. They were glad to see carpenters, engineers and labourers come to Regina, but balked at the idea of paying them decent wages. They could quote scripture to prove that labour unions were sacrilegious. Most of all, they wanted it known that Regina was as good as—or better than—Winnipeg! And so they tried to keep secret anything that might cast a shadow on their prairie utopia. Newspaper reports about the Queen City of the West had to be glowing or else be considered a pack of lies. When a new minister had the cheek to suggest that Regina was blighted by the same sins that afflicted her neighbours, one indignant citizen wrote, "Regina is one of the most moral, religious and law-abiding towns in the Dominion."

Carrying the torch for Regina was Nicholas Flood Davin, a lawyer-turned-journalist who founded the city's first newspaper, the *Leader*. A hard-drinking master of wit and blarney, Davin used his editorial column to duel with the Winnipeg press, the Mounted Police (who had the gall to charge him with possession of half a pint of illegal whiskey), and Regina's hand-is-quicker-than-the-eye real estate agents. Of the latter, Davin wrote, "Last week we had a nice rain, and everybody who walked down Broad Street took a homestead on one foot and a pre-emption on the other." Davin's paper would run editorials about such things as the evils of boys playing marbles for keeps but remain silent on the fact that boys as young as fourteen were losing their virginity in local brothels.

Regina's contrasts, oddities, hypocrisies and the free-wheeling pursuit of money by the cream of its society often had outsiders shaking their heads in either derision or exasperation. "Typical!" they would exclaim, upon hearing of some peculiar, new wrinkle in the fabric of the Queen City. This exclamation was to hold true in the aftermath of the calamity that was about to strike on that final day of June 1912.

The weather had been oppressively hot for days, and on that humid Sunday afternoon the thermometer read 100°F (37.7°C). There wasn't a breeze to stir the Union Jacks and bunting hung out in preparation for the following day's celebrations. In St. Paul's Anglican Church women fainted from the heat. Sunday School classes were dismissed early so the children could get out of the stifling buildings. People sat in the shade of their verandahs, sipping cold drinks and fanning themselves with little effect. Mothers and daughters dreaded the prospect of going into sweltering kitchens to prepare supper on coal stoves. At Wascana Lake, the man-made reservoir beside the Legislative Building, people sought relief by bathing in the blue water or boating on the smooth surface. In one canoe were 12-year-old Bruce Langdon and his pal Philip Steele, 11. At the far end of the lake, in another canoe, was a young English actor named William Henry Pratt,

better known by his stage name, Boris Karloff. He had been tour-
ing Western Canada with a theatrical troupe and decided to take a
short holiday in Regina. On the surrounding prairie, fields of
wheat baked under the blistering sun. Anybody who was praying
in church that Sunday no doubt put in a request for some cooling
rain. What they got was more like the wrath of God

The attack began at 4:30 PM to the south of town. A pair of
ominous-looking dark clouds raced toward each other, one from
the southeast, the other from the southwest. There was a crash of
thunder as they came together over Wascana Lake. An eerie green
glow filled the sky. Reginians looking up thought that at last they
would get some rain and relief from the heat. Even when blue-red
flashes of lightning cracked above them, they had no idea what
was about to be unleashed. Regina had never experienced a tornado.

A tornado is formed when a cool, dry air mass moves over hot,
moist air near the ground. The hot air is lighter, so it rushes
upward into the stream of cold air, creating a violent swirl of
energy as winds spin counter-clockwise at 500 miles (804.5 km)
an hour. The phenomenon is usually accompanied by heavy pre-
cipitation in the form of hail or rain. The path of a tornado is
narrow, its duration short, and the destruction of all that lies in its
way total.

The "cyclone," as Reginians would incorrectly call the huge
funnel, touched down at Wascana Lake. It sucked water into the
vacuum at its core and instantly killed five people. A real estate
salesman named Vincent Smith, out for a paddle in his canoe, was
picked up boat and all, and hurled half a mile through the air. Man
and canoe crashed through a third-storey window of an office
building, and Smith was killed.

Bruce Langdon and Philip Steele paddled for their lives toward shore but could not escape the raging monster. The fierce wind swept the canoe from the water, spinning it like an amusement park thrill ride. Little Philip was thrown out and killed. Bruce, still in the canoe and clinging to his paddle, sailed through the air for three-quarters of a mile before coming to a gentle landing in Victoria Park. When rescuers found him later, Bruce was sitting upright in the canoe, still gripping his paddle. He was stunned and didn't know where he was or what had happened to him, but his only injury was a broken arm.

The devil wind pounced on the Legislative Building next. It did little real damage to that magnificent structure, aside from peeling some copper strips from the dome and destroying a few office partitions. But it carried away all of the examination papers for Saskatchewan schools from the offices of the Department of Education. There were no final exams in Saskatchewan that year, which thousands of schoolchildren no doubt thought a blessing. Then, like a wicked prankster, the tornado vacuumed up eight carloads of dry cement mix and spewed it into the air. Mixed with the torrential rains that the tornado spawned, this came back to earth as a gritty "fallout" that coated trees, livestock and people's hair.

Now the twister sliced into the helpless city with a roar like doomsday. It erased the whole south wall of an apartment building and out sailed furniture, pianos and a naked woman in a bathtub. On Lorne Street it carved up the mansion of Saskatchewan Premier Walter Scott. Then it slashed through to Victoria Avenue and blew a wall out of the mansion of Judge John Lamont. The judge was in his bathroom, about to shut a window against what he thought was merely a rainstorm, when he felt his house shake as though hit by artillery fire.

Judge Hannon ran to his home in the pouring rain and hurried his family into the cellar as his house shook and the furniture danced. He dashed to close a back door and, looking outside, saw an empty space where his neighbour's small frame house had been.

Churches came next as the shrieking banshee ripped into Victoria Square. The Methodist, Knox, and Baptist churches, among Regina's most imposing structures, were demolished. The great cupola of the Baptist Church was tossed aside like a cake ornament. The minister of that church, Reverend J.S. Farmer, had left only minutes earlier to go home for tea. He'd been considering staying to prepare for evening services. "I can only think it was a wonderful miracle that I did not stay in the church," he said later. "Had I done so I would most assuredly have been killed."

What was miraculous was that St. Paul's Anglican Church, the only one with a crowd inside when all hell broke loose, was untouched. Of course, this led to the boast that "God protected the Anglicans because only they are of the true faith."

Not finished with its rampage in this part of town, the tornado made rubble of the Masonic Temple, the Presbyterian Church, the Carnegie Library, the YMCA and the YWCA. Most of the girls in the Y escaped to a park where they crawled under bushes as though hiding from a human fiend. Several others hid in a closet and prayed.

The beast seemed to know where to strike strategically. It slammed into the three-storey Telephone Exchange and reduced it to a pile of bricks, splintered timbers and shattered glass. The 15-ton telephone switchboard dropped from the second floor to the basement. Regina's communication centre had been obliterated. Three telephone operators crawled out of the wreckage and ran to the nearby offices of the *Leader* crying out that the Telephone building had been flattened, and that there were people buried under the rubble. At first the newspapermen didn't believe them. But the young women were insistent. The men from the *Leader* were soon crawling through the piles of debris, digging out the shaken operators. Astonishingly, none of the women were killed.

The demon wind howled through Regina's business section, leaving behind something that looked like the town dump. Stores and offices were ripped to shreds and the streets and skies filled with their contents: rolls of wallpaper, land deeds, blankets, clothing, toys.

The storm went through the CPR yards like a pile driver. It tossed boxcars around the way a child throws playthings during a tantrum. Warehouses were blown to kindling. All but one of the grain elevators disintegrated. The storm picked up a livery stable and dropped it on the tracks. Mercifully, none of the 50 horses in the stable were seriously injured. Cattle in one of the shattered railway cars were not so fortunate.

Having wreaked indescribable havoc, the tornado sped out of town like a galloping outlaw and churned a furrow through 11 miles (17.7 km) of countryside, flattening every farmhouse and barn in its path. With its final gasps the tornado stripped a farmwoman of every stitch of her clothing, including her shoes. It pummelled the hamlet of Govan with hailstones the size of baseballs. Then it was gone. Its swath of destruction through Regina was three blocks wide and 12 blocks long, and it had taken just a little over five minutes.

Regina lay in chaos and shock after this visitation from "a black hand of God," as one witness called it. Fires broke out here and there in the stricken neighbourhoods, but pelting rain quickly dowsed them. Otherwise the remainder of the city might have gone up in smoke.

As it was, the devastation was as bizarre as it was heartbreaking. On one side of a street an entire row of houses would be gone, while on the other side there were only broken windows. One house was lifted up and then set back right on its foundations. Other houses were picked up and then dropped upside-down on neighbouring houses. A man whose house and barn had been blown to smithereens found that his car parked inside the garage was untouched. Out in the streets, cars and wagons lay overturned and smashed. Throughout the tornado's path there were dead and maimed horses, dogs and chickens. But on one fire hydrant sat a crowing rooster, plucked naked but for a few tailfeathers.

The human stories that emerged from those few terrible minutes were both astonishing and tragic. In one house, William Beelby, his wife and their 16-month-old son were upstairs. Downstairs were William's 11-year-old daughter Marion, and his younger brother Wilfred, who had William's two-year-old daughter Florence in his arms. The tornado ripped off the upper storey of the house and dropped it in a neighbour's yard. The Beelbys crawled out a window, unhurt. In the bottom part of the house, the wind tore the baby from Wilfred's arms before pushing the building back 50 feet (15.2 m) and collapsing the walls. Wilfred was bloodied, but not badly hurt. Marion landed belly down on a rug that had blown into the street. Baby Florence was found safe inside the oven, with only a few scratches on her legs. A bottle of brandy from the family's medicine cabinet landed upright in the street, unbroken and unspilled, with the cork out. Never was there a greater invitation for a stiff drink!

In one office building a clerk doing a little Sabbath overtime walked into the company vault to file some papers just as the tornado hit. When he looked out the door, he found himself staring at "bald prairie." A woman had a diamond ring sucked off her finger, but was otherwise unscathed. A beam fell on one man's leg and broke it—but it was a wooden leg. Two teenaged girls, Lindsay McGall and Peggy Smith, were in Peggy's home when the floor beneath them collapsed and they fell into the basement. Neither girl had a scratch. Five-year-old Kenneth Dunn was buried under rubble for five hours, his leg broken. When he was rescued he bravely said, "It was awful. But I kept saying to myself, 'I am a Boy Scout, and I must not cry.'" Harry J. Potts, a plumber, sat on a piano stool in the middle of the wreckage of his house. The stool was the only thing he owned that had not been destroyed. By a strange quirk the storm had blown him a book, *Business Hints for Beginners*. It would be a useful book, he said, now that he had to start all over.

For others the loss was much greater than that of house and furnishings. Paul McIlmoyle saw his wife killed right before his eyes. "We were trying to get into the cellar after seeing that the storm had taken such dimensions," he said. "With my wife I was within one second of being safely in the cellar beneath our little store. I was horrified to see my wife fall, struck by something, and myself made helpless to render any assistance to her by the debris which was piled all around me. It is indeed a very hard loss to bear, with three motherless small children."

Searching the rubble of a collapsed house on Lorne Street, rescuers pulled out Fred Hindson, dead; his father James, badly injured; and Fred's friend Bob Edgar, not hurt at all. Also among the dead were Isabella McKay and her two children, an infant named Clarence Loggie, a dairy inspector from New Zealand named George Craven, and "two Chinamen."

Reginians pulled themselves out of the wreckage and saw the devastation of their so recently bustling city. Flags and bunting hung for Dominion Day lay over the ruins in sodden shrouds. The brightly coloured electric lights strung for the celebration were a tangled mess, as were the telephone, telegraph and electrical lines. The empty windows of blasted buildings gazed down like dead eyes. There were gaping holes where minutes earlier homes had stood. Some of those houses had been carried miles out onto the prairie. Here and there a dog that had survived the carnage sat on a pile of debris and whimpered for the masters lying dead or injured below. Glass shards were imbedded in trees and poles, and wind-blown gravel had pockmarked brick and stone walls like bullets.

"The silence was what got you," Dora Hudson said later. Only 15 at the time, she had escaped with only a minor cut, but her brother Fred was dead and her father badly wounded. "The hurt ones were so hushed. No one wept, much less screamed in pain. Nobody who died did so noisily. Not even the children cried. It's the loneliest, most lost feeling in the world, when your landmarks are suddenly gone."

But the boomtown spirit of Regina could not be swept away, not even by a "cyclone." There was the rubble of more than 500 wrecked buildings to be cleared away. Arrangements had to be made for some 3,000 people who were suddenly homeless. Survivors had to be dug from the wreckage. Over 300 injured people had to be cared for. The dead had to be found, identified and properly buried.

Mayor Peter McAra declared martial law—which included closing all the bars—and the RCMP and soldiers of the 95th

Saskatchewan Rifles patrolled the streets to prevent looting. (There was actually almost no looting, but six men were given a year in prison for stealing six bottles of beer.) Electricians picked their way through the waste, looking for deadly live wires. Every able-bodied man was called upon to help with the cleanup. Boy Scouts were recruited as messengers to re-establish a form of communications. Makeshift hospitals were set up for the injured. Women volunteered as nursing assistants, holding up lanterns while doctors worked on patients. Boris Karloff found that the rooming house at which he'd been lodging no longer existed. The soft-spoken actor who would one day horrify audiences as the Frankenstein monster organized a benefit show to raise funds for the homeless. He even rolled up his sleeves and helped to clear away debris.

Aid was soon pouring into Regina from all over the country, as communities from Halifax to Vancouver called upon their citizens to help stricken Regina. Donations came from the Saskatchewan Provincial government, the CPR, and the governor general of Canada. Moose Jaw, Regina's sinful sister, sent 10 doctors—and two undertakers.

It was in this aftermath of disaster, however, that things began to occur in Regina that once again had outsiders shaking their heads and saying, "Typical!"

The city had suffered some $6 million in damages and had hundreds of wounded. The number of dead would never be established to everyone's satisfaction. But it seemed that the financial loss mattered more to advertisers in Regina's newspapers than the human cost. After the saddest Dominion Day in Canada's history, with husbands and wives, parents and children still numb with grief, real estate companies were advertising business and residential lots in the devastated parts of town on "easy payment plans." The Regina Board of Trade placed a full-page ad in the *Winnipeg Free Press* boasting of their city as now being in "The Eyes of the World," a "Wonder City" and "The City of Destiny." It was, they said, a city in which to invest. And while these members of the moneyed elite were taking advantage of the disaster to boost Regina, they tried to stop issues of the local papers from being mailed out of town. They were concerned that stories about the actual extent of the tornado damage would hurt Regina's image abroad. They issued their own souvenir booklets—a dollar each—that glossed over the number of casualties. This led to confusion over the real death toll. The number of dead was "officially" placed at 28. But one city administrator claimed that 28 bodies were pulled out of *one* building. A *Toronto Star* correspondent wrote that there were 45 dead, and a Regina diarist named George Watt claimed 65. In the days following the tornado another 13 would die from their injuries.

In spite of the good works of many people and organizations who helped those whose lives had been shattered, tornado victims ran into official avarice. For those homeless people who didn't find shelter in the houses of kind-hearted Reginians whose homes were still intact, the city made room in Albert Public School, and the RCMP erected 250 tents in city parks. But the cots in those shelters cost refugees 25 cents a night. Moreover, the city presented each owner of a wrecked home with a hefty bill for having the ruins cleaned up and taken away. There were claims that the city was much more attentive to the wealthy who had suffered losses than to the poor.

Even with all the fundraisers and donations, Regina had to borrow $0.5 million, at steep interest rates, from the Saskatchewan government. Not until 1959 was that loan paid off. The interest pay-ments alone exceeded $1 million—twice the amount of the original loan. A woman from Regina's poor quarter said of the disaster:

> We know you can always get dollars and cents, but lives
> you can't. These rich folks who died, they must have
> made God angry. They must have provoked Him to wrath.
> We had lots of folks here who got so high up in the world,
> they thought they owned it. Yep, it takes something like
> this to bring them down equal.

An outsider might have been a little less philosophical, and just said, "Typical!"

The "Big Blow,"
Great Lakes, 1913

IN THE 19TH AND EARLY 20TH CENTURIES, saltwater sailors tended to have a condescending attitude toward freshwater sailors, the men who sailed the "Inland Seas" of the Great Lakes. *Real* sailors, sneered the men of the oceans, sailed the vast Seven Seas, not the freshwater "puddles" in the heart of North America. It was an unfair judgment, and one that the saltwater men quickly abandoned whenever they had occasion to sail the Lakes themselves. For the Great Lakes have always had their own particular dangers, and the thousands of wrecks that litter their bottoms are grim evidence of that fact. Storms blow up seemingly out of nowhere. Fog banks as thick as any along a seacoast roll in without warning. Iron-laden hills make magnetic compasses useless. Shifting winds and unpredictable currents test the most seasoned navigators.

Moreover, a ship caught in a storm on the ocean has thousands of square miles of open water in which to maneuver. Great Lakes vessels in similar circumstances have no such luxury. There is the danger of being dashed against a shoreline, an island, a reef, or some deadly hidden shoal. On each of the five Great Lakes there are areas that have deservedly been nicknamed "graveyard." One 19th-century skipper who had spent a lifetime sailing the Atlantic and had expressed scorn for his freshwater colleagues, admitted after a single day of battling Lake Ontario's tricky crosswinds that he had a whole new respect for the men who sailed the Lakes.

Storms can swoop down on the Great Lakes at any time during the navigation season, which lasts from spring thaw until winter freeze-up, but the very worst time of year is November. Cold Arctic air moves down, colliding with warm air masses and creating storms that turn the Lakes into foaming cauldrons. Blizzards cut visibility to zero, and ice coats everything above a vessel's waterline. "The witch of November," to use songwriter Gordon Lightfoot's metaphor, has claimed more ships and lives than any other hazard to Great Lakes shipping.

In the early 20th century there was one other factor—a man-made one—that put the lives of Great Lakes sailors in peril. That was the insistence of ship owners that their vessels make as many trips and haul as much cargo in the short navigation season as possible. Men who worked in safe, comfortable offices pressured captains to take risks. A ship's master who had a tendency to "heave to" and seek shelter every time bad weather threatened would find himself out of a job. When deadly November set in, the owners were especially adamant that their ships make "one more trip," no matter how foul the weather. Therefore, captains routinely ignored storm warnings.

To make matters worse, ship owners were notoriously tight-fisted when it came to spending money on their vessels to keep them safe and seaworthy. Lakeboat owners were not bound by regulations that applied to owners of ocean-going vessels. There were no laws against overloading lake freighters. Nor were the holds of the lakeboats divided into compartments by water-tight bulkheads, as they were on ocean freighters. There were only barriers of wire mesh to keep bulk cargo—usually grain or ore—from shifting.

All of these factors made commercial sailing on the Lakes a high-risk calling indeed. They were occupational hazards that were philosophically and grimly accepted. Ships sank, sailors died. But no one could have foreseen the disaster that would befall the ships of the Lakes in November 1913.

The first week of that November had been unseasonably warm. Nobody had to consult a meteorologist though, to know that it wouldn't last. Not that people paid much attention to what the weather forecasters said anyhow. Given the technology available to them in 1913, forecasters could at best make educated guesses. Since there was still no radio, information on weather conditions was passed along by telegraph. There was no way to communicate with ships out on the Lakes except by signal flags on shore.

It was not a question of *if* the November gales would come, but *when*. As was their seasonal custom, skippers up and down the Lakes were in a mad rush to get their ships loaded and under way, especially on Lake Superior, where the "big blows" always struck first. As those first November days passed, meteorologists were tracking an intense low-pressure system that was moving across the Canadian prairies from Alaska, and another that was rolling across the American plains from the Rocky Mountains. They predicted, quite accurately, that the two would collide over Lake Superior on November 7 and create a whopper of a storm. Subsequently, at Canadian and American ports from the Lakehead to the Soo, and on down to the St. Clair River the storm-warning signal was raised; a square red flag with a black square in the centre. Below it was a white pennant, which signified that the storm was coming out of the southwest. As was usually the case, Canadian and American skippers who saw the signal paid it little heed. Just another storm that they would have to ride out for a few hours. Ships already far out on the Lakes had no warning at all.

What *nobody* was counting on was a third low-pressure area advancing up through the Southern states from the Gulf of Mexico. This moisture-laden air mass would merge with the other two to create not a storm of a few hours' duration, but a five-day-long hell of 50-mile-an-hour (86.4 km) winds and blinding blizzards that would wreak havoc on land and water alike. It would cause sudden and diabolical shifts in wind direction, and throw captains the double whammy of winds coming from one direction and violently running seas from another. Those sailors fortunate enough to survive the carnage on the Lakes would remember it as the worst storm they had ever experienced. The Big Blow of 1913 would spawn legends and mysteries, and take scores of people to watery graves.

The dreadful fate of the luxury liner *Titanic*, which had gone down not quite a year and a half earlier, was very much on the minds of the passengers aboard the equally luxurious Canadian cruise ship *Huronic* when the first savage winds of the gale struck. The *Huronic*, downward bound on Lake Superior from Port Arthur (now part of Thunder Bay) to Sarnia, was carrying 50 passengers on a late-season, cut-rate cruise. Ironically, one of them had lost a relative on the *Titanic* and had only reluctantly agreed to accompany her granddaughter on the cruise. Over the next three days, the vacationers would get more than they had bargained for.

As Captain Malcom C. Cameron and his crew fought to keep the *Huronic*'s bow into the wind, waves pounded her hull with such ferocity that rivets popped out like bullets. Rigging wires snapped like elastic bands and the forward glass of the bridge exploded inward, exposing the captain and his officers to the shrieking wind and driving snow. A terrified woman asked the purser, "Sir, what is to happen to us?" The tactless man replied, "Madam, I fear that we are about to be drowned."

Probably realizing that panic among the passengers was the last thing the crew needed, the purser said a little later to another frightened woman, "The worst that will happen to you, dear lady, is that you may have some difficulty keeping your dinner down."

Wrapped in life jackets, the passengers all huddled together in the lounges, fearful that if they went to their cabins they might miss a call to the lifeboats. One man cried in dismay, "How could such a thing happen on a goddamn lake!"

By the time the *Huronic* limped into the relative safety of Whitefish Bay, she was battered from bow to stern, her pilot house had been demolished, and Captain Cameron was almost frozen to death. But the sturdy vessel and the veteran skipper had made it through a tempest of Biblical proportions without losing a passenger or a crew member. However, the exhausted captain had bad news to report when the *Huronic* docked at Sault Ste. Marie. He had seen a ship he believed to be the *Leafield* on the rocks at Angus Island, northwest of Isle Royale.

The *Leafield* was a 248 foot (75.5 m) ore and grain carrier that also carried steel railway rails on her deck. Half of her crew of 18, including Captain Charles Baker, were from Collingwood, Ontario. The *Leafield* was reputed to be an unlucky ship. Two of her sister ships in the Algoma Central Steamship fleet had sunk in previous years, and superstitious sailors believed that she was doomed to the same fate. Only a year earlier she had very nearly fulfilled the prediction when she tore her bottom out on a shoal. This time destiny caught up with her. The *Leafield* left the Canadian Soo for Port Arthur with a load of steel rails. She never arrived. A search was later made of the waters around Angus

Island, but no trace of the *Leafield* was ever found. The unlucky ship and all her men had simply been swallowed up by Lake Superior. The *Leafield* was the first Canadian ship to be lost in the Big Blow. More would follow.

Before moving down from Superior to ravage the other Great Lakes, the gale gave the crew of the 257 foot (78.3 m) Canadian freighter *Turret Chief* a horrifying ride. The ship was on her way from Midland to Fort William (now part of Thunder Bay) and was near Passage Island when the furies struck. Captain Tom Paddington and First Mate Joseph Phillips proved themselves to be woefully inadequate officers in the emergency.

The winds literally spun the *Turret Chief* around, and after a few hours in the storm the skipper had no idea where they were. He later testified that he knew only that they were being driven south. That meant that sooner or later they would have to strike the American shore—which they did. The *Turret Chief* ran aground on Michigan's rugged Keweenaw Peninsula.

The men easily scrambled ashore and made a rough camp. They shivered there for three miserable days before Captain Paddington decided that they had better find a settlement before they froze to death. They hiked along the shore, and by sheer good luck found that they had gone aground only six miles (9.6 km) from the town of Copper Harbor. Later, when the captain and first mate were asked why they hadn't adjusted their course to take the *Turret Chief* away from the American shore, they only shrugged.

The gale swept down into southern Ontario and the Great Lakes states. Cities and towns on both sides of the water became isolated as snow blocked roads and railroads. Telephone and telegraph lines broke down. There were blackouts as electric lines snapped. Communities ran short of coal, milk and food. Along waterfronts small boats were smashed to kindling. Wharves were ripped away, and with them went piles of merchandise awaiting shipping. Lakefront cottages and boathouses were swept away or pushed many feet inland from their original locations. In Chicago two men were drowned when the wind picked them up and tossed them into the Chicago River. Hospitals were overwhelmed with injuries from car accidents and other mishaps. Two men drowned trying to cross Lake St. Clair in a small boat. A train accident near Sarnia killed three more. Storm-related accidents killed five men in Cleveland. And just when the beleaguered citizens of both countries thought that the gale had blown itself out, it came roaring back with even greater intensity. For those unfortunate souls still out on the Lakes, the wail of the wind was a death knell.

At Kincardine, people watching the lake through binoculars saw distress flares fired by two unidentified ships. The tug *Onward* tried to go out to their assistance, but such was the violence of the storm that the little boat couldn't even clear the harbour. It was a valiant attempt, but not even the determination of heroes could prevail against the raw power of nature that day.

James McCutcheon was one man to whom fate had chosen to be kind, though he didn't know it as he fretted over missing his train. McCutcheon was first mate on the 250 foot (76.2 m) packet freighter *Wexford*. He had left the boat a few days earlier to visit some friends in Detroit. He planned to catch her at Sarnia but missed his train in Detroit. When he finally arrived in Port Huron—across the St. Clair River from Sarnia—he found that the boat had gone without him. McCutcheon was angry over his own tardiness. Missing his ship like that would result in a loss of pay and would not look good on his record. He was soon to discover that things could have been worse—much, much worse!

The *Wexford* had a young skipper, 26-year-old Captain Bruce Cameron of Collingwood, and a young crew. Only one of the 17 men aboard was over 30. One crew member was James Glenn, a homesick Scot who was making his last trip before returning to Scotland to bring his wife back to Canada.

While the *Wexford* loaded up with wheat in Fort William, Captain Cameron also picked up a couple of passengers, Murdoch and Donald McDonald, a pair of cousins from Goderich who needed a ride home. Murdoch had been working on another ship, but had become shore-bound by illness. Donald had been on a holiday but had to get back in time to start his new job as engineer on a train running between Guelph and Hamilton. The *Wexford* was bound for Goderich, and it was not uncommon for ship's officers to give a free ride to fellow lakemen in need. Cameron welcomed Murdoch and his cousin aboard. With her hold full, the *Wexford* sailed for Goderich. She almost made it.

The *Wexford* steamed down Lake Superior, passed through the Soo locks and into Lake Huron. On the morning of the 9th she was sighted by the steamer *Kaministiqua* about 40 miles (64.3 km) from Goderich. By that time the gale was raging over Lake Huron. At about two in the afternoon a resident of Goderich claimed to have heard a ship's whistle blowing out on the lake. The snow was blowing so thick that visibility was nil, and the wind was whipping the surface water a frothy white. The Goderich harbour foghorn should have been sounding, but it wasn't. The person responsible for that navigational aid did not turn it on until 11:00 PM. Asked later why he didn't turn it on earlier, he replied that he just didn't think of it.

It was never determined if the *Wexford* was the ship whose whistle had been heard on shore, but there was no doubt as to her fate. A few days later wreckage and bodies began to wash ashore. Among them were the homesick Scot, James Glenn, and the two McDonald cousins. Captain Bruce Cameron's body was never found, but ten days after the wreck, a board washed ashore near Goderich, with a message on it. "I am with the boat, lashed to the wheel.—B". The young captain had apparently gone down with his ship. Some of the dead who were washed ashore were identified by a badly shaken James McCutcheon, the first mate who had missed his train at Detroit.

One of the unsolved mysteries of the Great Lakes resulted from the dual loss of the Canadian freighter *Regina* and the American freighter *Charles S. Price*, one of eight American ships lost in the Big Blow. The *Regina* was a 269 foot (81.9 m) package freighter that hauled general merchandise up and down the lakes. Because of her shallow draft she could make calls at the smaller harbours that could not accommodate the big freighters. In November 1913 the *Regina*'s captain, Ed McConkey of Barrie, was completing his first season as a ship's skipper. Among the crew of 20 was Dave Lawson. He had recently signed aboard the *Regina* for just one voyage to Fort William, intending to go from there to Winnipeg. Then for some reason he changed his mind and decided to stay with the *Regina*. It was to be a fateful decision.

Missing from the crew was a man who, like James McCutcheon, had been handed a gift by the gods, though he hardly would have thought so at the time. Three weeks earlier George Gosby had fallen into the cargo hold and broken his leg. "Just my luck!" he moaned. "I break a leg and miss the rest of the season." It would turn out to be the most fortunate accident he could possibly have suffered.

Early Sunday morning, November 9, the *Regina* sailed out of Sarnia with stops scheduled at several ports along the Canadian shores of Lake Huron and Lake Superior. In her hold were thousands of cases of canned goods. She was also carrying on deck a heavy load of steel sewer and gas pipes. Added to the deck cargo was 140 tons of baled hay, which was covered with tarpaulins. One observer on the Sarnia dock later said that the deck cargo looked dangerous and that the *Regina* appeared top-heavy.

Hours passed, and the storm that everyone thought would blow itself out in a few hours steadily increased in violence. At about 1:30 PM the captain of the *H.B. Hawgood* sighted the *Regina* on Lake Huron about 15 miles south of Harbour Beach. He reported that she had "seas breaking over her." The estimated velocity of the winds on Lake Huron that afternoon was almost 70 mph (112.6 km). Waves were said to have reached an astonishing 35 feet (10.6 m). The *Hawgood* sighting was the last anyone ever saw of the *Regina*.

Investigators later theorized that Captain McConkey probably attempted to turn around and run for the safety of the St. Clair River, and was caught in a trough. The top-heavy ship foundered and sank. The wreck of the *Regina* has never been located. When one of the owners of the lost freighter was asked where he thought she might have gone down, he replied, "The whereabouts of the *Regina* will forever be a mystery."

That was not the only mystery connected with the *Regina* tragedy. At the same time that the little Canadian freighter was fighting her losing battle with Lake Huron and the gale, the 524 foot (159.7 m) American freighter *Charles S. Price* was in an equally perilous situation. The *Price*, her hold full of coal, had left the St. Clair River and entered Lake Huron sometime after the

Regina. She, too, was seen by the captain of the *Hawgood*. Quite likely the *Price*'s skipper, Captain William A. Black of Cleveland, tried to turn the big ship about when he realized just how ferocious the gale was. The ship was no doubt rolling dangerously on the heavy seas, and her cargo of coal shifted. Suddenly the *Charles S. Price* capsized, drowning all of her crew of 28. Tons of coal crashed through the deck, forming a black mountain on the bottom of the lake.

For several days the *Price* drifted upside-down on Lake Huron, with only the bottom of her hull visible above the waves. Sailors spotted the capsized wreck soon after the storm, and for many days she was referred to as "the mystery ship" by the press, because no one was sure which of several lost vessels the derelict might be. A diver was finally able to go down and read the name on her bow. Eventually she sank, joining the remains of countless other victims of Lake Huron on the murky bottom. But that was not the end of the string of mysteries.

Days after the big storm, bodies and debris began washing up on Lake Huron's Canadian shore at Thetford, Kincardine and Goderich. There were cases of canned fruit and vegetables that scavengers quickly swooped down on and carried off. Some of these looters did not stop at helping themselves to beached cargo. They went through the pockets of drowned sailors, stealing money and other valuables. This was not only a despicable crime—undoubtedly committed by wretches who were not from the port communities—but it also made identification of the dead all the more difficult because wallets were missing from pockets.

Dead men from several ships littered that stretch of shoreline. Most had been drowned. A lifeboat held the bodies of five who had died from exposure; one of them David Lawson, whose last thought might have been regret that he hadn't gone to Winnipeg. Another victim was Second Mate Robert Rowan of the American freighter *Argus*. Rowan was a native of Kincardine who had moved to the United States. His corpse was found on the beach not far from his family's lakeside property. It was as though, in death, he had come home.

Bodies from the *Regina* and the *Charles S. Price* were mixed together. A story circulated that men who were known to have been aboard the *Price* were wearing life jackets from the *Regina*. If this were so, just what had happened out there on the storm-tossed lake? Had the ships collided in the gale, with men scrambling from one doomed vessel to the other? Or had the *Regina* come upon men from the *Price* already struggling in the water, and being unable to stop to pick them up, tossed them life jackets in a desperate but hopeless gesture? No one from either ship survived to tell the story, and the question has puzzled Great Lakes historians for over 90 years.

John Thompson of Hamilton was another sailor who would have good reason to thank his lucky stars. He made a spur-of-the-moment decision that saved his life, and then turned his good fortune into a cruel prank. Thompson had been working on the freighter *James C. Carruthers*, a 550 foot (167.6 m), brand-new steel ship. A berth on the *Carruthers* would have been the envy of just about any Canadian sailor on the Lakes, but for some reason he could not explain, Thompson left the gleaming giant and signed aboard an old scow hauling coal on Lake Ontario. He hesitated to inform his family that he had changed ships, fearing that his father would disapprove of such an irrational move.

The *James C. Carruthers* was dubbed the "All-Wright Boat" because her skipper was Captain William Wright and one of her managers was A.A. Wright. She was making but her third voyage when on Saturday, November 8, she cleared the Soo locks and the St. Marys River, and steamed onto Lake Huron, downward bound for Midland with a cargo of grain. In the narrow St. Marys passage the *Carruthers* had passed the upward-bound *Midland Prince*. Wheelsman Angus McMillan spotted his friend Jack Daley on the *Prince* and called out to him, "We're going to Midland this time, Jack. I'll tell your father we passed you." Daley waved to Angus in acknowledgement, not knowing that he was waving a final farewell.

Captain Wright had taken the *Carruthers* through the horrendous gale on Lake Superior and the new ship had stood up well. While passing through the Soo he had commented to somebody that he doubted they would ever see a storm like that again. Considering the rough time they'd had, he was probably glad that his wife, who had originally planned on accompanying him, had stayed home. He expected to see her in Port Colborne in a few days.

At De Tour, Michigan, the *Carruthers* took on a load of bunker coal. The operation was supervised by First Mate Bill Lediard. He expected to be given the command of the *Carruthers'* yet-unnamed sister ship, then under construction at Collingwood. For that reason he had shaved off his moustache. Captain Wright sported a bushy moustache, and Lediard did not want to appear to be a copy of the older skipper.

With her bunkers full, the *Carruthers* steamed out into Lake Huron, heading for Georgian Bay. Somewhere on the storm-ravaged lake the big, new ship was probably caught in a trough and slammed broadside by mountainous seas. The *Carruthers* was never seen again. A few days later the bodies of some of her crew began washing up around Point Clark, south of Kincardine. Captain Wright was easily identified by his grand moustache and his initialed ring. Bill Lediard was more difficult to identify, because those who knew him had not seen him clean-shaven in ten years.

Fifty-six bodies from Canadian and American ships were found on the Ontario shore, and several factors frustrated accurate identification. Some faces had been badly disfigured by water and ice. A few had identification stolen by looters. Many freshwater sailors were drifters who just went by names like Mac, Blackie, or Slim; not even their shipmates knew their real identities. Shipping companies were very casual about keeping crew lists, and sometimes were not sure exactly who was on their boats. And there was always that matter of men hitching free rides, with no documentation of it. As a result of all this, some bodies never were identified, and in that grim November there was one terrible case of mistaken identity.

One of the dead men found near Goderich bore an incredible resemblance to John Thompson, the sailor who had not told his family that he had left the *Carruthers* for another ship. The body now lying in a Goderich morgue had similar (though battered) facial features, the same missing teeth, the same scars, even the same tattoo. Only the hair colour was different. Thompson's was dark brown, and that of the deceased was light brown. But an undertaker said that could have been caused by several days in the water.

Informed that the *Carruthers* had been lost with all hands, and believing that his son had been aboard the ship, Thomas Thompson, John's father, went to Goderich and mistakenly identified the body as that of his boy. He took it back to Hamilton, where John's grief-stricken mother and sister awaited.

Meanwhile, John Thompson was in Toronto. There he read in a newspaper about the *Carruthers* tragedy, and saw his name in the list of the dead. Instead of immediately telegraphing his family that he was alive and well, the young fool decided it would be "a really good joke" to let his loved ones think he was dead, and then surprise them.

When Thompson stepped off the train in Hamilton, his look-alike was lying in a coffin in the parlour of the Thompson house, surrounded by floral wreaths and mourners. His father had purchased a burial plot and arranged for a funeral mass. Instead of going directly home, young Thompson went to a bar to have a beer with the proprietor, his friend Ed Duffy. The stunned bartender, once he got over the shock of seeing a "ghost," told Thompson that he had better get home right away.

Thomas Thompson fainted when he answered a knock at the door and saw the son whom he'd thought was dead. When John's mother came to see what was happening, she, too, collapsed. When all the excitement over the young man's "resurrection" had settled down, the old couple were overjoyed that he was alive. But there was anger and embarrassment, too. "It's just like you to come back to attend your own wake," Thomas told the callous youth. The stranger in the coffin was sent back to Goderich, where he was buried along with five other unidentified men in graves without names.

The killer storm was not finished after sinking the *Carruthers*. It roared across Lake Erie and sank the *United States Lightship Number 82*, sending her six-man crew to their deaths. By the time the storm howled onto Lake Ontario, skippers were aware of its true severity and had kept their vessels in safe harbours. One ship, the *A.E. McInstry*, ran aground near Brighton, but with no casualties.

The Big Blow had sunk four Canadian ships and eight American ships on Lakes Superior, Michigan, Huron and Erie. Twenty-five other vessels had been driven aground or onto reefs. Between 250 and 300 mariners were dead. Communities like Collingwood, hometown to so many of the lost, were plunged into mourning. Americans made the sad journey to Ontario to see if their missing relatives were among the pitiful few the waters had given up.

As the funeral bells tolled and the astronomical financial losses were tallied, the hunt began for scapegoats. Ship owners and captains held the United States Weather Bureau and the Dominion Meteorological Department responsible, claiming that they had not properly warned anyone of the storm. But the weather experts pointed out, quite accurately, that the storm-warning signals had been flying at ports all around the Lakes, but that the captains, as was their wont, had ignored them. The real culprits, the weather experts said, were the ship owners who, for the sake of profits, discouraged captains from taking appropriate measures when bad weather threatened. The most seasoned skippers agreed that nobody could have predicted the unheard-of severity of that hellish storm. As was inscribed on a marker erected to the memory of the dead, "gales of cyclonic fury made man and his machines helpless."

The Newfoundland Sealing Disaster, 1914

B Y 1914 THE ANNUAL NEWFOUNDLAND seal hunt was more than 100 years old. Every spring men and boys from the outports would converge on St. John's, hoping to get a berth on one of the ships heading out "to the ice" where the migrating harp seals gave birth to their pups. It was the pups that the hunters were after. There was a great world demand for their pelts and for their fat, which was rendered into a fine oil. The "swiles," as the Newfoundlanders called them, were regarded as a vital source of income.

The Newfoundland economy was firmly in the grip of the wealthy merchant families of St. John's. This small clique ruled the island like robber barons, controlling almost every aspect of life in the city and in the outports. They determined what they would pay a fisherman for his cod, and what the fisherman had to pay for the supplies his family needed. The system was based mainly on credit, and the fisherman always came out on the short end—forever in debt to the merchants. The one chance the fisherman had to earn a little hard cash, perhaps as much as $50, was the seal hunt.

Hunting seals was one of the most dangerous jobs in the world. Sailing out on the North Atlantic amidst fields of ice was extremely hazardous to begin with. Getting off the ship to walk across those treacherous, heaving, groaning, booming ice pans was practically inviting the chill hand of death. Indeed, over 1,000

Newfoundlanders died in the seal hunts over the decades. Many a ship that cleared St. John's harbour to go to the ice never returned.

If the natural conditions of the hunt weren't bad enough, the ship owners and many of the captains did their utmost to make them worse. Profit mattered much more than the well-being, or even the lives, of the men. Many of the ships were leaky old tubs bought for a song. If such a ship returned to port with a hold full of pelts, it meant a huge return on a small investment. If she went to the bottom, it was of little consequence. As for the drowned men, they knew the risks when they signed on.

Conditions aboard the ships were appalling. The crews' quarters were filthy and cramped. The men lived on a diet of hardtack biscuits and tea. Medical facilities were practically non-existent. No special clothing was provided to protect the men from the murderous cold. They were dressed in the rough, well-worn cotton and sealskin garments they showed up in. Even the drinking water, stored with no consideration for sanitation, quickly became foul. For the use of his "crop," the tools needed for the hunt, a man had a deduction taken from his meager share of the profits.

Nonetheless, to the outport men a successful hunt was the stuff of song and legend. The most successful sealing captains were national heroes. For young Newfoundlanders the seal hunt was a rite of passage. A boy sailed away on his first trip to the ice, and a man returned.

The senior captain of the sealing fleet preparing to sail in March 1914 was Abraham Kean, known to one and all as Captain Abe. He was as hard and ruthless a ship's master as ever walked a bridge. A staunch Methodist, sanctimonious teetotaller and iron-willed slave driver, Captain Abe was a self-made man who had risen from the ranks of the outport fishermen. He was as powerful ashore as he was aboard ship, having been a Cabinet minister in the Newfoundland government—a position one did not achieve without the help of friends in high places. Kean was a man crossed at one's own peril.

Captain Abe had little regard for the illiterate, superstitious men from the outports. He did not believe in "pampering" his crew. Good food and comfortable quarters would make the men soft and lazy, he said. As if the conditions on board a sealing vessel were not already Spartan enough, Kean would gut the ship of every scrap of furniture and equipment he did not consider essential to the voyage.

But as fearsome a skipper as Captain Abe was, he had a reputation for finding the big seal herds and for bringing back record numbers of pelts. He had even set a record in taking a ship out and bringing her back with a full hold in a mere 11 days. To any tough fisherman from the outports, the promise of a tidy reward at the end of such a voyage was worth a couple of weeks under Captain Abe's harsh command. This season, though, Captain Abraham Kean's narrow, unbending policies would play a key role in a disaster.

The men of the Newfoundland outports were strong believers in fate. If a man lived to a ripe old age, that was the will of God. But if he were marked for an early death, nothing could save him. It was a way of dealing with the fear that was always in the back of a man's mind when he boarded a ship; the fear that he might not return home. The basic philosophy was that one would not die until one's time had come.

But until that time came, a human being was entitled to a degree of dignity. Such was the belief of William Coaker, the leader of the Fishermen's Protective Union. Coaker was the bane of the St. John's merchants and captains like Abraham Kean. With thousands of impoverished fishermen behind him, he had fought tooth and nail to improve the outport men's lot. One of his targets was the notorious treatment of men on the sealing ships. He had managed to press the government into passing the *Sealing Bill*, which required the provision of decent food, proper cooking facilities and experienced cooks on the ships. This year Coaker was going out with the fleet himself, on the *Nascopie*, to see that the new regulation was observed. As it turned out, only on that ship was the law obeyed.

One skipper who dismissed the new law was Westbury Kean, 29-year-old son of Captain Abe, in charge of the *Newfoundland*, a wooden steamer that was over 40 years old. Wes had been to the ice before, but his experience was limited. He did not even have a master's certificate, and so had to have Captain Charles Green aboard as navigating officer to comply with maritime law. Captain Green was a veteran seaman, but young Wes had no intention of taking advice from him. Captain Abe himself had warned Green not to interfere with his son's command.

The men of the *Newfoundland* would get hardtack and tea. There was, of course, better fare for the officers, as well as a cook to prepare it. When they got to the killing grounds the men would have seal meat, but without a galley for their use, they would have to cook their meals in the hold in little coal stoves called "bogies." When the hold filled up with pelts so that even this space was denied them, they would eat the meat raw. If the hunt proved successful, every bit of space, including the crew's bunks, would be used for the storage of pelts. This meant that the men would sleep on top of the stacks of bloody, greasy, smelly sealskins.

The *Newfoundland* had no deck thermometer. Even more important, she had no wireless. Her owners had taken it out, considering it an unnecessary expense. Every other ship in the fleet had a wireless. What the *Newfoundland* did have on board as she cleared harbour on March 12 were two stowaways—young men who had been unable to obtain berths but were anxious to join the hunt anyway. When they were found, an angry Wes Kean put them to work shovelling coal in the stoke-hole. Other men grumbled. Stowaways were bad luck.

Among the *Newfoundland*'s crew were Reuben Crewe, 49, and his son Albert John. Reuben had barely escaped with his life on a sealing expedition three years earlier when his ship sank. He had sworn never to go to the ice again. But 16-year-old Albert John was determined to go "swilin'" for the first time, and Reuben thought it best that he go along and look after his son.

Another crew member was young John Howlett. A few weeks before leaving his home to go to St. John's, Howlett had suffered a terrible nightmare in which he was freezing to death alone on a mountain of ice. Upon awakening he had been deeply disturbed by the dream but then had dismissed it.

Also making their first trip to the ice were teenaged cousins Cecil, Art and Ralph Mouland with a group of other boys from their town. Cecil had been given some practical advice by his grandfather. The old veteran had told him that if he ever got caught out on the ice, he should chew on something to keep his face from getting frostbitten. Cecil did not expect to get caught out on the ice, but as a precaution he kept some plugs of chewing tobacco on him.

On the sealing ships the first mate was called the second hand. The *Newfoundland*'s second hand was George Tuff, 32, a veteran sealer and a survivor of the *Greenland* disaster. Sixteen years earlier, in the very waters the *Newfoundland* would be visiting, the *Greenland* had encountered a series of horrendous mishaps and had returned to St. John's with 25 dead men on deck and 23 missing. It was a grim introduction to sealing for young Tuff, but he had developed into a reliable second hand. The Keans thought highly of him. But Tuff, like everyone else, had a fear of Captain Abe.

Captain Wes Kean ran into trouble right from the start. Bad ice conditions forced him into harbour and he wasn't able to sail for the icefields until Friday 13th, another ill omen. Then the *Newfoundland* became ice-bound and couldn't move. The men found few seals, but at least had a little meat to make a stew. As they ate, the younger men spoke of the disaster that had befallen the *Greenland*. The older men scowled. It was bad luck to talk of death aboard ship.

While the *Newfoundland* was grinding her way in an almost futile attempt to get through the ice, other ships were having better luck. One was the *Stephano*, a steel-hulled steamer commanded by Old Abe himself. As always, Captain Kean had found seals, and his men were busy killing, skinning and loading the pelts on board. The ice and snow around them were red with blood, as were the men themselves. The air was filled with the barks and squeals of the adult seals and their pups. The ice pans were littered with skinned carcasses. The sealers took the flippers, which were considered a delicacy. Most of the meat was left for scavengers.

Other ships were also "in the fat" as sealers called it when they found a herd. Having "cleaned up" one batch of seals and skinned their kills, the men would mark the pile of pelts with their ship's banner and trek across the ice to another group. This in itself was perilous, because the ice was not smooth, like the surface of a frozen pond. It was a tortuous gauntlet of ridges and clefts that could, in an instant, bring down the strongest, most careful man and leave him with broken bones and torn flesh. And in their haste to pile up the profits, the ships' masters did not allow the men time to be careful. Nor would they hurry back to St. John's just because a man was critically injured.

While the men worked their way through the seals on an ice pan, their ship could be miles away, dropping off or picking up other groups of hunters. It was not unusual for a party of men to be left out all night, with just some torches and a fire fed by seal fat to ward off the cold. It was also not unusual for a captain coming across a pan of sealskins belonging to another ship to simply cast away the owner's banner and steal the pelts. Captain Abe, in fact, was notorious for it. His Methodist piety did not get in the way of avarice. No one, of course, would dare to confront him on the matter.

Peering through his glass from his lookout on the *Newfoundland*, Wes Kean could see the men from other ships "in the fat." Men from steel ships like his father's; not old, wooden tubs like the *Newfoundland*. Those steel ships could slice through the ice with ease, reaping the harvest, while he—a Kean with a name to live up to—sat stewing. He had but a few hundred pelts in his hold. His crew should be out there where the swiles were thick, taking the "whiteheads" (pups) by the thousands. Another few days and the young seals would be big enough to take to the water. Then the season would be over.

While Captain Wes fumed and stewed, hundreds of miles to the south a storm was brewing. It was moving north, and by the time it hit the seas off Newfoundland it would have grown into one of the worst blasts of cold, snow and fury Nature had ever thrown against the Rock.

On the morning of March 31 Wes Kean told his men to go out on the ice and walk to the *Stephano*, about six miles (9.6 km) away. There they were to take their orders from his father. Second Hand George Tuff volunteered to lead them, though as a ship's officer he was not obliged to go out on the ice. Over the side of the ship went 166 men. They were divided into four groups, each under the command of a master watch. A master watch had authority only out on the ice, and on this occasion the four master watches were subordinate to George Tuff. As Tuff left Wes Kean's cabin, the captain told him that he and his men were to stay the night on the *Stephano*. Evidently, Tuff did not hear him. But Robert Green did.

The weather was clear and calm as the long column of men started out across some of the worst ice the veterans had ever encountered. Robert Green, however, had misgivings. Reflections of light called "sun hounds" were showing in the sky. They were considered a bad omen. But Wes Kean trusted in his barometer, an old one that had not been checked in years. It read "Fair." But Green wished they had a deck thermometer.

The men carried their "gaffs"—the long poles used to kill the seals—as well as their other hunting gear, ropes and heavy flag poles for marking their pans of sealskins. Each master watch was supposed to have a compass, but one, Arthur Mouland (no relation to Cecil, Art and Ralph) had forgotten his. George Tuff didn't have one either.

Since the day promised to be relatively warm, many of the men left their heavy coats on their bunks. Indeed, as they struggled over ridges of pressure ice, some of them stripped to the waist. They blazed their trail by having two men who had been working in the stoke-hole blacken ice peaks with soot from their mitts. Meanwhile, 100 miles (160 km) to the south, St. John's was getting the first snowflakes of what would be the worst storm of the year.

The going was rough, and some of the men dropped their flag-poles. They came across a small family of seals that yielded six pelts. By now there were definite signs of bad weather in the sky, and some of the men demanded that they return to the *Newfoundland*. There were heated words and the accusation of "cowards." Finally, 34 men turned around and started back. There might have been more, but there were a few men who chose to remain with brothers or friends.

At about 11:00 AM the *Newfoundland* men passed one of the *Stephano*'s flags. The sky was now full of storm signs and the sealers looked forward to getting aboard the *Stephano*. They reached it at about 11:20, just as a light snowfall began. All were certain that they would spend the night aboard the beautiful steel ship, or that Captain Abe would take them back to the *Newfoundland*. The *Stephano*'s steel prow would make short work of the ice it had taken them four hours to cross.

But Abraham Kean didn't have time to waste on the *Newfoundland* men. He had his own hunting parties to pick up, as well as pans of sealskins. The *Stephano* was moving as the men approached and barely slowed down for them to get aboard. They had to run alongside and grab hold of her ladders. Once they were aboard Kean gave them some hardtack and tea (a few didn't get their tea because there weren't enough cups to go around). Then he told Tuff that he would drop them at a place where they could get at a herd of 1,500 swiles. His orders were that they were to kill seals, then return to their own ship. The weather was fine, he said. Just a little snowfall that would soon blow over. They still had plenty of hours of daylight and, in fact, said Captain Abe, he was letting them off just three miles (4.8 km) from the *Newfoundland*. (There was later to be much controversy over this, as many men believed Kean had taken them farther away from the *Newfoundland*, not closer to her.)

George Tuff was concerned about the weather, but Wes Kean had told him to take his orders from the Old Man. Captain Abe said that the weather was fine, and *no one* argued with Abraham Kean. At 11:50, a scarce half hour after they'd boarded the *Stephano*, the *Newfoundland* men were back on the ice. So great was his haste to get back to his own men, and especially his pelts, that Kean very nearly ran them down.

As they left the ship, most of the men thought that Captain Abe would be coming back for them. They were stunned when Tuff said that they were to kill seals and then return to the *Newfoundland*. Dissention broke out again. Didn't Captain Kean know there was a storm coming? Some men wanted to start back for the *Newfoundland* immediately. They just *might* make it before the storm hit! They certainly didn't have time to kill seals. George Tuff wavered a bit, then put his foot down. Captain Abe had ordered them to kill seals, and by God that's what they were going to do. John Howlett—he of the nightmare about a frozen death—actually tried to strike Tuff, but other men held him back. Mutiny was a serious offence.

The men reluctantly set off for the herd that Kean had told Tuff about. He had said to use a flag he'd left on an ice pan as a directional guide. There were actually *two* flags out there, causing Tuff to inadvertently lead his men *away* from the *Newfoundland*.

The sealers found a small herd and fell to the work of slaughter, but all the while the dissenters argued that they should be getting back to the *Newfoundland*, which they couldn't even see now. The snow fell more heavily, and the wind blew harder. Finally Tuff relented and said they were going back to the ship. The sealers formed a long line—132 men—with Master Watch Tom Dawson in the lead and Tuff taking the rear to make sure no one fell behind. Everything was now in place for a catastrophe.

Back on the *Newfoundland* Wes Kean was furious with the 34 men who had returned to the ship. He had seen the rest of his crew board the *Stephano*, which had then sailed out of sight. He assumed they were all aboard her right now. It angered him that there would be 34 fewer men from his ship killing seals in the morning.

All around the ice pack ships were picking up their men as the weather deteriorated. Wes's brother, Captain Joe Kean of the *Florizel*, had seen the *Newfoundland* men on the ice earlier in the day, and wondered if they were safe. He wired his father aboard the *Stephano*. Captain Abe assured him that they were aboard their own ship. But other men on the *Stephano* weren't sure. They grumbled among themselves that the Old Man should not have put those men back on the ice with a storm coming. They felt that instead of cruising around the pans picking up piles of pelts, as they were doing now, they ought to be looking for the *Newfoundland* men. But no one would raise the matter with Captain Abe. Joe Kean wished that the *Newfoundland* had wireless.

Out on the vast icefield, with no ship in sight, the men walked and stumbled across the ice pans and climbed over the pressure ridges. The cold, black water of the ocean lapped the edges of the ice at places where they had to step from one pan to another, and if a pan dipped under their weight, the men's feet got soaked. Wet snow blew into the faces of the tired sealers. Their pace was painfully slow.

Tuff called a halt and divided the men into two columns, one to walk parallel to the other. He thought they would make better time that way. There was confusion over who should go with which group. A veteran sealer named Jesse Collins muttered prophetically, "The *Greenland* disaster will be nothing compared to this one."

They were looking for the path they had made on the journey out from the *Newfoundland*; a trail marked by discarded flagpoles and sooty ice peaks. But the wind and the movement of the water combined to turn the pans around, making the path increasingly difficult to follow. They kept losing it and used up precious time finding it again. The men at the heads of the columns had to break trail through the newly fallen snow and were getting exhausted. George Tuff did not rotate the men to relieve them. It must be remembered that on a ship or on the ice, the senior officer's word was law.

A man named William Pear began to lag behind. He was not an experienced sealer and lacked the stamina of the others. His thick glasses became coated with snow, blinding him. But if he took them off, he was almost sightless.

Tuff called another halt so that Pear could catch up. Then he sent five or six men ahead to find the *Newfoundland* and bring back help. When the columns started forward again, Pear could not walk without assistance.

On the *Newfoundland* Bo'sun John Tizzard was worried. It was customary for a ship's whistle to be blown at regular intervals during a storm, just in case anyone was lost out on the ice. No one was blowing the *Newfoundland*'s whistle. Tizzard went to Wes and asked if he should blow the whistle. Kean said it wasn't necessary, because his men were on the *Stephano*. Then he told the bo'sun to give it "a blow or two" if he liked. Tizzard did exactly as the captain ordered. He blew the whistle once. Then 15 minutes later he blew it again. Two blows were all that Wes had authorized.

Out on the ice the cold hand of death touched its first victim. Young Art Mouland fell into the water. His cousin Cecil and another man hauled him back onto the ice, but the teenager was soaked to the skin. Shivering and in shock, he began to fall behind. Not until later did anyone notice that he was missing. He was never seen again.

Up ahead, the advance party found evidence that the *Newfoundland* was near: discarded flagpoles and a pile of rubbish from the ship. Then, through the howling blizzard they heard a ship's whistle. It was the *Newfoundland*! But in the storm they could not tell from which direction the sound had come. Arthur Mouland cursed himself for forgetting his compass. The men shouted, but their voices were lost on the wind. Fifteen minutes later they heard the whistle again. If only it would keep blowing, they could locate the ship. But that second, tantalizing blast was followed by silence, save for the shriek of the gale.

Their shouts brought George Tuff and the others hurrying to them. Tuff thought that they had found the ship. The news that they hadn't was crushing. Tuff had to admit that they were lost. If the *Newfoundland* were but half a mile away, in that blizzard it might just as well be 100 miles. Darkness was falling, and they would have to spend the night out on the ice. Many of them thought longingly of the warm coats they had left on the ship.

The men divided into three groups, there being too many of them to stay on one pan. Master Watch Arthur Mouland put his men to work building a "shelter"; a wall of ice and snow 30 feet (9.1 m) long and over 6 feet (1.8 m) high. Then he made them build wings on each end. This structure would give them some protection from the wind, but that was all. The men were dead tired and numb with cold, but Mouland drove them. Even so, not everyone helped with the work. The men on the other pans also built shelters but not as complete as the one Mouland bullied his men into constructing. They would regret it before the night was over.

Huddled in the shelter of their ice walls, the men tried making fires with wood shavings from their gaffs, but the little campfires soon burned out. Men who had worked on the shelters quarrelled with those who hadn't lifted a finger to help. The wind kept shifting, and only Mouland's men had some degree of protection. Then Nature dealt her cruellest blow. The snow turned to rain, thoroughly drenching everybody. Then the rain became sleet as the temperature dropped to 14°F (–10°C). With the wind chill it was more like –22°F (–30°C). Captain Wes Kean's barometer still read "Fair."

Jesse Collins made up his mind that he was going to get himself and as many men as he could out of this icy hell alive. He told men to get moving, to dance, to march; *anything* to keep the blood flowing. When men wouldn't move, he shook and prodded them until they did. He made men repeatedly go through the motions of jigging for cod, as though they were out in their dories. When men had their eyes frozen shut because of ice in their lashes, Collins chewed the ice off, freezing his own lips in the process. If a man lay down on the ice from exhaustion, Collins hauled him to his feet, yelling "Up, b'y! Up!"

Cecil Mouland remembered his grandfather's advice and chewed tobacco to prevent his face from freezing. Cecil had a girl-friend back home whom he intended to marry. Keeping her in mind, he told himself that he would not die. He was determined to keep his young cousin Ralph alive, too. Not far from Cecil, a sealer named Edward Tippett sat with his arms wrapped protectively around his two sons, Abel and Norman. Some men prayed and sang hymns, but if any god was listening, he did not see fit to relieve their suffering.

Instead, the storm intensified as a killing Arctic gale came sweeping down from the north. In spite of the efforts of heroic Jesse Collins, men dropped to the ice and did not get up again. One man fell off the ice pan into the water. His companions pulled him out, but within minutes he was dead.

By dawn William Pear was dead. So were many others. Edward Tippett was sitting upright, his frozen arms lovingly embracing the frozen bodies of his sons. Arthur Mouland's pan had fared best with only two dead. The other pans were littered with corpses. Still the storm raged. The passing of the night did not mean that death was finished with the men of the *Newfoundland*.

Men aboard the *Stephano* grumbled. They were certain that the *Newfoundland*'s crew had been left out on the ice, in spite of Captain Abe's insistence that they were on their own ship. But still no one had the nerve to contradict the Old Man. On the

Newfoundland Wes Kean felt that the ice had loosened up enough for him to break free and sail over to the *Stephano* to pick up his men. But as the old steamer was about to get under way, her steering chains broke.

Hunger pangs added to the misery of the lost men. Those who still had some hard tack shared it with the others. Some stumbled around, looking for better shelter. Deep snow made the going difficult. Where the ice was open and clear, the wind blew men across it like rag dolls. A few mistook a layer of snow for solid ice and went through into the water.

To have any chance of staying alive, a man had to stay on his feet and keep moving. To lie down and sleep was to die, and many did just that. Those still alive were certain that the whole sealing fleet must be searching for them, that rescue was at hand if they could just hold on a little longer. On frozen limbs they walked around and around, stepping over the bodies of their shipmates. When Ralph Mouland tried to lie down, Cecil told him, "You keep movin', b'y." He gave Ralph a piece of hardtack, but the boy didn't have the strength to bite it. Cecil chewed a morsel himself, then put it in Ralph's mouth. The tiny bit of nourishment gave Ralph the will to go on for at least a little longer.

But it was hard! So, so hard! Reuben Crewe, the man who had broken his pledge to never go to the ice again because he had to look after his son, now lay down on the pan with Albert John. They died in each other's arms. John Howlett stayed on his feet. If he fell asleep, he'd fall and be jarred awake. Then he'd get back up. The man's will to survive was unbreakable.

Some of the men took clothing from the dead to add to their own. Others couldn't bring themselves to do it. Bitter accusations were directed at George Tuff. The second hand wept and said it was Captain Abe Kean's fault. Arthur Mouland again pushed the men to build shelters. He was sure they'd be rescued before dark, but making the men work kept them moving.

At that moment Captain Abe was worried about the piles of sealskins still out of the ice, pelts he couldn't get to because of the bad weather. He might lose them altogether, and Abraham Kean hated to lose a dollar.

The hopes of the stranded survivors suddenly skyrocketed when they saw the sealing ship *Bellaventure* coming toward them. She was far off, but weaving her way through the ice pans in their direction. Rescue at last!

But no one on the steamer saw the men, over 2 miles (3.2 km) away and almost invisible against the background of ice and water, with the wind still blowing snow. The *Bellaventure* turned around and sailed away. With her went the last shred of hope for many of the *Newfoundland* men. They simply dropped to the ice and died.

Then George Tuff thought he saw smoke from the *Newfoundland*. He and several others started walking in that direction, hoping to find their ship and send back help. They were sure that the *Newfoundland* was still stuck in the ice. But by this time Wes Kean had repaired his steering gear and was free enough from the ice to sail to within 2 miles (3.2 km) of the *Stephano*. He still expected to pick up his men from her. With the *Newfoundland* still heartbreakingly beyond reach, Tuff and his companions returned to what was left of the main group. Night was falling again.

The first night on the ice had been hell for the lost men. Now they were about to descend into the lowest depths of the human soul's worst nightmare. They were freezing and starving. Their

bodies and minds begged for sleep to which they could not suc-
cumb if they wanted to live, and for one after another the will to
live was dead and gone. A man could not move without stumbling
over the corpse of a relative or a friend. Men lost their reason, hal-
lucinated, heard the voices of wives and children. A few stepped
off the ice pans and into the oblivion of the sea. Some knelt in
prayer, and froze to death there on their knees. One man cut his
arm so he could drink his own warm blood. There were men who
lay down to die, and men who died where they stood. Master
Watch Tom Dawson, his legs and feet frozen solid, lay on the ice
and went to sleep. John Howlett covered him with corpses to protect him from the wind. Off in the distance, those whose vision
had not been impaired by cold, exhaustion and near insanity could
see the lights of a ship. Nine men decided that despite the dangers
of walking across the ice at night, they would try to reach her.
They all perished.

Even the valiant Jesse Collins seemed to have reached the limit
of his endurance. "We can't live through this night, Josh," he said
to a friend, and then fell to his knees. But a few minutes later he
was back on his feet, moving amongst the other men, encouraging
them not to give up.

Cecil Mouland had visions of the *Newfoundland* coming to
their rescue. He shouted to his cousin, "Ralph! There's our ship!
There's the *Newfoundland*!" Ralph looked, and he saw the ship,
too. Then in a blink the vision was gone, and there was nothing
but the ice and the cold blackness of night.

On the morning of April 2, George Tuff, Arthur Mouland and
a few others decided to try once more for the *Newfoundland*. As
they struggled across the ice the weaker members of the party fell
behind. Those who could continue on came at last within sight of

the ship. She appeared to be frozen in again. The pitiful human wrecks on the ice only hoped that this time she would stay put. They couldn't raise a shout. They could just keep staggering and crawling and hope someone saw them.

At the other side of the icefield the *Bellaventure* hove into the sight of a decimated flock of survivors. It was plain that the watch on that ship could not see the stranded men, so Jesse Collins and a man named Ben Piercey set out to try to get their attention.

It was Wes Kean himself who first spotted the gaunt figures lurching across the ice. He sent a party of men to get them, and soon George Tuff and Arthur Mouland were aboard the *Newfoundland*, telling the awful tale. Wes hoisted a distress signal to alert the *Stephano*, whose wireless operator would send the message to the other ships. By the time the news reached the *Bellaventure*, Jesse Collins and Ben Piercey were already aboard her.

The *Bellaventure* was nearest to the cluster of survivors, so her skipper, Captain Robert Randell, sent men across the ice with food, rum and stretchers. They could get there faster than the ship, which had to ram its way through heavy ice. What the crew of the *Bellaventure* found was appalling!

The dead were everywhere, frozen as solid as the ice they lay upon, in grotesque, life-like poses. Legs frozen in mid-stride as though walking. Hands frozen in prayer. Arms embracing a son or a brother, or reaching out toward heaven-knew-what! Those who were still alive ranted, wept, babbled like madmen. The toughest men who had ever trod the deck of a ship looked upon the scene, then broke down and cried.

On the *Newfoundland* Wes Kean heard the story: that Captain Abe had put the men on the ice when a storm was brewing. "Oh my!" he sobbed. "What has Father done?" Too distraught to carry on, he handed command of the *Newfoundland* over to Charles Green.

The men from the *Bellaventure* built fires and poured rum into the survivors. Some of the stricken men died in the arms of their rescuers. Of those who lived, many would be crippled for life. As the gaunt forms were placed on stretchers and taken aboard the *Bellaventure*, crews from the *Stephano* and the *Florizel* combed the ice field for bodies and any survivors who might have wandered off. In all, 55 men were rescued, one of whom would die later in hospital. Seventy-seven had died on the ice. The bodies of all but eight were recovered.

News of the disaster was sent by wireless to St. John's, stunning the Newfoundland capital. The *Bellaventure* was on her way home with the survivors and the dead, but the city was further stunned to learn that the ship owners had left to the captains the decision of whether or not to continue the hunt. William Coaker on board the *Nascapie* called this "heartlessness in the extreme." The ship owners told him, "Don't interfere." Abraham Kean was one of those captains who chose to continue the hunt. He did not head back to St. John's until April 8!

St. John's was a city in mourning as the *Bellaventure* steamed into harbour with her sad cargo. The survivors, Cecil and Ralph Mouland and John Howlett among them, were carried to hospital. Tom Dawson had made it, too. The bodies Howlett had piled on him as he slept had saved him. Now these men experienced the agony of flesh that has been frozen and then thawed.

An official inquiry into the disaster found Wes Kean innocent of any wrongdoing. Captain Abraham Kean was self-righteousness personified when he took the stand. He had done far more than his duty, he said. He had fed his son's crew and placed them near a herd of seals at a spot only 3 miles (4.8 km) from their ship. There was no indication of a coming storm, he insisted (though the testimony of other men said otherwise). Captain Abe said that he had acted "with the very best motive and the very best intention."

Much of Kean's testimony was contradicted by other witnesses, and there was considerable confusion over distances and specific times involved. But in the end the captain's bluster won out and he was acquitted. It was judged that the calamity was "an Act of God."

The people of St. John's, however, held Captain Abraham Kean morally responsible for the deaths of 78 men. They demonstrated in the streets, and 6,000 citizens signed a petition to have him charged with criminal negligence. But it all came to nought.

In March 1915 Captain Abe was given command of the *Florizel* for that spring's trip to the ice. Hundreds of sealing men converged in the street to prevent him from boarding the ship. Kean boldly walked through the crowd. Neither hand nor voice was raised against him. He continued to hunt seals for another 20 years. In 1934 he was awarded the Order of the British Empire for being the most successful seal hunter of them all.

Nobody thought of bringing charges against the ship owners who courted disaster by sending men into harm's way ill equipped and so poorly provided for. The widows and orphans of the dead men received but a pittance in compensation. But for those who, out of economic need, continued to risk their lives at the ice every spring, conditions would improve. Every ship had to have a wireless and a wireless operator. Ships' officers had to be certified. No

The *Empress of Ireland*: Unlucky Lady

MENTION THE WORDS "SEA DISASTER" and the first image that comes to mind for most people is that of the *Titanic*, going down after striking an iceberg in the North Atlantic on her maiden voyage in 1912. The "unsinkable" ship took 1,513 people to their deaths. Others might immediately think of the *Lusitania*, torpedoed by a German submarine off the coast of Ireland in 1915. That tragedy cost 1,198 lives. The sinkings of those two liners have been the subject of documentary films, books and movies. Yet, in the time between those catastrophes, there was a Canadian maritime disaster equally horrendous, which has been largely forgotten.

The *Empress of Ireland* and her sister ship the *Empress of Britain* were the pride of the Canadian Pacific Railway, which had commissioned both ships for passenger service in 1906. The *Empress of Ireland*, 14,191 gross tons, 570 feet (174.1 m) in length, and 65.6 feet (19.9 m) in the beam, was just slightly larger than the *Empress of Britain*. But the latter was a little more luxuriously fitted out. The *Britain* made the regular run between Liverpool and New York, and therefore was more likely to carry passengers with celebrity status, while the *Ireland* made the less glamorous trip between Liverpool and Quebec City.

Still, the *Empress of Ireland* lived up to the name "floating palace," for first-class passengers anyhow, and for eight years she faithfully plied the North Atlantic, earning a reputation as a fine, fast, reliable ocean liner. Literary giant Rudyard Kipling was aboard for her maiden voyage, and in July 1913 she participated in the Mersey Royal Review, presided over by King George V and Queen Mary.

However, it could be that the *Empress of Ireland* carried the seed of her ultimate demise right from the beginning. According to maritime lore, it is bad luck to change a ship's name. It had originally been planned to call the ship the *Empress of Austria*, but at some point the name was changed.

Or it could be that a curse boarded the *Empress* in the form of the man who was her skipper the night she met her untimely fate.

In 1910 Henry Kendall was captain of the Canadian Pacific Steamer *Montrose*. On a voyage from Britain to Canada, the sharp-eyed skipper spotted among his passengers the notorious dentist, Dr. Hawley Crippen, wanted by police in England for murdering and dismembering his wife. Crippen was travelling with his mistress, who was disguised as a boy, the pair passing themselves off as father and son. But Captain Kendall thought there was something decidedly girlish about the "boy." It was his wireless message to Scotland Yard that led to Crippen's arrest at Father Point, Quebec, when the *Montrose* stopped to pick up a pilot for the last leg of the voyage up the St. Lawrence. Before Crippen was taken away by police, he glared at Kendall and said, "You will suffer for this treachery, sir." Crippen was shipped back to England and executed, but not even the hangman could dispatch a murderer's curse.

On May 28, 1914, the *Empress of Ireland* sailed out of the harbour of Quebec City, downward bound on the mighty St. Lawrence River for the open sea. Strangely, just as the vessel was about to cast off, the ship's mascot, a cat named Emmy, leaped off the ship to the dock. The animal had made the crossing many times, and was abandoning a litter of kittens, but nothing could induce her to get back on board before the gangplank was raised.

All was festive aboard the *Empress* as she moved out into the river at about 4:30 PM. Among the 1,067 passengers were 170 members of the Salvation Army, on their way to a convention in London. Amid all the fanfare of the departure, their band— looking for all the world like Mounties in their scarlet coats and stetson hats—played "Auld Lang Syne," "O Canada," and, ominously, "God Be with You Till We Meet Again."

The *Empress* actually had some celebrities aboard for this trip. The popular English actor Laurence Irving and his actress wife Mabel Hackney were returning to Britain after a triumphant Canadian tour. The famed big-game hunter, Sir Henry Seton-Karr was also going home to England after a successful stay in Canada. In British Columbia he had bagged several fine specimens to add to his trophy room. In one of the most expensive staterooms was Ethel Sabina Grundy Paton of Sherbrooke, Quebec. She was the diamond-loving, socialite wife of one of the wealthiest men in the province. Ethel was just paying a little social call to London and Paris. Also enjoying elegant, VIP accommodations were 60-year-old Major Henry Herbert Lyman, president of a Montreal pharmaceutical wholesale firm, and his young bride. They were off on a European honeymoon.

Down in the bowels of the ship, hurling coal into the fire that kept the vessel's powerful steam engines roaring, was a man for whom celebrity had come and gone. Former boxer Ted Fitchett, on a downward slide after having been one of the best-known names in the ring, was working his way back to England, where he hoped to make a comeback.

In comfortable, if not ostentatious, surroundings in Second Class were Louise Gallagher of Winnipeg and her 19-year-old son Cedric, known to family and friends as "Ritchie." Young Gallagher had just completed his second year as a medical student at the University of Manitoba, and his mother was taking him on a holiday to Germany as a reward.

Second class was full of Salvationists. In one cabin were David Rees, Commander of the Canadian Salvation Army, and his wife and three children. In another was Eddy Dodd, editor of the Salvation Army's publication *War Cry*. He was going to write a series of articles about the trip under the column heading "Travel Jottings." He would mail the first installment at Rimouski, Quebec, when the *Empress* sent ashore the French Canadian river-pilot who had guided her down from Quebec City.

Also among the Salvation Army contingent were Teddy Gray, an editorial cartoonist for the *Toronto Star*, who had made his will and taken out a $2,000 life insurance policy before embarking. And there were Salvationists George and Hattie Attwell. George wrote in his diary that evening, "It looks as if we are going to have an excellent journey. Everything seems favourable."

By far the greatest number of passengers were in third class on the lower decks. These were working-class people like Abe and Pearl Cohen, recently of Toronto, but now going home to London where they intended to open a fish and chip shop. Pearl was expecting, and wanted her baby to be born in England. Of the 148 children on the *Empress of Ireland* that May day, all but a few were far down in the warrens of third class.

Presiding over all from the bridge was Captain Henry Kendall. The 6 foot (1.8 m), 39-year-old Kendall was a veteran of the North Atlantic crossing and had tasted a little celebrity himself after his part in the capture of Dr. Crippen; his name and picture had been in all the newspapers.

It had been four years since the now-dead murderer had uttered his dire threat, and Kendall had no reason to believe that anything would ever come of it. He had a fine record, as did the ship he commanded. A million dollars worth of silver bars, now secure in the ship's vault, had been entrusted to his safekeeping. Lessons had been learned after the *Titanic* disaster two years earlier, and the *Empress of Ireland* had enough lifeboats for all of the passengers and crew. In the unlikely event of an accident, her watertight bulkheads could be closed quickly, sealing off any stricken part of the vessel. Kendall had put the crew through a tough lifeboat drill at Quebec City, and they had responded admirably.

On the evening of May 28, first class passengers in the ship's ornate dining salon listened to a five-piece orchestra play "The Funeral March of a Marionette" as they enjoyed their supper. A 17-year old steward from Lancashire named Billy Boy Hughes, a lad with an infectious sense of humour, advised social butterfly Ethel Sabina Grundy Paton and Great White Hunter Sir Henry Seton-Karr not to eat too much or they'd get seasick and miss out on breakfast. Down in second class, some of the Salvation Army passengers were playing a game called "Dead Man," in which a man tried to fall down while those encircled around him tried to keep him upright. Irony seemed to be playing a morbid game that knew no class distinctions. At 1:20 AM, May 29, the *Empress* let the pilot off at Father Point, then proceeded downriver to her appointment with destiny.

Heading upriver for Montreal was the Norwegian freighter *Storstad*. She was carrying a full load of Cape Breton coal and moving at top speed, which meant that she was cutting through the water like a sharp-prowed ram. Her skipper, Captain Thomas Andersen, had gone to bed, leaving the bridge in the hands of First Mate Alfred Toftenes. The mate had instructions to wake the captain if he encountered fog.

At about 1:50 Captain Kendall saw the *Storstad* off to the starboard. At the same time First Mate Toftenes saw the big liner off his port bow. The two ships had plenty of room to pass each other. Then a thick fog that is peculiar to the St. Lawrence in spring; a fog created when the warm air meets the cold water, suddenly enveloped both vessels. Disregarding the orders he'd been given, Toftenes did not immediately call his captain.

No one is certain just what happened next, because there was so much conflicting testimony at the subsequent inquiry. But it seems that both vessels, in maneuvering to give each other wide berth, actually put themselves on a collision course. Uncertain where the freighter was in the dense fog, Captain Kendall ordered a full stop and blew the ship's whistle. The *Storstad* responded with a blast of her own, and it sounded to Kendall that the freighter was well off to the starboard. But fog can distort sound, and the *Storstad* was in fact bearing right down on him.

Only now did First Mate Toftenes call Captain Andersen through the speaking tube. He said it was getting hazy, and did not mention the big liner he had seen just before the fog rolled in. He had ordered a sharp turn to the starboard, assuming that the big ship had turned to port. When Captain Andersen reached the bridge, the first thing he saw was the hull of the giant *Empress of Ireland* looming out of the fog, only 800 feet (243.8 m) away. He immediately ordered "Full speed astern!" But it was too late. The *Storstad*'s momentum, powered by tons of coal in her hold, carried her forward like a torpedo.

When Captain Kendall saw the masts of the collier coming toward him through the fog, he instantly ordered a hard turn to starboard. He hoped that he could swing his ship around so that the other vessel would miss the *Empress* altogether, or just glance off the side. But this maneuvre, too, was too late.

The impact, when it came, was surprisingly gentle. This was because, as one chronicler put it, the bow of the *Storstad* "had gone between the liner's steel ribs as smoothly as an assassin's knife." It tore a hole both above and below the waterline, 23 feet high and 16 feet wide (7 by 5 m). The *Storstad* backed out, and water poured into the great ship.

Captain Kendall tried to make a run for the shore to beach the *Empress*, but the ship's boilers exploded, killing stokers like Ted Fitchett. Tons of water poured into the ship's belly through the gaping hole. Then as the *Empress* began to list, it rushed in through portholes that, contrary to regulations, had been left open. Ronald Ferguson, the ship's wireless operator, managed to get out one distress call before the electricity was knocked out. With no power, the watertight bulkhead doors could not be closed. The lower decks were quickly submerged, and few of the souls trapped down there in the darkness had any chance to escape. On the bridge Chief Steward Augustus Gaade said to Captain Kendall, "Well, this looks to be about the finish, sir."

"Yes," Kendall replied, "and a terrible finish it is."

The ship was already listing so badly that getting lifeboats away was almost impossible. The crew succeeded in getting only four of them into the water. Some of the lifeboats broke free from their davits and crashed down onto the mass of shrieking people on the deck below.

On the *Storstad*, Captain Andersen's wife, who had accompanied him on this voyage, hurried to the bridge. She thought that the freighter was sinking and wanted to be at her husband's side. But though the *Storstad* had damage to her bow, she was not taking in any water. Captain Andersen had his ship's four lifeboats lowered to start picking up survivors.

On the *Empress of Ireland* death was reaping a grim harvest. Of the 717 passengers in third class, 584 died. In second class, 205 out of 253 perished. In first class, 51 out of 87 were killed. Some were trapped in the ship and drowned; others died of exposure when the ship keeled over on her side and they were hurled into the frigid water.

Yet, there were acts of heroism and gallantry amidst the pathos. Sir Henry Seton-Karr forcibly put his own lifebelt onto a man who didn't have one. He went back to his cabin, possibly to get another belt, and was never seen again.

Survivor F.E. Abbott of Toronto was the last person to see the actor Laurence Irving and his wife alive. Irving's face was bloody from a fall he'd taken when the ship lurched, and he was trying to console the weeping Mabel. He put a lifebelt on her and carried her up the stairs to the deck. Abbott later said, "I said, 'Can I help you?' And Irving said, 'Look after yourself first, old man. But God bless you all the same.' I dived overboard, and I clung like grim death to a deck chair. I looked back, and saw two figures on the sinking deck. Irving was kissing his wife as the ship went down, and they were clasped in each other's arms."

When Irving's body was found, a piece of Mabel's nightdress was still clutched in his hand.

Many of those who had been in bed when the collision happened escaped stark naked. One was Dr. James F. Grant, the ship's doctor. He managed to squeeze out through his cabin's porthole, and found himself on the side of the ship with hundreds of other people. As the ship rolled, people would slide off the hull and into the St. Lawrence. Grant was taken in a lifeboat to the *Storstad*. When he had recovered somewhat from shock and the cold, he asked for a pair of pants so he could tend to the injured.

Wireless operator Ronald Ferguson was another who arrived on the *Storstad* in shock and without a stitch of clothing. He was walking to the engine room to get warm, when he encountered Mrs. Andersen. He said later, "She said something in Norwegian that sounded sympathetic, and took off her long blue scarf and gave it to me. I tied it around my neck and carried on."

Captain Andersen's wife was one of the heroines of that terrible night. She tended to people who were injured and in shock, giving them whiskey, Benedictine and coffee. She tore up tablecloths, curtains and her own petticoats to make bandages and provide the naked with simple covering.

It was a night, too, for the bizarre. When a steward told Ethel Sabina Grundy Paton that the ship was sinking and she'd better get up on deck if she wanted to live, the darling of society first put on her finest dress and her diamonds. She took along a little sewing bag with her spare glasses and her nail scissors. She went out on deck and stepped right into a lifeboat without so much as getting her feet wet. Aboard the *Storstad* she pitched right in, helping Mrs. Andersen with those survivors whose condition was more desperate. When Ethel saw eight-year-old Florence Barbour naked and shivering, she used her nail scissors to cut holes in a pillow case to make a smock for the girl. Florence was one of only four children aboard the *Empress* to survive. She had lost both her parents and had made it to safety by clinging to the back of Robert Crellin of British Columbia as he swam away from the sinking ship. Crellin and his wife later adopted the orphaned child.

Salvation Army bandsman Herbert Booth Greenway later recalled that when the ship lurched, he was thrown right into a gentleman wearing an ornate dressing gown. Greenway gasped, "Excuse me, sir. I'm awfully sorry. I slipped."

The man replied, "Oh, that's jolly well all right. Accidents will happen, old chap." Then the man in the gorgeous dressing gown dived into the water and disappeared.

After the collision, Richie Gallagher and his mother made it to the promenade deck, and saw that their only chance was to jump and swim for it. Louise Gallagher put her wedding ring on her finger. Then, hand in hand, mother and son jumped from the doomed ship. By freakish bad luck, Louise's neck became ensnared in broken rigging swaying from the mainmast. Her hand was torn away from Ritchie's, and she was dragged down with the sinking ship. "Poor Mother was swallowed up," a grief-stricken young Gallagher said later as he assisted Dr. Grant with the half-frozen survivors on the *Storstad.*

Abe Cohen and his pregnant wife had also decided to jump together. But before they could make their leap, an explosion hurled them apart. Abe, who survived, heard Pearl's last words: "Oh God! Save me for the sake of my unborn son!"

Steward Billy Boy Hughes found himself on deck in the clutches of a half-dressed teenaged girl who was in hysterics. She had him by the throat, her fingernails digging into the flesh, while she screamed wildly. Suddenly they were both in the water and the girl let go. He never saw her again. Billy swam through corpse-strewn water until he saw a lifeboat full of people. He caught hold of a rope hanging over the side and cried, "Please, pull me in."

A big man sitting near him tried to push Billy off, growling, "Go away! No room! No room!"

At that a ship's officer stood up and barked, "I'm in charge of this boat! And you're a murderer. I sentence you to death!" He struck the big man with an oar, knocking him over the side. Then he had Billy pulled in. The big man disappeared beneath the black water.

For several long minutes it seemed that the capsized ship would remain afloat. Then suddenly the stern rose slightly, and the *Empress of Ireland* slid beneath the surface, taking with her many of those who'd been perched on the side of the hull, waiting to be picked up by lifeboats. It had been but 14 minutes since the collision.

When the *Empress* lurched over onto her side, Captain Kendall was thrown from the flying bridge into the open water. He was picked up by a lifeboat, of which he immediately took command. Kendall delivered about 50 shivering survivors to the *Storstad*, many of them naked and almost dead from shock and exposure. On the *Storstad* Captain Kendall told Dr. Grant, "Doctor, there is only one thing that I am sorry for...that they did not let me drown."

Then Kendall got back into the lifeboat to search for more survivors. The tugboat *Eureka* and the Canadian government ship *Lady Evelyn* had responded to the distress signal from the *Empress of Ireland*, but most of the people they were fishing out of the cold, dark waters were dead.

Back on the *Storstad* Captain Kendall angrily confronted Captain Andersen. "You have sunk my ship!" he charged. "You were going full speed, and in that dense fog!" Andersen argued that it was the liner that had been at fault.

While the two skippers exchanged the first of what would be many verbal broadsides in the debate over who was responsible for the accident, the shattered remnants of the crew and passengers were taken to Rimouski. There the kind-hearted people of the town took them into their houses, providing food, warmth and clothing. The count of the dead would reach 1,012. Fate, as always, had been capricious in determining who would live or die.

George and Hattie Attwell jumped hand in hand from the ship, and survived. Major Henry Herbert Lyman and his young bride perished. There was a child who survived by floating on the body of her drowned father, and a man who clung to a corpse being buoyed by a lifebelt. There was no such twisted gift from the gods for Eddy Dodd, Teddy Gray, or David Reese and his wife and three children.

Tom Greenaway and his wife Margaret had become separated in the chaos on the stricken *Empress*, and each thought the other dead. They were reunited in a house in Rimouski, where Tom found Margaret in bed, badly burned but alive.

The chief investigator of the tragedy was Lord Mersey, who had conducted the investigation into the sinking of the *Titanic*. At the hearing that was held in Quebec City in June, most of the blame fell on First Mate Toftenes for being neglectful in carrying out his duties. But a later inquiry held in Norway found the captain of the *Empress of Ireland* at fault. When Sir Arthur Conan Doyle, creator of Sherlock Holmes, visited Montreal on a lecture tour, he was asked if he could solve the mystery of just what had happened out on the fog-shrouded river. (People frequently asked the author of detective fiction to unravel real-life mysteries.) Doyle said that he was as baffled by it as anyone else.

In England, author Joseph Conrad was asked to write an article about the accident for the *Illustrated London News*. He wrote, "It seems to me that the resentful sea gods never do sleep, and as long as men will travel on the water, the sea gods will take their toll."

The Quebec courts seized the *Storstad*, and the ship was sold to partially compensate Canadian Pacific for the loss of the *Empress of Ireland*. There was no compensation for the survivors or for the families of the dead, aside from a fund set up in England, which received contributions from, among others, King George V, the Prince of Wales and English stage actor Sir Herbert Tree.

Within weeks the world sank into the cataclysm of what would be called the Great War. Men died by the tens of thousands in the trenches. Scarcely a year after the *Empress of Ireland* disaster, the *Lusitania* was ambushed and sunk, providing a huge anti-German propaganda opportunity for the British. The tragedy on the St. Lawrence faded from the public mind, if not from the memories and nightmares of those who had survived it

The hulk of the once regal *Empress of Ireland* now lies in 170 feet (51.8 m) of water at the bottom of the St. Lawrence River. A salvage crew recovered her treasure of silver bars, and today scuba divers visit the wreck. It is still a tomb for the bones of many of those hapless souls who, on a May night in 1914, had the bad fortune to be aboard an *Empress* whose luck had run out.

The Parliament Building Fire, Ottawa, 1916

IT WAS CONSIDERED THE FINEST "pile" of Gothic architecture in North America. Canada's Parliament Building, rising in all its grandeur from a hilltop 150 feet (45.7 m) above the Ottawa River, was more than just an impressive sandstone structure housing the federal government. It represented the very founding of the Dominion of Canada, and the growth of the nation as new provinces joined Confederation's original four: Ontario, Quebec, New Brunswick and Nova Scotia. Ottawa (formerly Bytown) had been selected as the new capital by Queen Victoria. The cornerstone had been laid on September 1, 1860, on what would become known as Parliament Hill, by the Prince of Wales, later Edward VII. Here, though the building was not yet completed, the first Canadian Parliament under Prime Minister John A. Macdonald sat in 1867. Lying before the Speaker of the House in all its regal splendour was the House of Commons mace. This symbol of the power of the democratically elected representatives of the people already had a colourful history behind it. In 1849, when rioters set fire to the Legislative Building in Montreal (then the capital of the United Province of Canada), the mace was stolen. It was soon recovered, though in a somewhat damaged condition.

The imposing building, which was the pride of the young nation, was 472 (143.8 m) feet long. In 1878 a great iron crown on its tower was completed, and a clock added a year later. Called the Victoria Tower, the structure was 252 feet (76.8 m) high, and a great favourite with tourists who climbed the winding staircase to enjoy the spectacular view. At night, the crown glittered with lights.

The principal room in the Parliament Building was the House of Commons, 88 feet (26.8 m) long and 47 feet (14 m) wide. From that chamber came the laws and policies that steered the course of the nation. In that room Canadian leaders had squabbled, and spoken with eloquence. Its walls had echoed the voices of Sir John A. Macdonald, Sir Wilfrid Laurier and the silver-tongued Thomas D'Arcy McGee.

The Senate Chamber, though of lesser political importance than the Commons, was of equal dimensions. It, too, had a mace and a Speaker. Behind both chambers were suites of apartments for the families of the two Speakers. There were also apartments for such Parliamentary officers as the Sergeant-at-Arms for the Commons, and the Gentleman Usher of the Black Rod of the Senate. The latter was (and still is today) the official who carried the Black Rod, an ebony cane that was the symbol of his authority. He presided over certain ceremonial events, and was responsible for security in the Senate. The original Black Rod was Canada's oldest piece of Parliamentary regalia.

For Canadians in 1916, the Parliament served one other extremely vital function. The world was embroiled in the unprecedented havoc of what would be called the Great War. The massive stone structure on Parliament Hill was the nerve centre of Canada's huge war effort. Decisions were made there that affected not only the soldiers fighting in the trenches of France, but also every household in the country.

On the evening of February 3, 1916, the House was in session. Newly appointed Deputy Speaker Edgar N. Rhodes was in the Chair as the members discussed ways to improve the marketing of

Canadian fish. At about 8:45 Prime Minister Sir Robert Borden was in his office catching up on some correspondence. The Leader of the Opposition, former Prime Minister Sir Wilfrid Laurier, was attending a concert. The Governor General, the Duke of Connaught, was at his official residence. In the apartment of the Speaker of the Commons, Albert Sevigny, his wife was entertaining three guests: Mme. Florence Bray of Montreal, Mme. Mabel Morin of St. Joseph-de-Beauce and Mme. H. Dussault of Quebec City. The women were enjoying their own little piano concert— one that was to be cut short.

In the Reading Room of the House of Commons, Member of Parliament Francis S. Glass was reading a newspaper while a few other MPs came and went. The Reading Room was at the back of the Centre Block and adjacent to the Library of Parliament. It was 70 feet (21.3 m) by 36 feet (10.9 m) and contained six large, wooden reading desks. All of the walls, the ceiling and the shelves were made of white pine. The shelves, which went all around the room, were stacked with newspapers, magazines and books. As everywhere else in the building, the furniture and fittings were well-shellacked and polished.

Shortly before 9:00 Glass was startled when Mme. Verville, wife of an MP from Quebec, suddenly ran from the room. As he looked around to see what had frightened her, Glass felt a wave of hot air. He saw that a fire was burning on a shelf under one of the desks. Glass did not panic. This was not the first time there had been a small fire in the Parliament Building. There had, in fact, been 13 of them between 1913 and 1916; the most recent one only two days earlier. They had all been quickly and easily extinguished by Dominion Police, who were responsible for security. The 14th would prove to be the unlucky one.

Glass called Constable Thomas S. Moore, who was on guard duty outside the Reading Room. Moore grabbed a fire extinguisher and aimed it at the flames, which were now consuming the desk itself. However, instead of smothering the blaze, the force of the spray from the extinguisher scattered the flaming papers around, igniting other stacks of paper. Soon flames were racing along the varnished shelves and walls. Two more constables dragged in a fire hose and tried to douse the fire, but it was already too big and moving too fast. The Reading Room was filling up with thick, black smoke. The men had to retreat, with the inferno right behind them. "The fire fairly chased us," Constable Moore said later.

The Parliament Building had a fire alarm connection with the fire department, plenty of extinguishers and a reservoir of water atop one of the towers that fed the building's fire hoses through gravity. But there was no sprinkler system and there were too few fire escapes. The windows had been recently painted, making them difficult to open. As a wartime security measure, all exits but one were kept locked. The interior of the building was a devil's delight of dry, well-oiled and polished wood. Even the ventilation system created currents of air in the Reading Room and the Commons that would cause a fire to burn all the more fiercely.

While the constables were fighting their losing battle in the Reading Room, Francis Glass and two other men, one of them Mederic Martin who was both MP and Mayor of Montreal, ran to spread the alarm. One of them—just who would be disputed—alerted M.C.R. Steward, Chief Doorkeeper of the House of Commons. At 9:00 Steward burst into the Commons and interrupted the session when he shouted, "There is a big fire in the Reading Room! Everybody get out quickly!" Steward later wrote a letter of apology for the sudden disruption.

The Deputy Speaker and the MPs rose and quickly headed for the exits. They hadn't even completely evacuated the inner sanctum, when the fire roared in. It had no regard for the hallowed memories within that room. Fire danced among the chairs that had seated Canada's greatest statesmen. It swept up the walls toward the galleries. There had been but a few spectators there, and a group of soldiers on guard duty. Three of the soldiers were almost immediately overcome with smoke and had to be dragged out by their comrades.

Some of the Members ran straight for the main exit, but others dashed for a door that opened into a corridor near the Conservative headquarters. It was locked. Edward Nesbitt smashed a pane of glass with his bare hand, cutting himself badly, but smoke poured in. The men joined hands so no one would be lost in the black cloud, and stumbled through the Chamber to the main exit. One was knocked over by a jet of water as someone tried vainly to fight the flames with a fire hose. The men made it to the outside, but some had been burned and all were choking from smoke inhalation. William Loggie of New Brunswick, who scant minutes before had been addressing the House, was barely conscious.

One of the last to get out was Clarence Jameson of Nova Scotia. He had heard a loud noise and then was thrown down the corridor by a blast of hot air. It was the result of the roof caving in. Jameson luckily escaped with only singed eyebrows and moustache.

Arthur R. Ford, a Toronto newspaper reporter, was in the press gallery when the alarm was spread. He ran to the press room to alert other newspapermen, most of whom had been less than thrilled at the assignment of covering a dull debate over fish-marketing. When Ford told them there was a fire, some of them thought he was joking. They changed their minds when they saw the haste with which he stuffed papers into his pockets. The reporters quickly abandoned the press room. Some got out through the front exit. Others went out windows and dropped 18 feet (5.4 m) into a snowbank. Fate had placed them on the scene to report on something much more sensational, and tragic, than the selling of fish.

Prime Minister Borden was still in his office when he heard shouts. Then a House messenger ran in and blurted the unbelievable news: the Parliament Building was on fire! Borden didn't even waste a moment to grab his coat and hat. He and the messenger hurried to a messenger's stairway. The prime minister had to crawl on his hands and knees to get under the thick, deadly smoke. When he reached the outside and the bitterly cold February air, an MP lent him a coat. The PM lost no time in arranging an emergency meeting of his Cabinet in the Chateau Laurier.

The automatic alarm went off in Ottawa's Number 8 Firehall at 8:57, and within three minutes the first firemen were on the scene. There was a great roar as the roof caved in and a pillar of fire 20 feet (6 m) in diameter and 100 feet (30.4 m) high shot into the night sky. Many people would swear that they heard the sounds of explosions coming from within the maelstrom. This was no doubt the sound of gases erupting. The Centre Block was clearly beyond saving, though firemen blasted tons of water at it. They had to concentrate on stopping the flames from spreading to other wings, and especially to the Library, which contained priceless and irreplaceable documents. And they had to get people out!

Fortunately, librarian Connolly MacCorman had possessed the presence of mind to close the fireproof iron doors between the

Parliament Building and the Library as soon as he realized there was a fire in the Reading Room. A new threat arose when flaming debris set the Library roof afire, but Fire Chief John W. Graham spotted it, and his men quickly put it out. For once, fortune was with them, as a switch in the direction of the breeze carried the sparks and embers southward, away from the Library.

While the Ottawa firemen battled the blaze, a call was put through to Montreal, where arrangements were hastily made for a special train of firemen and equipment in case their assistance should be required. Soldiers were quickly dispatched to the scene of the disaster. Colonel John A. Currie, with the help of some police officers and MPs, fought to save the Senate Chamber. Using hose connected to the emergency reservoir, they at least held the flames at bay long enough for some valuable relics to be saved. The Senate mace was carried out by police with an escort of soldiers. The Senate Speaker's chair and some of the Senators' chairs were also rescued.

One of the most valuable items saved from destruction was a portrait of a young Queen Victoria painted by the English artist John Partridge. Remarkably, this same painting had survived the 1849 riot and fire in Montreal. The art rescuers were also successful in taking out priceless portraits of King George III and Queen Charlotte. Unfortunately, smoke and fire gained mastery of the Senate Chamber before they could save portraits of King Edward VII and Queen Alexandra, and King George V and Queen Mary.

While crowds of people gathered outside the flaming capital building—among them Sir Wilfrid Laurier and the Governor General of Canada—inside, people were fighting for their lives. Some would succeed. Others would not.

Two MPs from Saskatchewan, Dr. Edward L. Cash and Thomas MacNutt, were in the men's washroom and were not aware of the fire. "I had not been in there three minutes when I opened the door and could see a mass of flames at the other end of the corridor," MacNutt said later. There was no chance of escape that way, so the two men made a rope of towels and hung it out the window. Cash went first, and had to drop 20 feet (6 m) into a courtyard that was already six inches deep in water from the fire hoses. Before MacNutt could follow, a French Canadian care-taker burst into the washroom in desperate search of escape. MacNutt helped him down the rope ladder while Cash found a ladder to spare them that 20 foot (6 m) drop. "This is how we got out," MacNutt said. "I never saw anything like it."

Albert Sevigny, the Speaker of the House of Commons, was not in the Chamber when the fire broke out, his place being filled by the deputy speaker. He was in his office dictating letters. When he heard the alarm, Sevigny ran upstairs to his apartment where his wife was entertaining Mme. Morin, Mme. Bray, and Mme. Dussault. He shouted for everyone to get out, and grabbed his five-year-old daughter Madeleine. One of the children's nurses picked up the Sevigny's ten-month-old baby. Another nurse was cut by flying glass as a window shattered. The family, their guests and servants were on their way down the stairs to safety when, astonishingly, one of the visitors said, "Wait a minute! Let's get our furs." Mme. Bray and Mme. Morin turned back!

Mme. Sevigny tried to stop them, but they ignored her. They were determined to rescue their precious fur coats, which were probably already being devoured by the flames. When Albert got outside and realized that the two women were not with them, he put his child down and went back. But he was overcome by smoke and had to be rescued himself by a fireman. Two firemen ran a ladder up to a window of the Sevignys' apartment in an attempt to get to the women. One of them collapsed from smoke inhalation and had to be carried down the ladder by his partner. Later, when the bodies of Florence Bray and Mabel Morin were found, they were clasped in each other's arms. Their hair and clothing were burned, but it was the smoke that had killed them. A nearby window had been broken and there was blood on the glass. Cuts on the dead women's hands told the story. They had tried desperately to open the newly painted window. Both women left behind husbands and children. Costly fur coats indeed!

The third guest of the Sevignys', Mme. Dussault, had not accompanied the rest of the group in their flight down the stairs. She had instead run into the master bedroom. Trapped by the smoke and flames, she climbed out the window and hung on by her fingertips to the window sill, 40 feet (12.1 m) above the ground. Albert Sevigny saw her from the ground and shouted to her to hold on until help came. She clung there between fire and cold, for ten minutes before firemen came up with a net she could safely fall into.

Alphonse Desjardins was a steamfitter for the Public Works Department. He successfully escaped from the flaming building, then suddenly dashed back in to save his favourite fur hat. He found it, and on his way back joined three men who were trying to fight the fire in a room below the Speaker of the Senate's apartment. They were a postal worker named Randolph Fanning, and police officers James Knox and another Alphonse Desjardins (the steamfitter's uncle). Just after midnight, Knox ran a short distance down the corridor to straighten out a hose. That action saved his life. He heard a great crash, and looked back to see that a huge ventilation tower had collapsed, crushing the other three men. When the bodies were dug out of the rubble several days later, the younger Alphonse Desjardins was still clutching his fur hat. "They lost their lives in the discharge of their duty," Prime Minister Borden said in his eulogy.

Walter Hill, private steward to the deputy speaker, was in a second-floor room and unaware of the fire, when he heard a noise outside his door. He opened it and saw Rene Laplante, assistant clerk of the House of Commons, stumbling around a smoke-filled corridor in terror and confusion. He grabbed Laplante and pulled him into the room. The only way out was through the window. The quick-thinking Hill tore down the curtains and knotted them into a rope that he hung out the window. Laplante, however, was afraid to even attempt to climb down. Hill pleaded with him, but Laplante stubbornly refused to go. Finally, the heat became unbearable and Hill had to get out. As Hill climbed out the window, Laplante was on his knees, praying. "For God's sake, send someone back for me," the doomed man cried.

Hill slid down the curtain-rope and had to drop the last 20 feet (6 m) to the ground. The impact of landing knocked him unconscious, and when he came to he was in hospital. Laplante's badly burned body was found two days later.

Shortly before the fire broke out, MP Bowman Brown Law of Yarmouth, Nova Scotia, had left the Commons to make a long-distance telephone call. He had then gone to his office on the top floor. Whatever happened to him in his last moments, he was unable to escape. His only mortal remains were a thigh-bone and a few smaller bones found near his locker between the Reading Room and the Commons. Law was the only Member of Parliament to die in the great fire, though others were badly burned. He was eulogized by the prime minister, by Laurier, and by the Honourable Rodolphe Lemieux who said that Law was a man who would have gone with great courage and confidence "into the valley of the shadow and meet the King of Terrors."

While in some parts of the building people were losing their lives to a more earthly "king of terrors," in other quarters there were narrow escapes. Some restaurant employees were trapped on an upper level at the southwest corner of the building and were about to take their chances with the high drop, when people on the ground spotted them at the windows. A hundred voices cried, "Don't jump! Ladders are coming." Firemen successfully took the people down.

MP Michel Simeon Delisle was in the barbershop below the Reading Room when smoke started coming through the ceiling. The barber was alarmed, but Delisle said, "There's no hurry. Give me a close shave." Suddenly flames shot down, and the barber ran. Delisle was right behind him. He later said that he wasn't as addicted to close shaves as he thought he was.

Some of the lucky ones were helped out of the furnace that had been the Centre Block by policemen, such as the MP who became confused and wound up in the basement, where an officer found him. Others were taken down firemen's ladders. There were heroes like Chief Engineer Thomas Wensley, who rushed down to the boiler room to shut off the steam and thereby prevented what could have been a devastating explosion. Two others were electrician Fred Wilson and contractor S. Marshall. When the lights suddenly went out, they courageously hurried into the basement and within ten minutes had the lights restored, enabling many people to find their way out.

Outside, firemen continued to pour water into the blaze. Because of the freezing temperature, the ground was soon covered with a layer of slippery ice that made conditions all the more hazardous. Great cascades of ice ran down the stone walls, giving the ruined Gothic architecture an especially eerie look. General Sam Hughes, the Minister of Defence and of the Militia, put a cordon of soldiers around the building to keep the crowds back. He also had army field kitchens set up to provide police and firemen with sandwiches and coffee. Here and there, soldiers stood guard over piles of furniture and other property that had been rescued from the building.

All during the calamity, the clock in the Victoria Tower struck the hour regularly and the great bell tolled: 9:00, 10:00, 11:00. But by 11:00 the fire was in the Tower itself and rising beyond the reach of the fire hoses. Almost as if some supernatural force were at work, the bell had just started to strike the knell of midnight when it went crashing down. At 12:30 the clock stopped altogether. Less than an hour later, the huge iron crown collapsed.

It was after 2:00 AM before firemen seemingly had the blaze under control. But at 10:00 AM a fresh breeze whipped up flames at the rear of the east wing. A stone tower toppled over, giving some firemen and soldiers what one soldier called "a near squeak."

Firemen poured water into the smoldering pile of stone and debris throughout February 4 and into the fifth. At 8:00 that night a draft from a dumbwaiter fanned a new outburst of flame on the Senate side of the main building. Firemen attacked it with hoses, and one of the most tragic fires in Canadian history was vanquished at last.

Seven people were dead. The Commons and the Senate were gutted. All that was left of the mace of the House of Commons were a few blobs of melted gold and silver (which were sent to

England to be incorporated into a new mace). The Library had been saved, but many of its contents were water damaged. All of the books and documents in the Reading Room were destroyed, including a collection of rare Bibles. Gone, too, were the historic Black Rod and the uniform of the Gentleman Usher who bore it.

The Prime Minister's Office was spared, but the Journal Room and other offices containing important documents were obliterated. Many MP's offices that had escaped the fire suffered heavy water damage. Arthur Hawkes, writing for the *Montreal Standard*, toured the ravaged building on February 7 and wrote, "It breaks your heart to venture into the place where the House of Commons has been changed into heaps of rubble."

While Canadians mourned the loss of their magnificent House, and messages of condolence poured in from around the world—including one from King George V—the question on everyone's lips was, "How did the fire start?" Even before the flames were subdued, there was strong suspicion that it was the work of German agents. A report came out of Providence, Rhode Island, that an informer from the German Embassy in Washington D.C. (the U.S. was still neutral) had told a newspaper editor three weeks earlier that German saboteurs had targeted the Canadian Parliament Building, the home of the Governor General, and some munitions plants in Ontario. Someone in the German Embassy had allegedly said that they would "give the people of Canada a few things to think about." News of the alleged plot supposedly reached the United States Department of Justice but was never passed on to Ottawa. There were grumblings in Canada that American laxity in keeping German nationals under surveillance was handicapping Canadian efforts to stop spies from entering Canada.

Fire Chief Graham was one of those who believed the fire had been started by incendiaries. He said that it was "set, and well set." But Colonel Percy Sherwood, chief commissioner of Dominion Police, did not agree. He said that no agent could have slipped past his security. General Sam Hughes was also of the opinion that the fire had been accidental; that it had been started by a cigar or cigarette carelessly left on a shelf in the Reading Room, or a match tossed into a wastebasket. The general was angry over "wild rumours of German plots" and defended Canadians of German background who, he argued, had shown absolute loyalty to Canada.

Nonetheless, there were unsubstantiated stories about "foreign-looking" characters lurking around the Parliament Building the day of the fire. A few suspects were picked up by the police and questioned, and then released. If Imperial Germany had indeed been responsible for the fire, the idea rebounded; enlistment in the Canadian army increased in the following weeks.

The Canadian government moved to temporary quarters in Ottawa's Victoria Memorial Museum. The business of running the country and fighting the war had to go on. The government would not sit on Parliament Hill again until February 1920. The shell of the old building was pulled down. Many of the stones were later used to build the "Abbey Ruins" on William Lyon Mackenzie King's estate of Kingsmere. The bell that so dramatically fell while tolling the hour of midnight can still be seen on Parliament Hill.

Canadians built a new Parliament Building, incorporating the cornerstone from the original. The vanished Victoria Tower was replaced by the Peace Tower, the cornerstone of which was laid by the Prince of Wales (later Edward VIII) on September 1, 1919. It

The Halifax Explosion, 1917

THE CITY OF HALIFAX WAS FOUNDED in 1749 as a bastion in the defence of British North America. From this port, with one of the best natural harbours in the world, British warships sailed out to fight the French in the Seven Years War, and Nova Scotian privateers ventured forth to raid Yankee shipping in the War of 1812. During the American Civil War, daring Bluenose skippers sailed from Halifax to run the Union naval blockade of the Confederacy.

Yet, for over 150 years the destructive forces of war were never visited upon Halifax. The guns of her mighty Citadel never fired a shot in anger. Men of Halifax had died in conflict on the high seas and on foreign soil, but the blood of war had never stained the streets of the Nova Scotia capital. That was to change on the morning of December 6, 1917.

Canada had been a major participant in the Great War for over three years, and Halifax played a vital role in the Canadian war effort. Through the city of about 57,000 passed most of the men, munitions and supplies destined for the front lines in Europe. In Halifax Harbour, located well down an inlet of the sea and out of the reach of German U-boats, men and materials were loaded aboard ships that assembled into convoys for the dangerous Atlantic crossing. When convoys were ready to embark, they passed through The Narrows, which separated Halifax from the small town of Dartmouth, and made for the open sea. Those same ships—at least, the ones that did not fall victim to German torpe-does—would return to Halifax with a sadder cargo: wounded Canadian soldiers from the trenches of France and Belgium.

Halifax was a city on a war footing. A nightly blackout was in effect so that German submarine captains would not be given a convenient beacon. An anti-submarine boom across the har-bour entrance was closed from sunset until dawn. Military emplacements at strategic locations protected the city and har-bour against any threat from the sea. The city was strongly garrisoned, and Britain's Royal Navy was there to assist the fledgling Royal Canadian Navy. There were regulations on the books to govern the movements of ships in what was, in 1917, one of the busiest harbours in the world. There were regula-tions, too, regarding the transport of munitions. But regulations on paper and regulations in effect can be two different things. A lethal combination of confusion, apathy and violation of law was about to bring the war home to Halifax with horrendous consequences.

On the evening of December 5, the French freighter *Mont Blanc* arrived outside Halifax harbour after the boom had been closed for the night. She would have to wait until morning to enter the harbour. Meanwhile, Captain Aime LeMedec welcomed aboard Harbour Pilot Francis Mackey and Examining Officer Terrence Freeman of the RCN. Freeman's duty was to examine the *Mont Blanc*'s shipping manifest.

LeMedec's cargo consisted of munitions: 2,300 tons of wet and dry picric acid, 10 tons of gun cotton, 200 tons of TNT, and 35 tons of benzol, a high-octane gasoline. There was also ammu-nition for the ship's 90-millimetre forward gun and 95-millimetre stern gun. Most of the explosive material was well packed and sealed in the ship's holds, but the drums of benzol were stacked on deck. LeMedec had picked up his volatile cargo in New York but had not been allowed to join a British convoy leaving from that port because the 330 foot (100.5 m) *Mont Blanc* was too slow. He had therefore made a perilous solo run up to Halifax to join another convoy. Regulations stated that ships carrying munitions fly a red flag. The *Mont Blanc* did not. LeMedec said that would only be sending a clear message to U-boats and German spies.

The *Mont Blanc* was a floating bomb, but many munitions-laden ships had sailed in and out of Halifax and other Canadian ports without incident. The *Mont Blanc* passed inspection, and Freeman left the ship to report to his superiors. He later admitted that he had never before heard of benzol. Only a few military men in Halifax knew what the *Mont Blanc* was carrying. Francis Mackey, a 24-year veteran pilot without a single black mark on his record remained aboard so he could guide the ship down the channel in the morning.

Inside the harbour, anchored in the Bedford Basin at the other end of The Narrows, was the 430 foot (131 m) Norwegian freighter *Imo*. Captain Haakon From was on his way from Rotterdam to New York to pick up relief supplies for Belgium, and had put into Halifax to refuel. Norway was a neutral country, but neutral ships suspected of carrying troops or war materials for the Allies were considered fair game by submarine captains, as had been the case with the ill-fated liner *Lusitania* two years earlier. The *Imo* had the words "Belgian Relief" painted on her sides to dissuade German vessels from attacking her.

By the time the *Imo* took on a supply of coal, the harbour boom had been closed. She would have to wait until morning to depart. There would be some dispute as to whether Captain From had actually been given official permission to leave Halifax Harbour.

December 6 dawned bright and cold. There were a few patches of low fog scattered across the water; what locals called "a barber on the harbour." There were from 80 to 100 vessels in Halifax Harbour that morning: freighters, troop transports, tugs, schooners, the ferry that crossed between Halifax and Dartmouth, and naval vessels. The latter included HMS *Highflyer*, a cruiser on convoy-escort duty; the Royal Navy tug *Hilford*; HMCS *Margaret*, an auxiliary patrol ship and HMCS *Niobe*, permanently docked and used for training.

In the North End neighbourhood called Richmond, life was beginning to stir in the rows of modest frame houses. People were getting dressed, stoking up the fires in coal-burning stoves and furnaces, preparing for work or school. Many Richmond residents worked in the nearby Richmond Printing Company, the Hillis and Sons Foundry, or the Acadia Sugar Refinery. Children attended St. Joseph's Roman Catholic School, the Richmond Public School and the Bloomfield School.

In a house at the corner of Kenny and Albert streets in Richmond lived the family of Samuel Orr Jr. Orr was part owner, with his father Samuel Sr. and his brothers David and William, of the Richmond Printing Company. The house was a new one— Samuel, his wife Annie, and their six children had moved in only days earlier—with a splendid view of the harbour. On this day the Orr children were not going to school. One of them had the measles, so they were quarantined. They spent much of their time looking out the window, watching the activity in the harbour. Watching ships was a favourite pastime among Halifax boys, and many of them had become quite expert at identifying the various types of naval and merchant vessels.

At 7:30 the boom protecting the harbour was opened. The first vessel through was an American freighter whose name has gone unrecorded. Close behind was the *Mont Blanc*, piloted by Mackey. Heading into the other end of The Narrows was the *Imo*, with another veteran pilot, William Hayes on the bridge with Captain From. If the *Imo* had not actually received permission to leave the harbour, Hayes was evidently not aware of it.

As the American freighter and the *Imo* approached each other, they should have passed port side to port side. But the pilot on the American ship decided it would be simpler to pass on the starboard side. He gave two whistle blasts to inform the *Imo* of his intention. The *Imo* signalled back her agreement. As the ships passed starboard to starboard, the pilot on the American vessel shouted through his megaphone that another ship was not far behind. Pilot Hayes acknowledged the information.

The *Imo* was now in her wrong channel, and according to some witnesses, going too fast. She might have returned to her correct channel, but now the men on her bridge saw that they were bearing down on the tug *Stella Maris*, which was towing two scows. When the *Stella*'s skipper, Captain Horatio Brannen, saw the *Imo*, he had to alter his course sharply to avoid a collision. The *Imo* had to stay in the wrong channel.

Now Mackey on the *Mont Blanc* could see the *Imo* in what was rightfully his channel. He quickly signalled his intention to maintain his proper course. This meant that the *Imo* had to swing to the starboard, toward Halifax. But to Mackey's amazement, she signalled that she was swinging toward Dartmouth. It would never be certain whether those decisions were being made by Captain From or Pilot Hayes.

Captain LeMedec had ordered "Dead Slow" when he saw the *Imo*. Now he ordered "Dead Stop." But a moving vessel weighing thousands of tons is not an easy thing to stop.

LeMedec swung to the left, trying to give the *Imo* room to pass on his starboard. But the *Imo* suddenly shifted her engines to "Full Astern," causing her bow to swing to the right. The *Imo*'s prow struck the starboard bow of the *Mont Blanc*.

Witnesses said the collision was almost soundless. The initial damage to the ships was not even very serious. But the *Imo* had cut into the *Mont Blanc*'s Number 1 hold where the barrels of picric acid were stored, right below the drums of benzol on the deck. Some of the drums had ruptured, and the sparks caused by steel biting into steel set the gasoline alight. The time was 8:45. The fuse of the floating bomb had been lit, and the seconds were ticking away.

The *Imo* pulled away from the *Mont Blanc* and turned toward Dartmouth. The French ship, though her engines were stopped, was being carried by momentum straight for Pier 6. What happened next aboard the *Mont Blanc* would be seen by Haligonians, by most Canadians, and by the world in general, as an act of supreme cowardice.

Captain LeMedec did not try to steer the ship away from Halifax. He did not order his men to fight the fire. He did not order the seacocks opened to sink the ship to the bottom of the 60-foot (18.2 m) deep harbour. He did not even have the red "danger" flag raised, which would have given people on shore and on other ships at least some warning. Instead, he immediately gave the order to abandon ship. Pilot Mackey had no choice but to join the tide of French sailors going over the side into the lifeboats.

The crew of the *Mont Blanc* rowed like madmen for the Dartmouth shore. They later claimed that they shouted warnings to other ships, but if so, they were not heard. Once they reached land they told some people to get away from the water, then they ran to take cover in some woods.

A ship on fire is quite a spectacle, and the people of Halifax turned out in droves to watch it. Spectators lined the docks and watched from rooftops. Sailors on other ships stopped work to look at the burning ship. They were amused at the sight of the Frenchmen rowing as though their lives depended upon it. Children on their way to school made sudden detours to the harbour so they could see the grand show. Children already in their schools lined up at windows so they could see what was happening. Indeed, in every room in Halifax that had human occupants and a view of the harbour, there were faces pressed against glass window panes in rapt fascination.

So it was in the Orr household, where Annie Orr, 14-year-old Barbara, 11-year-old Ian and six-year-old Isabel looked down at the incredible scene in the harbour. They saw the smoke and flames pouring out of the ship with a hole in its side.

"That's an ammunition boat," said Ian, who knew his ships.

"Will it explode?" asked Barbara.

"Oh, I don't think so," Annie replied. Nobody in the harbour was acting as though there was any big emergency, so there didn't appear to be anything to be alarmed about.

Barbara, Ian and Isabel asked if they could go down to the harbour for a better look. Their mother said yes. The younger children headed straight for the waterfront. Barbara wanted to ask a friend to go with her, so she cut through Mulgrave Park.

On the *Mont Blanc*, which was now within a stone's throw of Pier 6, there were small explosions as some of the shells for her guns began popping off. Captain Brannen anchored the scows the *Stella Maris* had been towing and brought his tug right up to the side of the burning ship. His crew trained their firehose on the flames, but to no effect. The *Stella Maris* backed off a short distance. Six men from the *Highflyer* came alongside in a rowboat, followed by a motor launch from the *Niobe* with approximately the same number of people. They spoke for a few minutes. Then one of the *Stella*'s crewmen went below to get a heavy cable. The *Mont Blanc* had by now hit Pier 6 and set the dock on fire. The men were going to attach a cable to the French ship and tow it out into open water. Then they could open the seacocks and sink it.

Meanwhile, the Halifax Fire Department had been alerted. Down to the harbour raced the city's only motorized fire engine, a spanking-new beauty the firemen lovingly called *Patricia*. Behind the engine was a car with Fire Chief Edward Condon and Deputy Fire Chief Edward Brunt. Following them was another car driven by *Halifax Echo* reporter Jack Ronayne.

On the British freighter *Curaca*, Scottish seaman Edward McCrossan was on deck with his shipmates watching the *Mont Blanc* burn. This was even better than the newfangled motion-picture show. But McCrossan craved a cigarette, so he went below to grab a quick smoke. Ironically, McCrossan's bad habit would save his life.

From the little flotilla of craft bobbing around the *Mont Blanc*, a group of sailors in one of the small boats went alongside the burning ship and began to climb up the Jacob's Ladder dangling over the side; the same ladder the French crewmen had scurried down not quite 20 minutes earlier. It was now 9:04. The brave men did not even reach the deck. They never knew what hit them!

In the Richmond Terminal Office overlooking the harbour, telegraph operator Vincent Coleman happened to look out his window and see the burning ship. He was apparently one of the very few who realized the full danger. Coleman did not run for safety. He sat down and tapped out a message to Truro, Nova Scotia. "Ammunition ship is on fire and making for Pier Six. Good-bye."

It was his last message, and the first that the outside world would have of the calamity that was about to shatter Halifax. At four and a half minutes past the stroke of 9:00 AM, the *Mont Blanc* exploded.

The blast that ripped the heart out of Atlantic Canada's largest city remains on record as the biggest non-nuclear, man-made explosion the world has ever known. It shot smoke and flames five miles (8 km) into the sky and created an ominous mushroom-shaped cloud over the city. Witnesses would later say they saw a human-like death's face in the billowing, dark cloud.

The *Mont Blanc* disintegrated, and steel plates and molten metal rained down on Halifax and Dartmouth. The harbour bottom was laid bare as the force of the blast sent a tsunami roaring inland. Rocks from the bottom of the harbour shot skyward, arced, and then fell on houses and people. The very bedrock of the peninsula upon which Halifax was built was shaken by the blast. The tremors were felt in Sydney, Cape Breton, 270 miles (434.4 km) away. The sound of the explosion was heard in Prince Edward Island. Birds were blown out of the trees 30 miles (48.2 km) from the blast site. The American cruiser USS *Tacoma*, 50 miles (80.4 km) out to sea, felt the blast and immediately turned toward Halifax to investigate and lend assistance.

The *Mont Blanc*'s anchor landed on the other side of the Northwest Arm (a branch inlet of the harbour) three miles (4.8 km) away. One of the ship's guns splashed down in Albro's Lake, three miles in the other direction. In rapid succession the explosion swamped Halifax with a tidal wave, rocked it with an earthquake, then flattened it with a massive air concussion. Richmond was hardest hit. Dartmouth, too, suffered, though to a lesser extent.

The carnage within the harbour itself was horrific. The *Imo* was hurled against the Dartmouth shore like a child's bathtub toy. Captain From, Pilot William Hayes, and five crew members were killed instantly. Several others were badly injured. The *Stella Maris* was thrown into the place where the now-disintegrated Pier 6 had been. Only five of her 24 men survived. Captain Brannen was among the dead.

On the freighter *Curaca*, 32 out of 55 men were killed. Ed McCrossan, who had gone below for a smoke, was one of the survivors. Of the men who went out in the *Highflyer*'s rowboat, only one survived. On board the *Highflyer* herself, three were killed and 15 injured. All of the men in the *Niobe*'s launch were killed. The *Niobe* caught fire, but her remaining crew were able to extinguish the blaze.

The British freighter *Calonne*, which had been loading horses at Pier 9, was bowled right over on her side. Thirty-six of her crew died. The tug *Hilford* was blown right out of the water onto Pier 9. Only two of her crew survived. HMCS *Margaret* was broken loose from her moorings, and two of her crew killed. The

Canadian schooner *Lola R.* and a South American schooner, *St. Bernard*, were both completely destroyed, the latter with the loss of all hands.

At least two other vessels in the harbour, the British freighter *Picton* and the Canadian minesweeper *Musquash*, had substantial stores of munitions threatened by fire. Courageous men risked their lives to neutralize the danger. Their heroism no doubt prevented further lethal explosions.

In drydock the Norwegian ship *Hovland* lost five crewmembers. One hundred and twenty men who had been working on the vessel were killed. Many of the passengers on the *Halifax II*, the ferry, were injured but here there were mercifully no fatalities.

Two unidentified men in a rowboat had a remarkable escape. The blast tossed the rowboat into the air, and for a split second they were high above the water, their oars rowing empty air, as though in a scene from a cartoon. Then they dropped back down to the water, still sitting upright in their boat, not even slightly hurt.

Two square miles (5.1 sq. km) of Halifax had been wiped from the face of the earth. More than 1,600 people had been killed instantly, and of the 9,000 injured, hundreds would die. The total death toll would exceed 2,000. Some of the worst injuries were caused by flying glass. All those faces at windows, looking right at the explosion! More people—many of them children—were blinded by shards of glass from the explosion than the number of soldiers blinded in action during the Great War. One nurse later recalled seeing a doctor in a Halifax hospital carrying a bucketful of eyeballs.

Telegraph operator Vince Coleman was dead. So were Fire Chief Condon, Deputy Chief Brunt and the men who had been on the *Patricia*. The new fire engine was now just a twisted piece of junk. So was the car with the body of reporter Jack Ronayne in it.

With the Fire Department all but wiped out, Halifax was now easy prey for the flames. Fires blazed everywhere, started either by the molten hell that rained down from the sky, or by the hundreds of overturned stoves and furnaces with fires roaring in their bellies. Many victims who had survived the blast but were trapped in wreckage were roasted alive.

Barbara Orr was in Mulgrave Park when the *Mont Blanc* exploded. She flew through the air like a leaf on the wind and hit the ground a quarter mile away. She tried to rise, but one leg and foot had been shattered. All around her was devastation. Houses had been flattened as though made of cards. From under the debris came cries and screams. People dragged themselves out of the rubble and staggered around, injured, shocked and senseless. Some had had all of their clothing blown off and were oblivious to the fact that they were naked.

Barbara started to crawl toward home, but the way was blocked by smoke and flame. She dragged herself in the opposite direction, toward the home of her aunt and uncle on Gottingen Street. It was a hellish ordeal, but she made it. The house was badly damaged, but Barbara's Aunt Edna was alive. She did not recognize Barbara at first because the girl was so covered with soot and oil that her red hair appeared black. The only other survivors in Barbara's family were her grandfather and one uncle. The rest were all dead.

Before anyone could even begin the work of rescuing trapped victims, a new danger arose. Fire threatened the Wellington military barracks, where large quantities of munitions were stored. Soldiers moved through the chaos of blasted neighbourhoods, sending people who were on their feet to the safety of Point

Pleasant Park, the golf course, and Citadel Hill. There the survivors huddled in the chill December air, many of them naked or
dressed only in nightclothes. They had cuts, burns and fractured
bones. Some thought that Halifax had been bombarded by a
German fleet, or bombed by German zeppelins. They cringed in
terrified anticipation of the next explosion.

It didn't come. Bravely placing themselves in harm's way, but
working with discipline, the soldiers flooded the munitions dump,
and ended the threat from that quarter. Then soldiers and sailors
battled the flames throughout the stricken neighbourhoods, while
the fire departments of other communities raced to the disaster
area. At last people could start finding their way back to their
homes—at least, those who still had homes to go to.

More than 1,600 buildings had been completely destroyed,
and many more were damaged beyond repair. Ten thousand people were homeless. Gone were Oland's Brewery, the King
Edward Hotel, the Acadian Sugar Refinery, the Hillis Foundry
and the Richmond Printing Company, along with scores of people who had been in them. One hundred children lay dead in the
rubble of the Richmond Public School, their young lives snuffed
out in an instant. Another 27 children died when the Protestant
Orphanage was levelled. Even in those parts of Halifax that were
far enough from the blast not to be seriously damaged, or were in
the protective lee of Citadel Hill, not a pane of glass remained
in a window or door.

Pier 6 was gone, and others were heaps of twisted rubble.
Dozens of railway cars were now mangled wreckage. Gas and
electricity had been knocked out, so when night came Halifax
was a city of darkness. Then, as if Nature had decided to add her
own privations to those caused by human folly, the worst bliz-

zard in 20 years struck the mangled city. People who still had houses put boards and blankets over empty windows to keep out the cold and snow. The less fortunate shivered in tents the army had set up in parks. They had no means of heating the feeble shelters.

All over the city were people with stories of tragic loss or unbelievable good luck. One little girl survived because she had gone into the cellar to feed her cat. Two soldiers rescued her after she had been trapped in the darkness for days. Another girl saw her pregnant aunt dragging her six-year-old son by the hand, telling him to hurry. The aunt's eyes had been blown out, and in her shock and pain she did not realize that her boy was dead. A mother was bent over her baby's crib when the explosion blew in the windows. Dagger-like shards of glass flew over her and stuck in the wall. Had the mother been standing up straight, she'd have been cut to pieces.

One man was only 50 yards (45.0 m) from the *Mont Blanc* when she exploded. He landed in a pile of ashes two miles away. He was stark naked but for his boots. His fingernails were gone, and he had a badly injured arm, but he was miraculously alive.

One of the most incredible stories was that of 18-month-old Olive Henneberry. The child's father, Private S. Henneberry of the 63 Halifax Rifles, had been wounded in France and had just returned home. After the explosion, some of the men from his regiment found Henneberry frantically digging in the pile of rubbish that had been his house. It did not seem possible that anyone could be alive in that jumble of shattered timbers, but Henneberry insisted that he had heard a child's cry. The men helped him claw through the splintered boards and chunks of plaster, and to their astonishment found baby Olive, alive and

THE HALIFAX EXPLOSION   165

squalling, under the stove. She had been protected by the pro-
truding ashpan. Olive soon became known across Canada as
"The Halifax Ashpan Baby." Sadly, Henneberry's wife and other
five children had all perished.

As usually happens in such disasters, fate was fickle in its
selection of victims and survivors. Forty Micmac Indians were
killed in their shoreline community, but in the nearby black
ghetto called Africville, there was only one death. A minister
was in the parlour of his house, listening to his wife play the
piano and his son sing, when the blast hit. The clergyman was
relatively unhurt, but all he could find of his family to bury were
his wife's backbone and his son's collarbone. At the funeral he
was heard to mutter, "Rot all this praying business!" A fellow
minister nodded and said, "Those are the first natural words I've
heard since the disaster."

In the days and weeks following the explosion, relief poured
into Halifax from across Canada and from the United States. The
state of Massachusetts, with whom Nova Scotia had always had
close ties, was especially generous. It sent a trainload of medical
supplies and a small army of glaziers to make badly needed glass
to fill all those empty windows. Dr. M. Darrell Harvey, a Halifax-
born eye doctor who had moved to Providence, Rhode Island,
and was reputed to be the best specialist in his field in the United
States, did not forget his hometown. He went to Halifax to help
tend to the many eye injuries.

As rescue workers dug out the dead and the wounded, social
agencies tried to reunite parentless babies and small children
with relatives. Soldiers and police patrolled the streets to dis-
courage looting which, shamefully, became a problem. City Hall
issued a request for out-of-town visitors to stay away unless they

had urgent business. Doctors advised the public to eat only canned food, as other foodstuffs might contain slivers of glass. There was a crackdown on unscrupulous merchants engaged in price gouging. One soldier punched out a grocer who tried to charge a boy the unheard of price of thirty cents for a loaf of bread. Then the soldier generously gave the boy a fistful of the greedy grocer's candy.

A special request went out to the Nova Scotia countryside for horses. Horses were still very much in use in urban areas as draft animals, and most of the horses in Halifax had been killed or maimed.

As the people of Halifax buried their dead, tended to the wounded, and cleaned up the wreckage, they were asking the inevitable question: why had this happened? Many believed that German agents were behind it, a suspicion that persists to this day in spite of the absence of evidence. The German press, reporting on the disaster, said in effect that while the Halifax explosion was tragic, it was better that the explosives had killed Canadians rather than the peace-loving Germans for whom they had been intended. Men suspected of being "Hun spies" were arrested and then released due to lack of evidence.

Only one of the sailors from the *Mont Blanc* was hurt in the explosion (he died from his injuries) and public feeling against Captain LeMedec and his crew was bitter. The French captain insisted that the collision had been the fault of the *Imo*, and that once the *Mont Blanc* was on fire there had been nothing he could do except get his men out of there.

Captain LeMedec and Pilot Francis Mackey were charged with manslaughter. The series of hearings and appeals went from Halifax to the Supreme Court of Canada to the Privy Council in

London. In the end, the court ruled that the *Imo* and the *Mont Blanc* had been equally at fault. The charges against the men were dismissed.

If there had indeed been a German plot to cripple the port of Halifax, it failed, because only five days after the explosion a convoy sailed out of the harbour. Whether accidental or the result of a conspiracy, the explosion was a consequence of war. The enormity of that split second of earth-shattering violence would not be equalled until the coming of the atomic age in 1945. Not a soul who was in Halifax or Dartmouth on December 6, 1917, would forget that moment when, as one British seaman put it, "Death then advanced, roaring over the water."

The Spanish Influenza Epidemic, 1918–1919

DISASTER DOES NOT ALWAYS STRIKE in a few world-shattering seconds, minutes, or hours. It need not take the violent form of fire, be as awesome as a tornado, or as dramatic as a sinking ship. Disaster can stalk a land quietly, invisibly, and ultimately fatally, in the form of disease. Tiny monsters, the bacteria and viruses that are often lethal to the human host, are borne from one unsuspecting body to another by every means imaginable; the wind, animal species, tainted water and the many forms of human touch.

Throughout history the human race has reeled before every demon of sickness that escaped Pandora's box. Plagues savaged the empires of the Egyptians, the Greeks and the Romans. The Black Death swept across Medieval Europe like a killing wind, wiping out millions. When Europeans first landed in the Americas, they brought with them "white man's" diseases, most notably smallpox. These contagions, against which the Natives had no immunity, carried off far more lives than the guns of the conquerors could ever have done. The Natives of the Caribbean, Mexico, and Central and South America got payback of a sort when they passed on syphilis to the Spanish Conquistadores. The Spaniards carried the disease back to Spain, and from there it made its malignant way across Europe.

For centuries no one from any race knew what caused the massive outbreaks, epidemics that lasted months or years. They blamed witchcraft, evil vapours from the earth, and the anger of God. They clutched their talismans, said their prayers, buried their dead and burned at the stake any individuals whom they judged responsible.

By the early 20th century, medical science had, of course, long since discovered the actual causes of disease, and doctors knew it had nothing to do with the supernatural. They had discovered preventative measures against certain illnesses and cures for some others. But the science of medicine was still very much in its infancy, not far removed from the days when doctors bled patients to get rid of "bad blood." There were no antibiotics. Many patented "miracle" medicines were useless concoctions brewed up by chemists with an eye on a fast dollar. In households that could not afford the services of a physician or the local apothecary, the "doctoring" was done by a mother using traditional home remedies. Sometimes they worked; often they didn't. Thus, Canada, along with the rest of the world, was ill-prepared for the great Spanish Influenza Epidemic of 1918–1919.

The epidemic did not actually begin in Spain. It most likely had its origins in China, and from there spread to India and eventually Europe, travelling military and commercial routes like a murderous stowaway. In Ceylon it was called Bombay Fever. Japanese called it Wrestler's Fever. In Hong Kong it was "Too Much Inside Sickness." Persians called it the Disease of the Wind. To Poles it was the Bolshevik Disease, and to Hungarians, the Black Whip.

It reached wartorn France and Belgium in the spring of 1918, descending like a vulture on the hapless soldiers of two great armies; men who were already mired in the squalid trenches of the Great War. The malady swept across the battle-fields like a devil dancing through hell, laying low soldiers already suffering from trenchfoot, bad food, foul water, cold, lice, mud, rats and the ongoing insanities of the war. It favoured no flag. It tore into the ranks of the Germans, who called it *Blitz Katarrh*—lightning cold—sending 180,000 troops to their sickbeds. It fell upon the Allies, the French, British, Canadians, and the newly arrived Americans. It crippled the mighty British fleet by rendering 10,313 sailors too sick for duty. Nor did it respect rank. King George V of England caught it, as did Crown Prince Maximillian of Baden, the imperial chancellor of Germany. British Prime Minister David Lloyd George also fell ill. Colonel John McCrae of Guelph, Ontario, the Canadian doctor who wrote the poem "In Flanders Fields," died of pneumonia but almost certainly had the flu first. Victims of the epidemic frequently developed pneumonia in the latter stages of their illness.

Neutral nations were not immune to the invisible killer; Prince Erik of Sweden died from it. It penetrated the mountain strongholds of Switzerland to ravage the towns and villages. Spain, too, was hit hard. Belligerent nations kept quiet about how badly they'd been affected by "Flanders Grippe," as the British called it at first. But in Spain, where there was no wartime censorship, the press openly reported on the devastation the epidemic was wreaking in the country. It became convenient, therefore, for the Royal College of Physicians in London to officially call the contagion "The Spanish Influenza." The worldwide disaster has been known ever since as the Spanish Flu.

The name "influenza" comes from the Italian *influenza di freddo*—"influence of the cold." Mankind had known of the disease for centuries before 1918. The symptoms were a fever, cough, sore throat, headache and muscular pains. It generally made one feel ill for a few days and then went away. It was occasionally fatal to the very young and the elderly. The strain that emerged in 1918, however, took the world completely by surprise.

The epidemic that killed anywhere from 22 million to perhaps 100 million people worldwide, sent some 60,000 Canadians to their graves—a number greater than of those who had been slain on the battlefields of Europe. There is no doubt that it was brought to Canada by returning soldiers, though there were claims that the illness was brought to North American in vials by German spies.

The soldiers unwittingly brought the disease to a country that was a perfect playground for pestilence. There was no federal ministry of health; sanitation and hygiene were municipal and provincial matters, and once the country realized it was in the grip of an epidemic, no one could agree on how best to fight it. Most of the country's doctors and nurses were overseas or working in military hospitals. Doctors couldn't even agree on what the illness was. Some thought it was the cholera. A vaccine was developed, based on the belief that the sickness was caused by a bacillus. (Influenza is caused by a virus.) The vaccine had to be injected deep into muscle tissue by means of a very long needle, and so was quite painful to receive. It ultimately proved ineffective. Most frustrating to the medical community was that the Spanish Flu did not follow the familiar patterns of influenza.

The epidemic did kill many children and elderly people, but its principal targets were healthy, young adults. People aged 26 to 30 seemed to be at the greatest risk. In a three-generational household, grandparents and children might be fine, but both parents seriously ill. Some patients were bedridden for days or weeks, then either died or recovered. Other victims would wake up one morning, seemingly in perfect health, and would be dead by nightfall. A community would go through the terrible throes of the epidemic, then after several weeks with no new cases reported, people would sigh with relief that the danger had passed. And just as they were trying to return to some form of normalcy, the killer would return with a vengeance. Isolation was no guarantee of protection, because remote communities that had no contact with the outside world were hit just as hard as the urban centres.

The Spanish Flu was 25 times more lethal than any influenza Canadian doctors had previously dealt with, and its symptoms in those most badly affected were horrifying. The victim would first complain of the usual flu symptoms, but then would be carried into agonies beyond sore throat, coughing and slight fever. His (or her) temperature would shoot up to 104°F (40°C), and he would shiver uncontrollably. He would become delirious. His face would turn a dark, brownish-purple colour and his feet would turn black. There would be heavy bleeding from the nose, and he would cough up blood. He would finally die, gasping for breath. An autopsy would reveal lungs full of a thin, bloody fluid.

The Spanish Flu arrived in Canada in June 1918 when hospital ships carrying infected soldiers landed at Halifax, Quebec City and Montreal. Throughout the summer there was no indication that the disease would run rampant, and soldiers who had been ill and recovered, or who had been in contact with sick men, boarded trains to go home. The first major civilian outbreak came on September 8 at Victoriaville College in Quebec City. First, two boys were sick, then 400! An alarmed college administration put all students who were well enough to travel onto trains and sent them to their homes all over the province of Quebec. The next day nine sailors on American ships docked at Quebec City died, and there was an outbreak of flu at a military camp near Niagara Falls, Ontario. Neither the government nor the military deemed it necessary to alert the general public. They considered it to be a minor flare-up of a contagious but not very serious ailment. Any action on their part, they concluded, would only needlessly alarm people.

The weeks passed, and the number of communities reporting influenza grew steadily. By the end of September it was in St. John's, Newfoundland. Within two weeks it had spread to the outports. Hundreds of people were sick. Eight died within one 24-hour period. Schools, churches and other public places were closed. A mail boat carried the flu to Labrador, where it wreaked havoc amongst the helpless Native population. Entire families were wiped out. In the settlement of Hebron only 70 people out of a population of 220 survived. At Okak, 217 of the village's 266 people died. In some places the survivors did not have the strength to bury the dead, so they dropped them through the ice into the sea. An eight-year-old girl who miraculously survived for five weeks all alone, watched in horror as dogs devoured the bodies of her mother, father and two siblings. The child herself was attacked and bitten by the ravenous animals, but somehow managed to escape.

The desperate people of Labrador appealed to the government for medical aid. They received nothing, the excuse being that there was no coal available to send a ship north, and no one willing to cover the insurance costs of such an expedition. Not until the following June did a ship with doctors, medicine and lumber for making coffins go to Labrador. By that time, one third of the people of Labrador were dead.

The Spanish Flu rolled across the Maritime Provinces like a juggernaut. Halifax, still recovering from the disastrous explosion of December 6, 1917, had sent nurses to Boston to help with an outbreak of flu in September. By October 9 the Nova Scotia capital was calling the women back home. Keeping the ferry between Halifax and Dartmouth operating was difficult, because captains and crews were sick. An attempt by the city to placard the houses of stricken families failed, because no one would admit that there was sickness within. All over the province people were dying. Communities on Cape Breton Island looked like ghost towns.

Prince Edward Island had already been battered by months of exceptionally stormy weather when the Spanish Flu pounced on the tiny province in October. By the 16th there were 650 cases in Charlottetown. The government prohibited public funerals. Roads were so bad from the foul weather that it was almost impossible for doctors to get around. Captain John Read of the car ferry *Prince Edward Island* came down with the flu but was determined to keep that vital link with the mainland operating. He drank a concoction of hot lemonade, quinine and aspirin, and spent a night sweating it out. In the morning he dowsed himself with buckets of cold sea water, then dried himself, got dressed and took his place on the bridge of his vessel.

Not all, however, could shake the flu as Captain Read had done. The Cullen family, who lived on a farm near Charlottetown, had a family tradition of celebrating the November 9 birthday of the father, Timothy, with a big chicken dinner. This year, Cullen's four sons, two of his three daughters, and his wife Fanny were stricken with the flu. A doctor visited daily, and Cullen gave the sick ones sips of brandy and rum, and rubbed their chests with camphorated oil. The children recovered, but on November 10, one day after Timothy's birthday, Fanny died. Timothy Cullen never again permitted any sort of observation of his birthday.

In St. John, New Brunswick, a naval vessel, HMCS *Festubert*, sailed into harbour. Every officer on board, right up to the captain, was sick with the flu. Oddly enough, not one of the crew had been stricken. Ordinary Seaman George A. Davies went ashore and found a city wrapped in gloom. It seemed that every second house he passed had a black rosette on the door. He asked someone what they were for and was told that it was the sign that someone in the house had died of the flu.

Elsewhere in the province, at Doaktown on the Miramachi River, a family named Swim lost two sons—both in their twenties—within three weeks. The story was the same everywhere. Three thousand people were sick in Moncton, and 2,000 in Edmundston.

The flu went through Quebec like wildfire as infected soldiers and students returned to their hometowns. By September 30 there were 530 sick soldiers in an army camp at St. Jean. A military spokesman said the situation was under control and the epidemic would be over in "a matter of days." He was wrong on both counts.

The contagion reaped grim harvests in Sherbrooke, Trois Rivieres and Montreal. Factories shut down because there were not enough employees fit to go to work. McGill University was closed, as were elementary schools and high schools. Businesses were required to close in mid-afternoon, a ruling that drew protests from merchants in Montreal. Public gatherings were forbidden. Families living near cemeteries drew their curtains so they wouldn't have to see the endless parades of funerals. The dead were placed in rough wooden boxes and taken to the grave-yards in the backs of trucks, because there weren't enough coffins or hearses. In Montreal a special streetcar was converted into a funeral car that carried the dead to Bout de l'Ile ten at a time. Roman Catholic priests walked down streets bearing the Sacred Host and calling out the Mass, while their parishioners knelt in their doorways. Doctors were instructed to issue free death cer-tificates to the poor.

One retired man survived the plague, while his three sons—all strong, young men—died. Another man fell ill, and then appar-ently recovered. He went out and bought some groceries, returned home and had supper, and was dead before midnight.

The flu ravaged the Gaspe region, and for a time seemed to have spent itself. Then it came snarling back, this time with pregnant women as its particular targets. "It seemed like a witch's curse," recalled a survivor named Hazel Clark. "If you gave up, you died."

A young soldier named Arthur Lapointe, from Matane County, was in the front lines in France when he fell ill. In his delirium, he dreamed that his youngest sister, Martine, appeared to him. "She led me to a row of graves and named my brothers and sisters as those the graves enclosed. 'I, too, am dead,' she told me. 'But God in his mercy has allowed me to spend this day with you.' Then the dream faded and I awoke." When Lapointe returned home he found that two of his sisters and three of his brothers had died in the space of nine days.

The September of 1918 was the coldest and wettest Toronto had seen in almost a century. "It was as though a dark, sombre cloud had fallen over all," one survivor recalled. The Spanish Flu crept in. By the end of the first week of October all of the hospitals were filled, and two hotels were transformed into temporary clinics. A request came from Washington D.C. for 300 nurses to help with the flu crisis there. Toronto had to refuse, because so many of the city's nurses were sick themselves. As in other communities, schools and other public places were closed. The closure of theatres threw actors out of work, and they had to seek other employment. There were plenty of vacancies because so many people were sick, dead or just plain afraid to go to work.

All over Ontario it was the same, grim picture. Cabinet makers in Hamilton worked overtime turning out coffins. In London undertakers were making several trips a day to the cemeteries. One girl in need of a hearse whistled one down the way someone would a taxi.

A spokesman for the Ontario Board of Health refused to admit that there was any cause for alarm. He objected to the idea of closing schools, and said that health officers throughout the province should just carry on as usual. "They should not be moved from their duty by public clamour to adopt fussy and ill-advised measures which only serve to irritate the public and serve no useful purpose," he said, as the death bells continued to toll.

In Brantford, chairman T.J. Minnes of the Board of Health stated that there was no call for alarm. The rumours of epidemic, he said, were greatly exaggerated. Yet, even as he spoke, the Brantford hospital was filled to capacity and a local doctor died of the flu. By the second week of October there were 2,500 cases of flu in Brantford and people were dying at an appalling rate.

In the countryside around communities like Ripley and Guelph, doctors had difficulty convincing immigrant agricultural workers that if they felt ill, they must stop work and rest. These were, for the most part, strong men and women who believed that a little sickness was no excuse for not doing their jobs. They had to work, they said, for the sake of their children. As a result, many children lost one or both parents.

The list of public places ordered closed eventually included all churches. Most clergymen were cooperative, but a few were not. A Hamilton priest ignored the order and was fined. He appealed his case, claiming that the government was interfering with freedom of religion. Several Baptist and Anglican ministers agreed with him. But the government would not be swayed, and the churches remained closed.

The scattered communities of Northern Ontario were not spared. In the Indian village of Sand Point on Lake Nipigon, 58 people out of a population of 70 were stricken. Five of them died. A man in Sault Ste. Marie, delirious with fever, jumped out of an upstairs window and ran off into the bush. He died out in the snow. In some communities, other diseases joined the Spanish Flu in its deadly romp through frail humanity. There was scarlet fever in Port Arthur and Fort William, and diphtheria in Erin.

As news of the epidemic that was paralyzing the eastern provinces reached the prairies, Westerners tried to take measures to prevent it from spreading. Little did they know that the devil was already in their midst. Winnipeg banned public meetings and city health officials advised people to wear surgical masks. Spitting on the street carried a whopping $50 fine or a jail term. Churches were ordered to close, and almost immediately pamphlets appeared, condemning the order as showing a lack of faith in God. A Baptist minister blasted the authors of the pamphlet: "To pray for immunity from the plague while ignoring natural precautions is impiety itself."

One Winnipeg man died within three hours of noticing the first symptoms of flu. In The Pas, the local undertaker fell ill and had to ask a friend named Jean Mastai Poirier, who was not an undertaker, to fill in for him. Poirier was kept busy making caskets in his kitchen, while his nine-year-old daughter Florence made little satin pillows. A priest brought him the measurements of people who were still alive but not expected to live long. On Lake Winnipeg the boat *Majestic* had to go into harbour because most of her crew of 12 were sick. By the time the *Majestic* sailed again, only five of them were still alive. Residents of Brandon witnessed a sight reminiscent of the evil days of the Black Death; a cart rattling along a street collecting the dead.

Fate played a cruel trick on Alan McLeod of Stonewall, Manitoba. At 18, McLeod became the youngest Canadian ever to be awarded the Victoria Cross. He was a bomber pilot in the RAF, and on one mission he and his observer (machine-gunner) were attacked by eight German fighters. Thanks to McLeod's skillful maneuvring, the observer was able to shoot down three of them before both men were wounded and their plane riddled with bullets. McLeod crash-landed in no-man's-land and dragged the unconscious observer away from the wreck. After surviving the war and receiving the British Empire's highest military honour, young McLeod returned home only to die from the Spanish Flu.

After the first resident of Regina died of the flu on October 6, the province of Saskatchewan made influenza a reportable disease, which meant it was unlawful not to tell a health officer if someone in the family fell ill. The city had to cut back on streetcar service because so many drivers and conductors were sick. Canvassers going door to door for the Victory Loan campaign were instructed to collect information on any sickness at each home they visited and report it to the Central Health Bureau. By the end of the month there were 2,000 cases of the flu in the prairie capital.

All over the province the measures that were taken in points east were repeated. All public places were closed. Saskatoon schools were turned into emergency hospitals. The morgue in Rosetown was so full the undertaker had to put bodies in a lumberyard. A travelling salesman who was determined to make his usual calls found death at every stop. At Paradise Hill he found that a client and his wife were dead. At his next stop he discovered three dead Indians, and a young man who was digging graves for his mother, father, brother and sister. At Witchekan Lake the disease had killed an entire threshing crew. In some places there were outbreaks of scarlet fever, diphtheria and smallpox. The whirlwind continued moving west.

Calgary's medical health officer, Dr. C.S. Mahood, tried to keep the sickness contained when it rolled into Alberta. He had 15 sick soldiers taken off a train from Regina and sent to an isolation ward at Sarcee Military Camp. He then attempted to impose a quarantine when cases of flu broke out in the city. But many people would not cooperate. If they weren't too sick, they went to work. By the time it became obvious that they had the Spanish Flu, and not just a cold, it was too late.

On October 25 it became mandatory for Calgarians to wear gauze masks outside their homes. Officials advised them to sterilize the mask in boiling water after it had been worn for two hours, but few people did. As was the case with other communities, Calgary ran out of coffins and the dead had to be buried in rough wooden boxes. Also, as happened elsewhere, just when beleaguered residents thought that the infection had finally run its course, it came roaring back.

Edmonton native John Stewart had joined the Royal North West Mounted Police and was in Regina for training when he fell ill with the flu. He was expected to die, and a grave was dug for him. But he survived and was released from hospital, after losing 30 pounds (13.6 kg). When Stewart retired from the force in 1952 he requested, and was given, all papers relating to his service. Among them was a document of which he had no recollection; a will that he had signed while he was delirious with fever from the flu.

In Grande Prairie there was a $50 fine for not wearing a mask outdoors. Medical students were put on trains to make sure all passengers wore masks. In towns all over the province travellers were not allowed off trains unless they promised to stay put until the epidemic was over. The citizens of Alliance tried to quarantine their entire community. They set up roadblocks and would not allow visitors in. But it did no good, and the flu's first fatality was the town's only doctor. The invisible killer carried off more than 3,300 Albertans.

The Rocky Mountains were no barrier at all to the relentless spread of the contagion. British Columbia was, in fact, invaded on two fronts; by train from the prairies and by sea, as ships from the Orient entered the port of Vancouver. The city's hospitals, as well as emergency clinics set up in schools, soon filled up. Dr. Harry Milburn recalled seeing the rows of cots and the nurses, with their white uniforms, moving amongst them. "They looked like ghosts walking through a graveyard." The death toll in Vancouver would be almost 1,000.

In the town of Corbin, high in the mountains, people thought they would be safe from the epidemic. They weren't. The flu struck as savagely in the high country as it did at sea level. All it took was for one infected visitor, a peddlar, to step off the train. Within a day half the town was sick. Townsmen converted a dancehall into a hospital and then had to make do as best they could, because the only doctor had been laid low. Before he was overcome by delirium, he'd written, "Stay in bed, take Epsom salts, and more Epsom salts."

A logger known as Missouri Bill was one of the first patients in the makeshift hospital. He indignantly refused the Epsom salts and demanded moonshine whiskey, which was easily obtained in that era of Prohibition and bootlegging. He got the gut-burning firewater he wanted, and walked out of the clinic a well man. In his opinion, the best cure for the flu was to go to bed and drink rot-gut liquor until you saw double, and the hell with Epsom salts. For other people, however, alcohol proved to be a feeble defence.

The arrival of the flu in Kamloops showed that Canadians were not yet free of the taint of racism. Once the hospital was full, white patients were sent to the Patricia Hotel, while Natives were put in an army barracks. In Prince Rupert the mayor had to appeal to the public for spare beds to put in emergency clinics. In Victoria a firehall was used as a hospital, and girls were advised not to kiss sailors.

Among the Chinese residents of British Columbia a story spread that the sickness was the work of an evil spirit that had taken the form of a six-year-old white boy. It was said that the innocent-looking demon went barefoot and lurked in the dark, and that all who looked upon it sickened and died.

The Spanish Flu rampaged through Yukon and the Northwest Territories, where doctors were few and far between, and many people lived far from any kind of medical aid. Entire Native communities were wiped out. Men who had gone into the bush to hunt never returned home. Bodies went unburied because no one had the strength to do the job. People died along Arctic trails, trying to reach settlements where they might get help. Mounties made heroic efforts to get through to remote communities with food and medical supplies. But even their dedication could not slow the marauding disease. In the provinces to the south the Spanish Flu had run its course by the spring of 1919. In the far North it continued killing until well into the 1920s.

The medical community was simply stonewalled by the epidemic. Scientists did not know how to prevent the disease, nor did they know how to cure those who caught it. Nonetheless, doctors and nurses did what they could to try to ease the suffering. In urban centres they worked around the clock in hospitals, clinics, and people's homes. In rural areas they got around by whatever means available: automobile, horse and buggy, sleigh, dogsled. Retired doctors and medical students stepped forward to fill in for the many physicians who were in Europe. Always the health care workers were exposed to the disease, and many of them died. Their families, too, bore the brunt of the battle.

Ella Parsons, whose husband Richard was a doctor in Red Deer, Alberta, wrote to her mother of her concern that he would catch the disease, if he did not first drop dead from exhaustion. Dr. Parsons did not catch the flu, but a few days after writing the letter Ella did. She died in a matter of days.

Dr. James Collins of Prince Edward Island took his daughters with him as he made the rounds in Vernon River, Elliotvale and

Armdale. While he tended to the sick, the girls would clean houses, do dishes, prepare food—whatever the families needed. Their father also had them deliver rum from door to door.

A quarter of the doctors in Hamilton, Ontario, were sick, so the remaining physicians like Dr. Elizabeth Bagshaw were overwhelmed. Dr. Bagshaw and another woman MD came down with the flu themselves, and nursed each other back to health. They were so weak, she said later, that they could hold a cup of tea, but not the saucer, because that was too heavy.

Legions of other dedicated people joined the battle against the epidemic: the people of the Canadian Red Cross, the St. John Ambulance, the Victorian Order of Nurses, and the Salvation Army. Organizations like the Imperial Order of the Daughters of the Empire and the Council of Jewish Women took up the fight. Clergymen, nuns, police officers, firemen, and pharmacists all devoted their time and abilities to the struggle.

Where schools were not being used as hospitals, teachers turned their empty classrooms into soup kitchens, preparing food for people who were too sick to look after themselves. Other teachers did volunteer work in short-staffed hospitals and clinics. They did laundry, washed dishes, bathed patients and turned their hands to any other tasks that would help the beleaguered doctors and nurses. The people of St. John's, Newfoundland, were so grateful for the selfless work of teacher Ethel Dickinson, who died during the epidemic, that they erected a monument to her memory. Eleanor Baubier, a native of Manitoba, was teaching in a village in Saskatchewan when the flu struck. The 24-year-old teacher was a pillar of strength as she administered to the sick. Then she, too, fell victim to the disease and died. The village was re-named Baubier in her honour.

All across Canada ordinary people risked their lives to help the sick. They prepared and distributed food, cleaned houses, chopped firewood, cared for children and buried the dead. People who owned cars and trucks volunteered their vehicles for whatever good use to which they could be put. In farming regions neighbours who were still healthy looked after the livestock of those who were sick.

There were some, of course, who tried to capitalize on the disaster. Insurance companies advertised "Influenza policies." A bicycle manufacturer ran an ad telling people that they could protect themselves from the flu by buying a bike and riding it out in the fresh air. The Victory Loan organization said that people could beat the flu by doing volunteer work for them, "... as it is impossible to feel blue when you are enthused with the spirit of victory." Many of the gauze masks people wore actually had "Victory Loan" stamped on them. In Vancouver some pharmacists were guilty of price gouging on an astronomical scale. A Saskatchewan doctor asked exorbitant fees for services other doctors were providing free of charge. In Calgary a group of young women passed themselves off as "professional" nurses and demanded $25 a day for their work. Real nurses were earning about $2 a day. Such cold-hearted opportunism, however, was rare. For the great majority of Canadians, those dreadful months of 1918 and 1919 brought out the best in them.

People tried anything and everything to fight the contagion. Aspirin was readily available, but people preferred the old-fashioned powdered form that was dissolved in water. There was a suspicion that the new tablets, manufactured by the Bayer company in Germany, were deliberately infected with flu germs. Mothers and fathers applied onion and mustard poultices to sick family members. Others used goose grease and garlic. In the rural areas skunk oil was a prime ingredient.

Pharmacies sold out of camphor, a white substance with a pungent odour (used in the manufacture of mothballs) because people thought that a little bag of it worn around the neck would ward off germs. Others thought the best protection was a piece of salt herring. Still others put sulphur in their shoes, or drank coffee mixed with mustard. A great many swore by cinnamon. A daily dash of it in food, they said, and you wouldn't get the flu.

Smoke of just about any kind was thought to be a good germ-killer, so people fumigated their homes with sulphur, tobacco and shavings of various types of wood. Chain-smoking was encouraged. People sprayed curtains with creoline or hung up cheesecloth soaked in formaldehyde. Some people baked their mail in the oven in case the letters had flu germs on them.

In Native communities people made potions from wild ginger and ginseng, and the bark of wild cranberry and cottonwood. A Chinese doctor in Calgary claimed he could kill flu germs by penetrating the skin with a needle and then rubbing in a vegetable powder. A Chinese orderly in High River, Alberta, said that scratching the skin with a penny until it bled was a sure-fire preventative.

Since this was the era of Prohibition, there was a great controversy over the use of "medicinal" alcohol. Temperance advocates damned the use of alcohol for any purpose, but many doctors believed that alcohol used in moderation was beneficial. They were permitted, by law, to prescribe it. Pharmacists were allowed to keep it in stock. The Temperance people argued that not everybody who bought medicinal alcohol was sick. A resident of Kingston, Ontario, pointed out that among the elderly alcoholics in a ward of the Hotel Dieu Hospital, there was not one case of

Spanish Flu. Hundreds of people who were children during the epidemic testified in later life that they survived because their parents had dosed them with whiskey, brandy or rum. One New Brunswick man said that he was spared because he took two spoons of gin three times a day, and kept gin in his mouth whenever he left the house.

There was considerable debate over whether windows should be opened or closed. Nobody knew if the disease was spread only by direct contact between humans, or if it was carried on the air. Some said that open windows and lots of fresh air helped the sick to recover, with no danger of spreading the illness. Those who disagreed put their argument in a bit of doggerel:

There was a little bird
Its name was Enza
I opened the window
And in-flu-Enza

Some of the ideas individuals came up with for prevention were downright bizarre. One man suggested that people got sick because they wore clothing, which was not natural to the human body. Nakedness, he said, was the best protection—an idea that obviously did not catch on in the Canadian winter. There was a woman who claimed that having all of one's teeth pulled out would prevent the flu, and another who said that having an appendectomy would do the trick.

The Spanish Flu's greatest allies were ignorance and fear. If the best medical minds in the world did not know what the silent killer actually was, what were ordinary people to think? There were those who believed that God was punishing the human race because of the evils of the Great War. They waved their bibles and cried, "After war comes plague!" Some people thought that the trouble stemmed from mankind's growing use of electricity. Electric wiring in the streets and in buildings was "unnatural" they said. Many European immigrants were convinced that the epidemic was a return of the Black Death. When they fell ill, they just gave up hope and died.

To the health care workers who were fighting the odds to save lives, this fear, this surrender to hopelessness, was a sure ticket to the graveyard. Those who succumbed to the fear died. The patients who survived were usually the ones who had the strongest will to live.

The Spanish Influenza epidemic of 1918–1919 left desolation in its wake. Tens of thousands of Canadians were dead. Many more who had been sick but had survived were afflicted with heart trouble and respiratory weaknesses. A large part of the population now comprised widows, widowers and orphans. Juvenile delinquency rose because of the long periods of school closures. Businesses from small retail operations to heavy industry suffered inestimable losses. Insurance companies were hit hard, paying out more in influenza claims than they did in war-related claims. Banks, mines, transportation and the entertainment industry all suffered heavy blows.

As generally happens after such a calamity, measures were taken to ensure that the disaster would not be repeated. The streetcorner spittoon became a thing of the past. At public drinking fountains disposable paper cups replaced the familiar tin cup used by one and all. Most importantly, scientists went to work to track down the killer. In 1933 British scientists isolated an influenza virus for the first time. Eventually they would learn how to man-ufacture effective vaccines.

But viruses, like true monsters, are still very much a mystery to medical science. They mutate and adapt. They vanish, seem-ingly from the face of the earth, and then they come back, with new ways of breeching human defences. For all the vigilance of the men and women of medicine, there are no guarantees that there will not be another unholy plague like the one that in just a few months killed 60,000 Canadians.

The Laurier Palace Theatre Fire, Montreal, 1927

M ONTREAL'S ST. CATHARINE STREET EAST rang with
the shouts and laughter of children that cold, sunny,
Sunday morning of January 9, 1927. At least 800 of them were
converging on the old Laurier Palace Theatre for a day at the
movies. On the bill for that afternoon's matinee were a drama
entitled *Upstage*, starring Norma Shearer; *The Devil's Gulch*, a
western starring Bob Custer; and a comedy, *Get 'Em Young*. The
latter title would prove to be a grimly ironic one. Posters on
the front of the theatre told patrons and passersby that later in the
week the feature film would be *Sparrows*, starring Canadian-born
movie queen Mary Pickford.

For the majority of the children who lined up and waited for
the ticket window to open at noon, this outing to the cinema was
more than watching black-and-white images flicker across the
silent screen while they munched candy. There was the added
thrill of enjoying forbidden fruit.

Quebec law stated that children under the age of 16 were not
to be admitted to movie theatres unless accompanied by an adult.
A 1919 amendment to that law allowed theatre owners to admit
unaccompanied minors to showings of films that were made
specifically for children. However, none of the films being shown
at the Palace that afternoon were classified as children's movies.

But the children clutching their nickels and dimes for the 15
cent admission knew that such picky details didn't matter at the

good old Palace. At most other movie theatres in Montreal, kids had to hang around the entrance and pester adult patrons to "take" them in. Not at the Palace! The staff at the Palace let *everybody* in. But you had to get there early if you wanted a good seat. Latecomers had to stand in the aisles. It was even rumoured that the first 50 kids in line were sometimes let in free, though it seems this was never a policy at the Palace. Proprietor Ameen Lawand, a Syrian-born entrepreneur who had been in Canada for 15 years, was not the kind of businessman to hand out freebies.

No more than four of the youngsters who went to the Palace that day were accompanied by adults. Rene Roy and his brother were among the few who even had parental permission to be there. It was Rene's 14th birthday, and a day at the movies was part of his present. Twelve-year-old Philip Martel had permission to take his sisters Eva, 8, and Yvette, 7, to the movies; 14-year-old Loretta Francoeur not only had her mother's permission, but also was going to a movie for the very first time.

The parents of most of the young theatre-goers—as many as 75 percent of them—did not know their children were at the Palace. The three children of Montreal police officer Albert Boisseau—Germaine, 13, Roland, 11, and Yvette, 8—had told their parents they were going skating. Marcel Girard, 14, was there even though his father had told him he was not allowed to go. Joseph Metu had told his 10-year-old son Adrien that he had permission to go to the movies, but *not* the Laurier Palace. Joseph had been in the Palace and did not consider it safe. There weren't enough exits, he said. But Adrien was with the throng of boys and girls who surged squealing and laughing into the Palace, dashed for the best seats and waited for the magic to begin at 12:30.

The Laurier Palace Theatre was a two-storey brick and stone

building that had seen better days. It could have been closed down for any number of reasons. For one thing, it was a fire trap. There were exits at the front and back, but because it was in the middle of a block, there were no side doors. Two 30 foot (9.1 m) stairways led to the balcony. They were narrow, dark, and had sharp turns and no railings. The doors at the bottom were only 37 inches (93.9 cm) wide.

There were other problems. Owner Lawand was in violation of numerous regulations. He did not provide proper storage facilities for film, which at that time was made of a highly flammable material. The law stated that on the side rows of the auditorium, there could be no more than five seats between the side aisles and the walls. The Palace had six seats. Lawand had been warned on previous occasions for not keeping fire exits clear. His staff had, in fact, been told by a constable that very morning that the fire exits did not meet city standards. There had been small fires at the Palace in the past, as well as at the Maisonneuve, another theatre Lawand owned, and at a pool hall/bowling alley of which he was part owner. Moreover, Lawand had been fined for admitting unaccompanied children to the theatre, having people standing in the aisles, displaying unapproved posters and neglecting to charge the entertainment tax. There would later be accusations—though nothing that anybody could prove—that the Laurier Palace was not shut down because Lawand had political connections.

Lawand was not at the Laurier Palace that Sunday. He was at the Maisonneuve. At the Palace, which was packed with hundreds of children, were head usher Camil Bazzy and several of his assistants, some of whom weren't much more than boys themselves. In the box office was Annette Bordua, who later claimed that her employer had never told her about the law concerning minors.

Emile Masicotte was in the projection room, and assistant manager Michel Arle was in the office. Aside from approximately 30 men and women scattered throughout the audience, there were no other adults in the theatre. About 500 young people, mostly teenagers, were on the orchestra floor. From 300 to 350 kids, mostly younger children, were jammed into the balcony. There were children standing in the aisles because all of the seats were taken. Some kids were there with brothers and sisters or friends. Others had gone to the movies by themselves.

For a little more than an hour and a half the young audience sat enthralled by the action on the screen. Quite likely older children read the lines of dialogue for the little ones. They ate candy, and kicked off overshoes and wiggled out of winter coats as the room became too warm.

It was just after 2:00 and projectionist Masicotte had started to run *Get 'Em Young*, the comedy that most of the children had come to see. As the kids hooted at the slapstick antics on the screen, smoke began to curl up from under a seat at the centre of the balcony. Just what started the fire was never satisfactorily determined, but it was strongly suspected that the cause was a carelessly discarded match or cigarette that had ignited rubbish on the floor, the blaze then spreading to the dry old wood of the balcony. In days to come, ushers would be accused of smoking on duty, but the ushers said that children often sneaked cigarettes into the theatre. They said that children frequently asked them for matches so they could look under the seats but that the ushers always refused. Whatever caused the fire, the next ten minutes would show that ignored regulations, untrained staff, and a mob of terror-stricken children are potent ingredients for a disaster.

Usher Paul Champagne saw some of his colleagues trying to douse the blaze with water. He ran for a fire extinguisher, but by the time he turned it on the flames, it was too late. Now he and one or two other ushers shouted, "FIRE!"

The alarm had people on their feet and moving in an instant. While *Get 'Em Young* still played on the screen, the people in the orchestra seats made a dash for the exits. One man stopped at the ticket window and demanded his 15 cents back because he had not received full entertainment value for his money. To that Montrealer's credit, he returned to the theatre to help in any way he could, when he became aware of the true nature of the tragedy.

The audience in the orchestra seats escaped unhurt. But for the children up in the balcony, the next few minutes would be an ordeal of confusion, panic and death. With one exception, the ushers clearly did not know what to do. Some of them told the children to get out, while others told them to remain seated. As the smoke thickened and flames began to eat at the seats, the children fled in complete disorder down the two stairways. At the west stairway, usher Champagne told the frightened children not to rush all at once, and managed to get them down and out to the street. He tried to return to the balcony but was forced back by smoke.

On the east stairway there was chaos. When the children ran down and around the sharp corner, they were stopped at the bottom by assistant manager Arle, who had his arms outstretched. He told them to go back, that there was no danger. The children obediently went back up, against the tide of those trying to get down. They turned and started down again. By this time Arle had gone out to the street.

As the children tried to jam past each other to get out through the tiny door, someone fell, effectively blocking the narrow passageway. Somehow the door was pushed shut, and with the press of bodies against it, could not be reopened. More children fell as they tried to force their way forward. Once down, a child could not get up because of the mass of bodies on top of him or her. They were soon piled eight deep. Thick smoke was now pouring down the dark stairway. The stairway became, in the words of a Toronto *Globe* reporter, "a solid, suffocating, groaning, shrieking and dying mass."

Emile Massicote was quick to act when he realized what was happening. His projection room had a window that overlooked the theatre's marquee. Massicote hurried out to the throng of pushing, shoving children trying to enter the top of the stairway and tried to tell them there was another way out. But the hysterical, screaming children probably didn't even hear him.

Massicote started dragging them, two at a time, into the projection room. In spite of their struggles to get away from him, he managed to put 30 children through the window and onto the marquee. Finally, he too, was forced out by the smoke.

Firemen and police were at the scene quickly. Some rushed into the theatre, the front windows of which had been blown out, while others put up ladders to take the children off the marquee. There were bodies in the lobby; victims of smoke inhalation. A grown man, alive but unconscious, lay across the bodies of two children. Two little girls lay beneath a poster advertising the movie *Sparrows*. But the most horrifying, heart-rending sight awaited the firemen in the east stairway.

They could not get the door open and had to go into a washroom and chop a hole in a wall. Then they saw the pitiful tangle of little arms and legs, from which came only a few frail whimpers. The boys and girls were so tightly packed that just pulling them apart required herculean effort. One constable wrapped his belt around a small body, and it took the strength of several men pulling on it to dislodge the child.

Firemen rushed upstairs where they easily put out the fire. Police officers and other firemen pulled little bodies from the human tangle and carried them out to the sidewalk where they could begin the awful task of separating the living from the dead. One fireman who worked with a fury was Alphego Arpin. He knew that his eight-year-old son Gaston had gone to the movies that day.

Outside, police had set up a cordon. They allowed frantic parents through, but were "merciless" with the morbidly curious. The scene on the sidewalk in front of the theatre had even the toughest cops choking back sobs. There in a long row lay the little bodies, their faces blackened with smoke. Some had their clothes torn. Others had been battered in the crush in the stairway. One little girl still clutched a candy bar in her lifeless hand. Two little boys managed to gasp their names before they died. Distraught mothers and fathers moved from one child to another, praying, dreading. A priest was already administering last rites. A steady stream of ambulances and volunteer taxis carried children off to hospital—or the morgue. Gaston was not one of the children that Fireman Arpin carried out of the theatre. When he was free to leave the scene of the tragedy, Arpin searched all four hospitals to which fire victims had been taken. He finally found his son in the morgue.

Constable Albert Boisseau, whose children had told him they were going skating, was one of the first officers on the scene. To his horror, he found his 13-year-old daughter Germaine among the dead. He, too, made a frantic search of the hospitals for Roland and Yvette. He found them in the morgue.

The dead ranged in age from five to 16. They included Loretta Francoeur, Adrien Metu and Marcel Girard. Rene Roy, on his 14th birthday, was dead, though his brother escaped. In the crush on the stairway, Philip Martel had been separated from his little sisters. He had survived and was in hospital, but Eva and Yvette were dead.

Of the dozens of children rushed to hospital, 17 would die. The total number of dead reached a staggering 78. Some parents, like Constable Boisseau and his wife, lost all of their children on that terrible day. Most suffocated or had the life crushed out of them. Only one was reported as having been burned to death. Those in the hospital were treated for burns, smoke inhalation and injuries resulting from the crush in the stairway. Once the fire was out and the smoke gone, investigators found a pitiful collection of items in the stairway and on the balcony: overshoes, bits of torn clothing, a little coat.

Accounts related by survivors provided a frightful picture of those ten deadly minutes. Antoine Girouard, 16, told the press from his hospital bed, "I noticed flames shoot up through a crack in the floor and immediately everyone rushed from the balcony. I got safely down the stairway to within five steps of the bottom, when I was knocked down by the rush on the stairway and fell, with people piled over me. Three dead boys were beneath me when the police raised me, and above me five or six injured boys had to be removed before I could be reached."

Ernie Fitzpatrick, 14, had gone to the theatre with his friends Michael and Eddie Murphy, ages 11 and 12. They got there late, and only Michael was able to find a seat. Ernie and Eddie had to stand in the aisle.

"We saw flame and smoke coming from near the first row of the balcony in the centre," Ernie said. "Some men were pouring water on the fire with extinguishers and were telling everyone that it was not a serious fire. Smoke began to get in our throats and everybody began to shout and run. I said a prayer, and started to climb over the benches and over the other people. They were mostly children in the balcony. Then downstairs someone carried me in his arms and brought me somewhere."

Eddie continued, "I ran in the back of the balcony and I could not get out, but I climbed up on a ledge, and a man standing on a little roof there with a handkerchief over his mouth carried me out the window." Michael, the "lucky" one who got a seat, perished.

Roger Frappier, 13, escaped by means of a desperate action. "There were several men shouting for everybody to remain seated and there were some ushers trying to keep people quite. But there were others who stood up and cried, 'Fire! Fire!,' and told us to get out quick. I began to run up the aisle to the stairway in the rear, but smoke began to get in my throat and I couldn't get up that far. I ran back and jumped down into one of the aisles ... I suppose I hurt myself when I landed downstairs, but I was too excited to notice it."

Eighteen-year-old Romeo Colin was one of those who was initially stopped on the stairway by Michel Arle. "I had almost got downstairs, when this man held out his arms and told us to go back again," Romeo testified at one of the hearings after the fire. "When the man stopped us, we obeyed, for we thought it might have been a little joke. So we went up again. There was a mass of children rushing out. A girl had fainted and I picked her up and carried her downstairs on my back. I don't know what happened then, for I was pulled out myself." Romeo was commended by the chief of police for his gallantry in saving the unconscious girl.

Condolences from across Canada, from the United States, and from King George V poured into grief-stricken Montreal. Newspapers had mistakenly reported Mary Pickford's *Sparrows* as the film the children had been watching. An agent for the Canadian office of the film's distributor made a statement to the press that *Sparrows* was not the film being shown that dreadful day, not wishing the movie or the star to be associated with the tragedy.

One of the two large funeral services held for the dead children was presided over by the archbishop of Montreal. It was unusual for an archbishop to conduct a funeral mass, but it gave him an opportunity to address the crowd of 35,000 on the immorality of movie theatres being open on Sundays, and to call upon "upright spirits" to prevent children from going to cinemas.

Movie theatres throughout Montreal and in many other Canadian cities were closed for fire inspections. The Quebec law forbidding children under the age of 16 to attend movies unaccompanied by adults was vigorously enforced. This law would remain in effect until 1961.

At the inquest into the tragedy, it was revealed that when Ameen Lawand received a phone call at the Maisonneuve Theatre and was told of events going on at that very moment at the Laurier Palace, he went straight home and called his lawyer. He collected a large sum of money from the insurance on the theatre. Some bereaved parents tried to sue him for a portion of the insurance settlement, but through some legal manipulations he was able to dodge the lawsuits.

However, Lawand, Michel Arle and Camil Bazzy were charged with manslaughter and convicted in October of that year. Lawand was sentenced to two years, and Arle and Bazzy to a year each.

The Laurier Palace fire was the worst movie theatre disaster in Canadian history. It was made doubly horrific by the fact that the victims were children and because it could so easily have been prevented.

The Brockville Explosion, 1930

IT WAS A TRAGEDY THAT, UNTIL NOW, has seemingly escaped the attention of the chroniclers of Canadian disasters. Yet, in the blink of an eye, 30 men were annihilated in an explosion set off by the raw power of nature. Before the rumbling of the blast had echoed away down the St. Lawrence Valley, the town of Brockville, Ontario, would bear witness to acts of heroism, and some near-miraculous incidents of survival.

On the afternoon of June 26, 1930, Roderick McNeill of Brockville took his wife and five children to a picnic ground at Macdonald's Point, a spot on the St. Lawrence shoreline just across the Brockville Narrows from Cockburn Island. Mrs. McNeill and the three boys and two girls wanted to watch Dad at work. McNeill was the day foreman on board the drill boat *John B. King*. The vessel was planting dynamite charges out in the Narrows, and the wife and kids had never seen an underwater blast before.

Not that there was usually much to see. The *King*, 150 feet (45.7 m) long and 30 feet (9.1 m) in the beam (the largest drill-boat in Canada) could drill 12 six-inch (15.2 m) diameter holes at a time in the bedrock at the bottom of the river. The crew packed the holes with dynamite, which was connected by wire to a detonator aboard the ship. Then a layer of logs was placed over the blast site to absorb the shock and keep the main force of the explosion thrust downward into the rock. When all was ready, the *King* would move off about 1,000 feet (304.8 m) and trigger the explosion. There would be a heavy WHUMP, and the surface of the water would heave. Tons of shattered rock would then be ready for removal from the river bottom. This was part of a project to deepen the channels in the Thousand Islands and had been underway for a year. There had been no mishaps, though the owners of some nearby properties complained of damage done to their boathouses. They said that the men were using too much dynamite.

The *John B. King*, owned by John B. Porter and Sons of St. Catharines, was specially constructed for this work. She had a platform that extended out over the drilling site, a blacksmith shop, cookhouse and sleeping quarters for crewmembers who did not live in Brockville. Only eight of the crew, including Roderick McNeill and his brother Billy, were Brockville men. Most of the others came from various towns in Ontario and Quebec, though there were also four Nova Scotians and two men from Finland. The crew worked a day and a night shift, due to the shortness of the construction season on the river.

Among the men aboard the *King* that day were Public Works Inspector Leo Marion of Ottawa, Superintendent Luther Kuchenbecker of St. Catharines (whose rank was similar to that of ship's captain) and Brendon Killarney of Brockville. Killarney, a war veteran, had lost his previous railroad job due to the ravages of the Great Depression and had been hired aboard the *King* that very morning. There were also Jack Wylie of Brockville, and a German shepherd named King, the ship's mascot. A few months earlier, in March, Wylie had plunged through the ice on the river and would have drowned but for the courageous King. The dog leapt into the frigid water and dragged Wylie out. King's bravery was brought to the attention of the Spratt's Dog Hero Award

Committee of New York. On this very June day, as King kept vigil over his masters while they went about their jobs, the committee was making the announcement that he had been chosen to receive a medal for valour.

Another crewmember, Paul Lake, was a Brockville man who had earned local fame as a hockey star. Just two days earlier he had taken his wife to the river to show her the buildings that had been damaged by the blasting. It was never recorded whether or not he thought too much dynamite was being used.

At about 4:00 PM a tender brought a load of dynamite to the *King* from a storage facility on Big Island, two miles away. There would be disagreement later over just how much dynamite was now on the drill-boat. Everett Snider, the driver of the supply boat, went into the *King*'s galley. Superintendent Kuchenbecker had to inspect some dredging equipment ashore, so he and about 20 men left the *King* for Brockville. Fate had just dealt those men a very lucky hand indeed. Not so for most of the 41 men still aboard the *King*.

At roughly the same time that Snider arrived with the explosives, a thunderstorm began. The rain was a welcome relief from the heat wave that had been scorching the region for the past few days. No one was alarmed when streaks of lightning forked across the sky. The men had worked under worse conditions, one man would say later. There had not been a drill-boat accident on the river in 18 years, and there was no reason to expect anything to go wrong now. Besides, it took the better part of an hour to bring in the boat's drilling apparatus and get her ready for a trip to shore. By that time the storm would probably have blown over. The crew had drilled ten holes and were busy stuffing them with explosives. To quit now would just be a waste of valuable time.

It had just passed 4:45, and Mrs. McNeill and her children were watching the drill-boat from the verandah of a cottage they'd run to for shelter when the downpour started. Nearby, on another verandah, a Mrs. Easter was putting her baby to sleep while she and a friend, Mrs. Walklate, watched the men working on the water. Upstream from the *King*, the crew of an auxiliary drilling platform wondered if the blast the *King* set off would cause another big wave such as the one that had damaged the boathouses. Half a mile west of the *King*, on the American side of the river, Captain Garrett B. Lok, wheelsman E. Schulmeyer and Superintendent M.R. Rasmussen were on the bridge of the United States Coast Guard cutter *Succor* (CGQ-11). A few weeks earlier Captain Lok and his men had been involved in some commendable rescue work on Lake Ontario.

What these witnesses on land and water were about to see with their own eyes happened as instantaneously as the flash of a camera. A bolt of lightning shot out of the sky as though hurled by the unerring hand of a wrathful god, and struck the *John B. King*! In the blink of an eye the ship exploded and the water under her erupted as electricity sizzled down the wires to the dynamite charges packed into the riverbed. The blast shook the St. Lawrence Valley for miles. The concussion hit the *Succor* with such force that the engineer in the engine room thought that his skipper had run the boat into a dock. An observer on the auxiliary drilling rig remarked on the size of the rocks the explosion had thrown into the air. Then he realized to his horror that they weren't rocks. They were pieces of the *King*!

"I happened to look across the water in front of the cottage and saw the explosion," Mrs. Walklate later told the *Toronto Daily Star*. "There was a deafening report, a sheet of flame, then smoke, and that is all that was left of the boat."

Said Captain Lok of the *Succor*, "I saw the flash of lightning and a second later heard a terrific explosion. I immediately ordered full speed ahead, and at the time of the explosion the CGQ-11 was approximately half a mile distant from the drill-boat. The force of the explosion gave the revenue cutter considerable of a jar. On arriving at the scene of the tragedy I noticed several men in the water and others clinging to wreckage."

Captain Lok saw no sign of the *King*. She had vanished. "A thousand torpedoes couldn't have dealt such a deadly blow," said one witness. Ignoring the danger caused by the combination of poor visibility in the driving rain and the floating debris, Captain Lok launched a boat to look for bodies, while he put the crew of the cutter to work rescuing survivors. This was no time to worry about the niceties of seeking permission to cross the international boundary. One unidentified barge had already steamed past the men in the water without stopping to give assistance.

The Canadians would have nothing but praise for the gallant American captain and his crew. They pulled ten survivors from the water. An 11th man, whom they had missed and who was presumed dead for almost 24 hours, was picked up by another ship. The other 30 were dead. Gone were Paul Lake, Brendon Killarney and Jack Wylie. Gone, too, were the four crewmen from Nova Scotia. King, the beloved mascot who had saved Jack Wylie's life and whose name would appear in the papers as a Canadian canine hero on June 27, was also dead. The two Finns were among the survivors.

The injured men were suffering mostly from cuts, bruises and shock. There were relatively few broken bones. Everett Snider had severe lacerations on his hands and was somewhat stunned when hauled out of the river, but recovered sufficiently to act as pilot for the American cutter on the trip through Canadian waters into Brockville's harbour. From there the injured men were taken by ambulance to Brockville General Hospital and the St. Vincent de Paul Hospital. Some were only half conscious. Roderick McNeill (whose brother Billy also survived) was delirious.

Mrs. McNeill and her children had seen the boat explode right before their eyes. Eight-year-old Joseph McNeill told the *Toronto Globe*, "There was a great big ball of fire and a big noise. Then the boat split in two."

Mrs. McNeill immediately ran out into the storm and tried to launch a rickety old rowboat that was at the riverbank. She knew that her husband was out there in the water, probably hurt, possibly dead, and she was going to find him. She was having difficulty with the boat when an unidentified man—a total stranger—came to her assistance. He pushed the boat into the water and took the oars while the frantic woman peered through the rain in search of her husband. She learned from a man in another small boat that Roderick was alive and aboard the American cutter.

When the injured men recovered enough to talk to the press, some said they could remember nothing from the moment of the explosion to finding themselves struggling in the water. Others gave vivid accounts of their brush with death. Leo Marion, the Public Works Inspector from Ottawa, said, "I was in the cookhouse when a blinding flash of lightning lit up everything around. A terrific roar followed, and the next thing I knew I was high in the air with the debris of the boat and the rocks beneath. Although I was only in the air for seconds, it seemed like hours. The next thing I knew, I was screaming beneath the waters of the St. Lawrence River in an attempt to bring myself to the surface.

I must have been underneath the boat, for my lungs were bursting and I could hardly swim, I felt so weak. I finally saw daylight, but timbers obstructed my efforts to get to the surface. Pushing them aside, I finally found myself in open air." After a few minutes that he said also seemed like hours, Marion was picked up by the cutter.

"I sure had a merry old time on that mattress of mine," George L. Brown of Ottawa told the *Globe*. "I was asleep in my quarters on the deck below the cookhouse of the drill-boat when the explosion came. My bunk was situated directly over the second boiler and when it went, I went with it through the roof. As I went up, I remember thinking that I resembled the man in the Arabian Nights who had the magic carpet. When I came down I found myself in shallow water not up to my neck, with the window of my sleeping quarters around my neck like a frame."

Brown took the window frame from around his neck and crawled onto a large piece of the *King* that was still afloat. There he found the foreman McNeill pinned under a heavy door. Brown lifted the door off McNeill, and the two men were rescued by the Coast Guard cutter.

"It's a funny thing," Brown continued. "When I went up in the air, everything around me looked black, but when I was coming down, everything seemed white. When I was at the top of the ascent, I remember putting my hand beneath the mattress and feeling that the springs were there."

When Everett Snider landed in the water, he plunged so deep that he thought he would never reach the surface alive. He was on the verge of blacking out when he broke through to the air. Once he was aboard the American cutter, he found that his shoes had been blown off.

Initially only one body was found by searchers; that of Nova Scotian Reuben Arnold. The watch on his wrist was stopped at 4:50. As police and volunteers searched the river for more of the dead, a man in a small boat came out and asked them if they had any news of Archie Kerr. He was George Kerr, of Kemptville, 22-year-old Archie's father. A few days later Archie Kerr's body was found, along with that of George McRae, 26, of St. Annes, Cape Breton. A well-known diver from Quebec named Eddie Bouchard went down several times to look for the bodies of men who had been below deck when the *King* was destroyed but reported that "They are hopelessly imprisoned beneath 350 tons of rock." Searchers did find, washed up on the shore, two Valentine cards, one reading "To Daddy from John," the other "To Daddy from Donie," and a photograph of a small boy.

At an inquest into the tragedy, former Member of Parliament T.L. Church said that the *King* was an old boat and improperly equipped. However, an inquiry made by the Department of Public Works could find no evidence to support that charge. There was conflicting testimony over just how much dynamite had been packed into the riverbed, and how much was on the *King*. Survivors had told the press that 3 tons of explosive had been placed in the drill holes and that about 40 tons were on the boat. Superintendent Kuchenbecker said that was ridiculous. "Why, we do not keep as much as that on Big Island at any time." He did not think there was any surplus dynamite at all on the *King*. Roderick McNeill said that 700 pounds (317.5 kg) had been packed into the rock, and a case and a half—about 75 pounds (34 kg)—were still on the vessel.

Some witnesses on shore stated that they had heard three distinct explosions in the brief seconds it took for the *King* to disintegrate. The court of inquiry concluded that the blasts might have been from the dynamite in the river, the dynamite on the boat—if, indeed, there was any—and the ship's boiler exploding. Or the witnesses could have heard the explosions from the river and the boiler, and then an echo.

Each survivor was asked if anything could have been done to prevent the disaster. Each replied, "Not so far as I could say." In the end, the jury decided that no one was to blame for the accident. "Personally, I would have no fear of it happening again," said Kuchenbecker.

Two years later at nearby Alexandria Bay, on the American side of the river, a similar drilling accident—though one that did not involve lightning—killed seven men and injured nine others when the drill-boat *America* blew up. Deepening the channels of the Thousand Islands proved very costly, in terms of both money and blood.

The Knights of Columbus Fire, St. John's, Newfoundland, 1942

FIRE IS PROBABLY MAN'S OLDEST weapon of war, aside from the club. It is also one of the most convenient: it costs nothing to make, it does not have to be smuggled past watchful guards and in the hands of a saboteur it can wreak lethal havoc. Russian partisans used it effectively against Napoleon's occupying army in Moscow in 1812. Confederate arsonists tried (and failed) to set New York City ablaze during the American Civil War. And it is quite possible that an agent of Nazi Germany was responsible for a deadly fire that struck wartime St. John's, Newfoundland.

It was mid-December 1942, still dark days for the Allies. Europe was bleeding under Hitler's iron heel. Nazi U-boats, the fearsome "wolf packs" were devastating the Atlantic convoys from North America that kept beleaguered Britain alive. If the Allies were to have any hope of defeating Germany, they first had to win the Battle of the Atlantic.

Newfoundland, Britain's oldest colony, was sparsely populated and economically poor, but it was vital to the Allied cause. It was a storehouse of natural resources needed for the massive Allied war effort. But even more important was The Rock's strategic location.

St. John's is North America's easternmost port, which meant it was a convenient gathering place for ships making up the convoys bound for Britain. From Newfoundland's airfields the fighter planes of the Royal Canadian Air Force and the United States Air Force could provide at least short-range cover for the freighters, tankers and troop ships. Moreover, Newfoundland sat like a sentinel guarding the Gulf of the St. Lawrence and the entrance to the St. Lawrence River, the great highway to the heart of the continent. To get to the Gulf, U-boats had to slip past Newfoundland's defences. It is true that a few daring U-boat commanders managed to do that, causing considerable damage and loss of life. But they had such a hot time of it in those waters that they withdrew and were damned glad to get out. Still, one had the effrontery to torpedo the gates protecting St. John's harbour.

Because Newfoundland was obviously of interest to the Germans, it was heavily garrisoned with Canadian and American servicemen, as well as the island's own Newfoundland Militia (Newfoundland would not become a province of Canada until 1949). In coastal communities like St. John's a nightly blackout was in effect. All windows had to be covered so that no light would show to give a convenient beacon to prowling U-boats. Ironically, this necessary security measure would contribute to the tragedy about to befall St. John's that December night.

As in any harbour city in time of war, the civil and military authorities in St. John's had to be concerned about spies and saboteurs. The adage "Loose lips sink ships" was a serious warning to anyone with any knowledge about shipping schedules, routes, etc. to keep their mouths shut. The stranger at a nearby table in a tavern or restaurant, or a girl in a brothel, just might be an agent in the employ of the enemy. Not all of Berlin's agents spoke with German accents. Just two months earlier, in October 1942, a U-boat had landed a Nazi spy on Quebec's Gaspé coast. The German agent had been quickly discovered and taken into custody by the RCMP, but where there was one there were undoubtedly others.

Any Nazi agents skulking about St. John's would know that there were more ways than one of striking a blow for the *Fuehrer*. Anything that damaged Allied war facilities, killed Allied personnel, or hurt Allied morale was a step on the road to final victory. St. John's might have been a colonial backwater, but it was right on the enemy's front doorstep. Its destruction would throw a large wrench into the Allies' convoy system, especially with Britain hanging on by her fingernails. And St. John's had a long history of fires.

Historian Dr. Cecil R. Fay wrote, "St. John's has two claims to distinction: it is the oldest town in North America, and it has been burnt more often than any other capital city in the world." Wartime St. John's was a city constructed mostly of wood. Its frame buildings had risen from the ashes of other wooden structures that had been devoured by flames. Many North American communities, their residential and business sections thrown together with inexpensive pine and spruce lumber, could look back upon a "Great Fire" in their histories. Chicago had one. So did Toronto and Vancouver. St. John's had suffered *two*. The first, in 1846, started in a cabinet maker's shop. It gutted the town and left 12,000 people homeless. The second, in 1892, burst from a barn full of straw and raged for 16 days, levelling two thirds of the city. Miraculously, the human cost had been light; only two died in the 1892 conflagration. This time things would be tragically different.

The Knights of Columbus hostel in St. John's had been built by that Roman Catholic organization in 1941 with the best of intentions. Situated on Harvey Street, on a high point in central St. John's, it was meant to be a "home away from home" for

Canadian and American servicemen, and for Newfoundland Militia men from the outports who had been stationed in, what was for many of them, the biggest city they had ever seen. It was a place where lonely young men who were far from home could eat, see a show on stage, dance with the local girls to down-east music and find a comfortable bed in one of the upstairs dormitories. Soldiers, airmen and sailors on leave could play ping-pong in the recreation room, or sit back in the reading room with a book and forget the war for a while.

But the architects of this servicemen's oasis in foggy, wartime St. John's had made some serious mistakes; errors that were to prove fatal. Perhaps these mistakes would have been spotted if plans for the building had been submitted to the St. John's town council. But they were not. And the council, for its part, didn't inquire about the construction going on up on Harvey Road Hill. Remarkably, none of these errors should have gone unnoticed, because they were actually violations of the law.

First, the hostel's doors opened inward. There were only two emergency exits, each of which had a wooden door and a screen door, also opening inward. A crowd pressing from the inside would make opening the doors next to impossible.

Second, there was no straight, unobstructed route from the auditorium to the exit leading to the street. A person leaving the big hall had to go through a restaurant—usually crowded and cluttered with tables and chairs—and a lobby—also likely to be jammed with people. This exit had an inner and an outer door, with a small vestibule in between. It could not accommodate a large number of people needing to get out in a hurry.

Third, there was no separate emergency lighting system. All lights were connected to a panel in the movie projection booth at the rear of the auditorium. If the fuses in that booth were knocked out, the entire building would be plunged into darkness.

The hostel was constructed of clapboard, and was tinder dry. Because it was the Christmas season, the place was strewn with highly flammable decorations. Finally, in their enthusiasm to comply with the blackout law, the hostel's administrators had the windows covered not with blinds or heavy curtains, but with plywood. They also had all the doors but one locked from the outside, to prevent them being carelessly opened and letting out a tell-tale spot of light. The place was a fire inspector's nightmare, and an arsonist's dream come true. It wouldn't even require gasoline to ignite this fire trap. A few well-placed rolls of toilet paper would do the trick.

The night of December 12, 1942, was a cold one in St. John's—minus 10°C. Inside their warm homes, many of the little city's residents were listening to radio station VOCM's popular Uncle Tim's Barn Dance show, which was being broadcast from the stage of the Knights of Columbus hostel. It was a Saturday night, and over 400 people were packed into the popular centre. They were mostly Canadian, American and Newfoundland servicemen, but there were also local girls who were out with soldier boyfriends or who were just looking for someone to dance with.

Most were in the auditorium, watching Uncle Tim's show. "Uncle Tim" was 55-year-old William Patrick Duggan, a St. John's barber who loved to entertain. With his troupe were his three sons: Mickey, 32, a pianist; Gus, 20, a dancer; and Derm, 16, a drummer. Among Uncle Tim's biggest fans was his daughter Margaret Ryan, 28, who always tuned in to the show on her radio. She lived right across the road from the hostel. On this particular night her brother Mickey was performing at a different hostel, and a Canadian sailor named Ted Gaudet was filling in for him. Margaret was listening closely, comparing the stand-in's ability with Mickey's.

In the recreation room other servicemen and their girls played ping-pong and checkers. Two RCAF sergeants from Toronto, Max Goldstein and Bill Collis, had walked into town from their base at Torbay, 8 miles (12.8 km) from St. John's. They'd had a coffee and were waiting for a turn at a ping-pong table when Goldstein decided that it was too hot and sticky in the room, and that he wanted to step outside for a breath of fresh air. As the two men headed for the exit, they noticed the plywood-covered windows and commented that dark window-blinds would have been more sensible, as they would "let a little of God's air inside this sweat-box."

When they got outside, they met two girls with whom they were acquainted. Goldstein took one of the young ladies inside for a dance, while Collis and the other girl stayed outside to have a chat in the frosty night air. Before his friend went back into the smokey, humid building, Collis remarked, "It looks as though we'll have a hot time in the old town tonight after all." His words were to be cruelly prophetic.

The upstairs dormitories at the hostel had 350 beds. These were for the use of servicemen on leave, and for the overflow from the surrounding bases. The men who used them, besides the Canadians, Americans and Newfoundlanders, included Free French who had escaped when their government had capitulated to the Nazis, and some Chinese merchant seamen whose ship had been sunk in Newfoundland waters by a U-boat.

One of the Canadians spending a night in the hostel was Signalman Maurice Weldon of Toronto. At 22 he was already a veteran of Canada's corvette navy. The young man was enjoying a dance but planned on going to bed early. Nineteen-year-old Reginald Holwell of the Newfoundland Militia had been billeted at the hostel but had spent the last three weeks in hospital recovering from mumps. He'd been released that very Saturday and had orders to return that night to the Militia base at Shamrock Field. But first he had to go to the hostel to pick up a shirt he'd left behind. He considered staying for the dance, then decided that he wasn't up to it after his long illness. Instead, he paid a visit to his aunt and uncle. By an odd twist of fate, he would owe his life to a case of the mumps.

At about 10:30 that night, investigators determined later, an unknown arsonist opened a plywood storage cupboard on the second storey. The cupboard was next to one of the dormitories and was part of the loft over the auditorium. In the cupboard were cardboard boxes of paper towels and toilet paper, piled one on top of the other. The arsonist broke open one of the boxes and took out some rolls of toilet paper. He made a trail of toilet paper from the boxes to some point in front of the cupboard, then closed the door and set a match to the tissue. The fire raced toward the cupboard like flame along a gunpowder trail, leaving nothing behind but a bit of sooty residue on the floor that no one would notice. In seconds the boxes in the cupboard were smoldering.

Whoever the arsonist was, he must have had an opportunity to study the interior of the hostel. He knew just where to start the fire and was no doubt aware of the building's lack of escape routes. He must have known that the body count after this night's work would be high. Mass murder was most certainly his intention, because he pulled his act of sabotage on the hostel's busiest night of the week.

While the servicemen and their girlfriends danced below, and on stage a woman named Biddy O'Toole sang "I Met Her in the Garden Where the Praties Grow," the stack of boxes became a pillar of fire. The flames fed on the rolls of paper like so much cordwood. The fire burned through the wallboard above and spread into the bone-dry interior of the loft. Flames licked at the rafters and devoured the tarpaper insulation. The fire burned slowly, soundlessly, while below the music played and the people laughed. They had no idea that hell was right above them.

The loft was not ventilated, so the fire burned down to a blue glow as it consumed the oxygen. The loft was transformed into a big box full of carbon-monoxide gas; invisible, odourless, tasteless and deadly! Down below, a Canadian soldier named Eddy Adams was on stage. He was dressed in a cowboy outfit, and was playing a guitar and singing "The Moonlight Trail." In his dormitory, unsuspecting of the furnace that the cupboard within sight of his bed had become, Maurice Weldon was getting undressed for the night. In her home across the street, Margaret Ryan was listening to the program with her husband.

At 11:10 Weldon, stripped down to his underwear, saw a man in a Newfoundland Militia uniform open the door of the storage cupboard. Instantly a billow of flame roared out as the air hit the smoldering boxes. The fresh oxygen fuelled the blue flickerings in the loft, and pockets of combustible gas became roaring balls of fire. The man in the Militia uniform made a dash for the stairway and was gone.

As the steady boom of exploding gas reverberated down to the auditorium, tongues of flame licked out through the slots of the movie projection room. A woman screamed "Fire!" Then the hall full of happy people became bedlam.

Blistering hot gas shot down from the ceiling and set the stage curtains on fire. Joe Murphy, the show's master of ceremonies, grabbed the microphone and called on people not to panic. But terror already had them in its grip. They stumbled over tables, chairs and each other in a frenzied rush for the doors that wouldn't open. No one knew what to think or what to do as people who only seconds before had been laughing and talking, suddenly dropped in their tracks from lethal doses of carbon monoxide.

In her house across the road, Margaret Ryan heard the scream of "Fire!" on the radio, as did people all over St. John's. She and her husband rushed to the front window and pulled open the blackout curtains. The scene was one they would never forget. The Knights of Columbus hostel was engulfed in flames. Men in blazing pyjamas were jumping from the second-storey windows. Even above the roar of the flames, they could hear the pounding and shrieking of victims trapped behind the locked doors. The heat was already so intense that the windows of nearby buildings were starting to crack. Then the Ryans' radio went dead, as fire destroyed the fuse box in the hostel across the road. People in parts of the building not yet ablaze were left to try to find their way out through smokey darkness.

Even amidst all the terror and chaos, there were acts of heroism. Joe Murphy, already in pain from burns to his hand and foot, guided 20 members of the performing troupe to one of the plywood-shuttered windows. He ripped off the board with his bare hands, then smashed the window with a steel chair. Middle-aged "Uncle Tim" was the first to make the 10 foot (3 m) jump. He picked himself up from the snow, and then caught the others as they came down. Joe Murphy was the last one out. Just before he jumped, Murphy saw the ceiling above the stage explode and a blazing piano come crashing down.

Uncle Tim's son Gus was not with the 20. When he saw people clambering over each other in a mad rush for the locked doors, he joined a group of Newfoundland Militia men who were attempting to bring some order to the panic-stricken mob while their comrades tried to break down the door. Gus and all of those Militia men perished.

So did another troupe member, a Canadian signalman named Hector Wooly. He might have made it to safety with Murphy's group but instead went to the aid of his girlfriend, a singer who had jumped from the stage to the auditorium floor. Before Wooly could get her out, he was struck down by a flaming timber and pinned to the floor. A pair of sailors grabbed the girl and tossed her out through a window from which the shutters had been torn. They could do nothing for Hector.

Upstairs, Maurice Weldon rushed to the blazing cupboard even as the unknown Militia man was racing down the stairs. The heat was of volcanic intensity and forced him to duck to the side. Before he slammed the door shut, he saw the still-unburnt bottom boxes with the words "Toilet Tissue." One of them had been torn open.

Weldon had burned his arm and shoulder in his futile attempt to contain the fire. Now he roused the other men sleeping in the dormitory; four Canadians and two Americans. Then he ran for the stairs. Still dressed only in his underwear, he made it down to the lobby, where he blacked out. He awoke hours later in the hospital.

A teenager named Doug Furneaux found himself at the east side of the auditorium, in darkness and in front of a locked door.

He was jostled by fear-crazed people who hampered his attempts to break the door down. Then someone turned on a flashlight, and the people stood back and allowed Doug to kick in the door. The exit led to a lobby and another locked door. An air force officer knocked himself out trying to batter it down.

Pandemonium still reigned in the auditorium as Doug and others hammered at the door. The fire had been raging for only a few minutes, but already the floor was littered with the dead and with screaming wounded. Flaming Christmas decorations fell from the ceiling and set people's hair ablaze. A big St. John's policeman carried two men and two girls out of the smoke and flames. All four had had their hair burned off, and the girls had lost all of their clothing except their underpants. The policeman was trying to pull a fifth person to safety—a man as big as he was—when a gas explosion sent him sprawling.

Young Doug Furneaux helped rescue over a dozen people that night. He said later, "I'll never forget how many people suddenly remembered their prayers in their time of crisis." One of those he had tried to help was a Chinese sailor. But the man had lost both legs to the fire, and died.

Max Goldstein, who had gone back into the hostel with a girl after catching a breath of fresh air with his buddy Bill Collis, was swept up in a terror-stricken mob when the panic struck. The surge of bodies carried him to a locked door. Goldstein was a champion weightlifter, and with help from some other men, he battered the door down, using his shoulder as a ram. He had no idea where his friend Collis was and was afraid that he might be trapped in the building.

Collis had the same dreadful fear about Goldstein. Shortly after Max and his female companion had gone into the hostel,

Collis and his ladyfriend had been startled to see flames shooting from the building. Collis ran to a side door, and heard the pounding and the screams of people trapped on the other side. He tried to open the door, but it was locked tight. Collis slammed it hard with his boot, and the door sprang open. Six people tumbled out in a blast of flames and scorching air. One was an air force officer whose jacket was on fire. Collis yelled, "Hit the snow!" When the dazed man did not respond, Collis rolled him in a snowbank.

St. John's Central Fire Station was only 200 yards (182 m) up the road from the Knight's of Columbus hostel, and Fire Captain David Mahon had his trucks and men at the blaze by 11:17. But this was the fastest-spreading indoor fire that Newfoundland—or Canada—had ever experienced. Sir Brian Dunfield, who headed the official inquiry into the disaster, said, "I think everyone who was still inside the building was dead by 11:15."

So intense was the heat coming from the inferno that firemen with their hoses couldn't get within 50 feet (15.2 m) of it. If they did, their clothes caught on fire and their helmets became so hot they had to pour water into them. The building was clearly a total loss and there was no hope of any more survivors getting out. The firemen turned their attention to nearby buildings, hosing them down to prevent the conflagration from spreading. They were assisted in this by a pumper from the American base at Fort Pepperrell. If it had been the arsonist's intention to have all of St. John's go up in smoke, he was thwarted in that at least. There was absolutely no breeze that night to carry the sparks and flaming fragments over the wooden rooftops of the city. Nonetheless, any U-boat captain watching from out on the night-dark water must have smiled at the sight of the monstrous red glow coming from a hilltop above blacked-out St. John's.

A crowd of about 10,000 people watched in shock and awe as the flames devoured the hostel and everything in it. A cordon of American servicemen helped the police keep them at a safe distance. By 2:30 AM, December 13, the flames began to die down, but firemen had to continue pouring water on the smoking, smouldering mass until 8:30. Then, as if Nature had to have a cruel laugh at the trials of mere mortals, a blizzard roared in, covering the scene of horror in a mantle of virgin white.

Max Goldstein and Bill Collis found each other that Sunday and each expressed relief that the other was alive and well. "Gee, Bill, it's good to see you breathing," Goldstein said. "The gods were sure good to both of us."

But the gods had not been good to 99 others. Many of the human remains pulled from the ashes were unrecognizable. Bracelets, watches and rings had been melted. Servicemen's "dog tags" were embedded in roasted flesh. Many corpses could be identified only through dental records. When the city morgue became full, the bodies were laid out in the Catholic Cadet Corps Armoury and the Church Lads' Brigade Armoury. The stench of burned flesh hung over St. John's for days. Stray dogs, drawn by the smell, began skulking around the makeshift morgues, and sentries were instructed to shoot them. Prime Minister Mackenzie King sent his condolences on behalf of the people of Canada. The mayor of Boston sent plasma and a team of doctors who were experts in the treatment of burns to help with the 107 injured survivors.

The 19 dead civilians were buried with private funerals arranged by their families. The 80 servicemen were interred with military honours in mass graves. Each individual's coffin was draped in the colours of his branch of the service.

In the month following the disaster, Sir Brian Dunfield interviewed 174 witnesses. The arsonist was never identified, but Sir Brian had no doubt that the fire was "of incendiary origin." There was no evidence whatsoever that the blaze had been accidental; nor that it had been set for an insurance scam. Some people thought that it might have been the work of a pyromaniac, a "fire bug." But Sir Brian said that the blaze was "a classic case of the kind of flash fire which is built around a low-grade gas explosion. That, in my view, accounted for the great rapidity of the fire. It certainly looks as if an enemy agent was about."

His opinion seemed to be borne out within weeks of the Knights of Columbus fire. Rolls of toilet paper were found in the loft of the YMCA's Triangle hostel in St. John's, arranged as though in preparation for a fire. Then fire mysteriously broke out in the Old Colony Club, a spot frequented by servicemen. Four people died in that tragedy. Not long after, there was an attempt to torch the Knights of Columbus hostel in Halifax while servicemen were watching a movie. It was all just too much to be put down to coincidence.

In the end, the saboteur's grisly work that night was in vain. St. John's held fast as a front-line bastion in the Battle of the Atlantic. The convoys continued to sail out of its harbour, carrying to Great Britain the troops and war materials necessary for ultimate victory over Nazi Germany.

The Quebec Air
Disaster, 1949

IN THE OPENING SCENES OF THE 1959 motion picture *The FBI Story*, starring James Stewart, a young man (Nick Adams) escorts his mother to an American airport, takes out a life insurance policy on her and sees her aboard the plane. The old lady bids her son goodbye, little knowing that this will be a final farewell. Her not-so-loving boy has placed a bomb in her luggage. In midair the plane explodes, killing mother and everyone else on board. The villainous son is now a wealthy young man. Of course, the FBI suspects foul play and soon has enough evidence to arrest the killer. Agents slap the cuffs on him and haul him off, as he puts it, "to hell."

The actual incident upon which Hollywood screen writers based this scenario did not take place in the United States but in Canada, ten years before the film was made. It was, at the time, one of Canada's worst air disasters and the most diabolical episode of mass murder in the nation's history. It was a brutal crime that would be a predecessor for even greater acts of evil in decades to come. The perpetrator was a slender young French Canadian who wanted to get rid of his wife and make some money on the side. He didn't really give a damn who else got killed.

Joseph Albert Guay, born in 1917, the youngest of five children, grew up in Quebec City's tough, impoverished Lower Town. His father died when Albert was very young, but his widowed mother doted on him, spoiled him, in fact. What little Albert wanted, little Albert got. If a teacher dared to scold him for mis-behaving, Madam Guay would rush to the school and heap abuse upon the culprit. As a teenager Albert was more interested in pool halls than in school. He sold watches on commission so he would have money he could use to play the role of the big shot. Young Albert liked to talk big and present the image of a guy who could do anything or be anything. When he drove his Mercury sedan, it always had to be fast, with plenty of screeching tires, just like the tough guys in the movies. When he kissed a girlfriend on the side-walk—and he was very popular with the girls—it had to be a passionate public display so that everyone could see that cool Albert was "making out." If the car needed fixing, Albert would put on coveralls and strip down the engine, talking "shop" with anyone present, like a mechanic who knew his stuff. He didn't drink, but he had a taste for fine clothes and liked to strut around in them. He bragged that one day he would be rich. "You will hear more about me someday," he told his friends. "I will make some-thing of myself."

But it was all bluff and show. Behind the big-man facade, Albert Guay was a mediocre little man. He did not have much money. He was no dashing movie star. He was a gullible, easy mark for pool-hall louts who put the touch on him for the "loan" of a few bucks. After he had stripped down that car engine in a show for any friends looking on, he would leave the nuts and bolts on the floor for a real mechanic to put back together. Albert didn't care, as long as he came off looking good.

During the Second World War Guay worked in an armament factory, earning $40 a week. It was there that he met Marguerite Pitre, a heavy-set woman several years his senior. Because she always dressed in black, Marguerite was nicknamed "The Crow."

Guay and Pitre might have had an affair. What is certain is that she borrowed money from him. She eventually was so financially indebted to Guay that he became the dominant influence in her life, even more so than her husband Arthur. Marguerite felt obliged to do just about anything Guay demanded of her.

Before the end of the war Guay married Rita Morel, a raven-haired beauty who also worked at the armaments plant. Albert was dressed to the nines for his wedding, in a tuxedo and top hat, something rarely seen in a working-class Quebec City neighbour-hood. He and Rita settled into a home at 90 Rue Du Roi, and had a baby daughter. When his factory closed after the war, Guay went into the jewellery business, with a store in Quebec City and later branches in Baie-Comeau and Sept-Isles. He played the role of a successful businessman who knew the jewellery trade inside out. When a customer brought a watch in for repair, Albert looked it over with a careful, knowing eye. Then he told the customer that he could see just what the problem was and that he could fix it. Come back tomorrow.

In fact, Guay was barely making ends meet. And it was not he who fixed the watches. His friend Marguerite had an older brother, Genereux Ruest, who was paralyzed from the waist down, but was "a wizard with his hands" according to those who saw him work. Guay gave Ruest a job as watch repairman.

Guay soon found a solution to his financial problems: insurance fraud. He put in a claim for a "robbery" in which he said he'd lost thousands of dollars worth of watches, and to his delight the insurance company fell for it. He followed this up with further robbery claims, and each time the trusting souls at the insurance company sent him a cheque. A couple of "accidents" involving fires paid off nicely, too.

Meanwhile, Guay was getting tired of Rita, although he was very jealous of any attention shown her by other men. Once, when a neighbour gave Rita a ride home from the grocery store, Albert warned the man to never do that again. "That sort of thing can only end in tragedy," he told the man. But for Albert, being a husband and father just wasn't as much fun as being a skirt-chasing single man. In the spring of 1948 he met petite Marie-Ange Robitaille, a 16-year-old waitress. He was immediately smitten with the attractive teenager. Marie-Ange found the 31-year-old jeweller witty and charming. They began dating, even though Marie-Ange knew that Albert was married; the impressionable girl was sure she was falling in love. Guay bought her presents, and she took him home to meet her parents, introducing him as Roger Angers.

Rita, however, learned of the affair. She went to the Robitaille house and showed Marie-Ange's parents a wedding picture of herself and Albert. Monsieur and Madam Robitaille were stunned. Roger, as they thought his name was, had already asked for the hand of their daughter in marriage, and they had consented. He had even bought Marie-Ange an engagement ring. Now they forbade the girl to ever see the charlatan again.

Rita's interference in his romantic adventures infuriated Guay. Moreover, she would not even consider separating. It was probably about this time that Guay first started to think about murdering his wife. But first he had to make some arrangements for Marie-Ange, for whom he had developed an infatuation. She'd had a big row with her parents over the matter of her lover, so she was receptive to Albert's idea that she move in with Marguerite Pitre, who kept a rooming house. What she didn't know was that Albert had told the Crow to keep a close eye on "his" girl. When Marie-

Ange left home, her parents thought she was going to a job in Montreal.

Between sexual encounters with Marie-Ange at the rooming house, Guay was trying to think of a way to kill Rita without getting blood on his own hands. He was, in fact, afraid of the sight of blood. Rita liked cherry wine, so Guay offered a man $500 to poison her drink. The man laughed at him. Then Guay had the family car rigged with a bomb that was supposed to go off while Rita was driving it. Instead, the device exploded while a mechanic was doing a repair. The man was seriously injured. Somehow, Guay managed to escape suspicion. Rita didn't seem to be at all aware that an attempt had been made on her life. Albert even collected the insurance on the car.

Back at the rooming house, Marie-Ange, now 17, complained that she was uncomfortable with the Crow, who had been as domineering as a prison matron. Guay obligingly moved his child mistress into a small apartment on Richelieu Street in Lower Town. But if Marie-Ange thought that now she would have the free life of a "kept woman," she was mistaken.

Guay made her adopt the name Nicole Cote. He gave her only two or three dollars a day—just enough to live on. She was not to leave the apartment except to buy food and cigarettes. Marie-Ange was a prisoner in Guay's little love nest, but it would still be some time before, as she later put it, "common sense took the place of love."

After a few boring months on Richelieu Street, the long days punctuated only by Albert's visits for sex, Marie-Ange decided that her boyfriend wasn't such an exciting fellow after all. She borrowed $50 from a neighbour and went to the train station, where she bought a ticket to Montreal. Her plan was to phone her parents from there and say she was coming home, then get the next train back to Quebec City. She got aboard the train and was in the ladies' room in the Pullman when Guay burst in on her and seized her. Like an obedient puppy she followed him to his car. It was winter, so Guay took away her overshoes and shoes so she couldn't run away while he went back to collect her luggage.

Back in the Richelieu Street apartment that Marie-Ange had grown to hate, Guay slapped her, scolded her, and made red marks on her face with his lips; "hickies," as teenagers would call them. These would make her stay indoors out of simple embarrassment. Just to be sure she wouldn't wander, Guay kept her boots and shoes, and burned her gloves in a small stove.

Later Guay moved Marie-Ange to another apartment. He told her that she could leave anytime she wanted, but that she would need money, which she didn't have. She had by now grown afraid of Guay but was just as much afraid to leave him. She didn't know what he might do if she took such a step.

Guay took Marie-Ange to Havre Ste. Pierre and Sept-Iles, reg- istering her into hotels as Mrs. Guay. At some point she finally overcame her fear and decided to try again to escape from this frightfully possessive man. She telephoned her mother and said she wanted to go home. She was soon back with her mother and father, and had a job as waitress at the Monte Carlo Restaurant. "Things were going well again," she said later.

But things were not going well with Albert Guay. He was enraged over what he considered Marie-Ange's desertion. On the evening of June 24, 1949, as the girl was walking to work, she was startled by the sound of someone running up behind her. It was Albert, and he had a revolver! He told her how depressed he was without her, and gave the impression that he might shoot himself.

"Killing yourself is a lazy way out," she told him.

Guay replied darkly, "Maybe both of us will be lazy." Then a policeman approached and Albert fled.

The officer escorted Marie-Ange to the restaurant. He would have returned to his beat then, but the girl said she had a bad feeling that Guay was inside, waiting for her. She was right. When she went in, with the policeman right behind her, Guay burst out of the men's washroom with his gun. He was arrested, charged with possession of an unregistered firearm, fined and placed on probation.

Amazingly, a short time later Albert and Marie-Ange made up. He bought her some new clothes, and in August the pair flew to Montreal. There they quarrelled, and Guay slapped her around again. Marie-Ange telephoned her father for money, and that long-suffering parent sent her funds for a boat trip back to Quebec City. Guay was on the boat for part of the voyage, and he handed her a letter in which he had written that he would soon be free of his wife and that she (Marie-Ange) would be sorry that she hadn't listened to him. Marie-Ange had no idea what Albert Guay was plotting. Not until weeks after the crime had been committed would she realize that she had been the catalyst in a madman's decision to commit mass murder. All for her—and $15,000!

Albert Guay already had a $5,000 life insurance policy on Rita. Now he took out an additional policy for $10,000. After all, he had done well by the insurance companies in the past, leading him to believe that most people weren't as bright as a slick operator like Albert Guay. Then he turned his genius to the matter of explosives.

Guay told Marguerite Pitre that he would cancel her debt to him if, among other things, she would get him some dynamite. This she was able to do through an acquaintance in the construction industry—about ten pounds (4.5 kg) of it! Then Guay asked Ruest if he knew how to use an alarm clock to detonate dynamite. The "wizard with his hands" said that he could, but just to be sure, he got some professional advice. One day a man named Ovide Côté entered the jewellery store to have a watch repaired. Côté was a veteran of both world wars, an ex-cop and an explosives expert. Guay and Ruest asked him how much dynamite it would take to blow up "a carload of fish." He gave them some information on the use of blasting caps and fuses, but added, "There's no sense fishing that way. You'll only get yourselves arrested." In weeks to come Côté would regret going to the jewellery store that day.

All during this time Albert was playing the part of the suddenly devoted husband. He took Rita on a vacation to Gaspé. He brought her flowers and other gifts. He called her "darling" and told her she was the only one for him.

On the morning of September 9, 1949, Rita Guay boarded a twin-engine DC3 for the 8:00 flight from Quebec City to Baie-Comeau. She was flying Quebec Air, a branch of Canadian Pacific. Albert had persuaded her to take a day trip to pick up some jewellery for him. As Rita was settling into her seat, Marguerite Pitre arrived at the airport in a taxi. She had a 27-pound (12.2 kg) parcel that she wanted to send to Baie-Comeau. On it were a false address and a false return address. The Crow paid the $2.95 shipping charge and told the clerk to handle the package carefully. It was fragile, she said; a religious statue. Then she got into her waiting cab and went back to the city. At some point she stopped and phoned her home. Over the telephone, in the background, she could hear Albert Guay laughing.

The parcel was stowed in the DC3's forward luggage compartment. At 8:05 AM—five minutes behind schedule—the plane took off. There were 23 people on board. Fifteen minutes later a fisherman named Patrick Simard looked up from the riverbank near his home at Sault-au-Cochon, about 40 miles (64.3 km) east of Quebec City. The drone of the airplane passing overhead was suddenly ripped away by the ear-ringing blast of an explosion. Simard witnessed the horrifying sight of a plane falling from the sky nose first. It crashed into a wooded hillside. Twenty-three men, women and children were dead. Albert Guay had rid himself of his wife. Now he was free to marry little Marie-Ange.

But things were not going quite the way Guay had planned. When the plane crashed the fuel tanks did not explode, and the first people to reach the site of the wreck smelled the sharp odour of dynamite. Moreover, the fragments from the inside of the forward luggage compartment showed evidence of an explosion. Investigators quickly suspected the unthinkable. Someone had put a bomb on the plane! While the pieces of wreckage were gathered up and taken to the basement of the Chateau Frontenac for examination, and the shattered bodies were taken away for identification and autopsies, the RCMP, the Quebec Provincial Police and the Quebec City Police began the work of tracking down whomever was responsible for the foul deed. The trail, as it turned out, would not be a difficult one to follow.

Even as Albert Guay was making a great show of grief over the loss of his beloved Rita, and telling his five-year-old daughter that *maman* had gone away, police were looking into the personal backgrounds of all the victims. They questioned the baggage clerks at the airport, and found the record for one parcel with false addresses. A clerk remembered that it had been brought in by a "fat lady" dressed in black. The woman, he said, had come and gone in a taxi.

It didn't take the detectives long to find the cab driver who had brought the "fat lady" to the airport. He remembered her because she had been "fussy." She'd told him that her parcel contained a very fragile religious statue, and that he was to drive slowly and not hit any bumps. At the airport he had carried the parcel to the counter for her. Top reporter Edmond Chase of the Montreal newspaper *Le Canada* also spoke to the cabbie, and the next day his article about the "mysterious woman in black" was being read at breakfast tables all over the province of Quebec.

Albert Guay saw it and got scared. He called Marguerite Pitre and warned her that the police would soon be at her door. If she were caught, he said, she'd hang. He told her that she'd be better off if she took her own life—but first write a note claiming sole responsibility for the plane crash. In desperation, the Crow swallowed an overdose of sleeping pills but instead of the graveyard she landed in hospital. While she was recovering from her failed suicide attempt, the taxi driver was showing the police where he had picked up "the fat lady"; Marguerite's rooming house.

When Marguerite was released from hospital she was officially charged with attempted suicide and questioned about the package she had taken to the airport. She admitted delivering the parcel but said that it was a religious statue. At least, that's what she had been told by Albert Guay, for whom she had simply run an errand. Marguerite was not jailed, but police kept a close watch on her house.

Now the police took a close look at the affairs of Monsieur J. Albert Guay, the jeweller who had a history of making insurance claims and had recently been charged with illegal possession of a firearm. They recalled the beautiful little waitress he had apparently been stalking and spoke to her. Marie-Ange told them all about her relationship with Guay, and that Albert had been telling her for a year and a half that he was going to be free of his wife.

The police examined Genereux Ruest's workshop and found evidence of bomb making. Ruest admitted that he had made a bomb for Guay but said that Albert had told him he was going to use it to blast some stumps on a piece of property he owned. On September 23, scarcely two weeks after the disaster, Guay was arrested and charged with murder. He denied everything.

As the story unfolded in the newspapers, like "half a dozen fiction thrillers," as the *Toronto Globe and Mail* put it, angry Quebecers gathered outside the Pitre house. Police were stationed there, out of concern that there might be an ugly incident of "mob justice." But the people just hoped to get a glimpse of the mysterious Crow. They also crowded into the Monte Carlo Restaurant, hoping to see the beautiful Marie-Ange, who was innocent of murder but whose unwise love affair had led to the tragedy. The one place the people stayed away from was Guay's address. They did not want to disturb the little girl. The child, people said, had been through enough.

As police continued questioning the prime suspects, the whole sordid business began to come out. At first they were led to believe that the bomb had been meant to kill Rita alone. It was supposed to go off in her arms while she was looking for a non-existent address, but had exploded prematurely. That story, however, didn't hold up. After checking flight schedules, the police noticed that the doomed plane had taken off five minutes late that morning. If it had left the airport exactly on schedule, as that flight usually did, the explosion would have happened over water, and the broad, deep St. Lawrence River would have hidden the evidence.

The trial of Albert Guay began in February 1950, and each day's proceedings made headlines across Canada. An explosives expert demonstrated in court how an alarm clock could be used to set off a bomb. A pathologist showed the jury pictures of Rita Guay's pulverized corpse. He testified that almost every bone in her body had been broken, her skull had been crushed and her lungs had burst. Albert Guay wept—or at least appeared to do so.

Marie-Ange, now 19, took the stand and told the whole story of her stormy love affair with Albert. She told about the note he had given her only weeks before the plane crash, in which he had written that he would soon be free of Rita. "I don't love him anymore," she concluded. "I am going around with a nice boy now."

Incredibly, Albert Guay was still trying to con people. He claimed to be a fourth-degree knight of the Knights of Columbus, making him eligible to receive financial help from that organization with his legal costs. The Knights actually started raising funds for him but then withdrew their support when they discovered that he was lying. He was, in fact, a third-degree knight but had been turned down for elevation to the fourth level.

It took the jury only 17 minutes to find Albert Guay guilty, with no recommendation for mercy. The judge sentenced him to be hanged on June 23. After his conviction, Guay confessed to everything, implicating Genereux Ruest and Marguerite Pitre in the murder plot. They had known about the bomb the whole time, he said and had gone along with it because he'd promised them a share of the insurance money. The execution date was postponed so Guay could testify at Ruest's trial. Further evidence confirmed Guay's claims.

On January 12, 1951, J. Albert Guay went to the gallows in the Bordeaux Jail. He did not meet death like a "big shot" but trembled so badly he could not walk without assistance. Ruest was hanged on July 25, 1952, and Marguerite Pitre on January 9, 1953. The victims of the Quebec Air disaster had been avenged. Ironically, as Guay had once predicted, the world had indeed heard about him.

The *Noronic* Fire,
Toronto, 1949

SHE WAS CALLED "The Queen of the Inland Seas." The Canada Steamship Line's luxury cruise ship *Noronic*, known affectionately as the "Norey," was the largest passenger ship ever to ply the Great Lakes. At 326 feet (99.3 m) and 17,000 tons, she was not as large as the ocean liners *Queen Mary* or *Queen Elizabeth*, but on the Lakes she was their equivalent; a floating pleasure palace for the well-to-do.

By 1949 the days had long since passed when Great Lakes passenger ships carried travellers for purely practical purposes. Planes, trains and automobiles had taken away that business. People boarded ships like the *Noronic* to cruise the waters from Lake Ontario to mighty Superior, enjoying the spectacular vistas of the lakes and surrounding countryside. They took meals in her elegant dining room where gourmet dishes were brought to tables set with fine china and genuine silverware. They drank champagne and danced in the ship's gorgeous ballroom while an orchestra played and ladies and gentlemen in fine attire posed like ornaments on the magnificent staircase. At night they would retire to plush staterooms that were furnished with full-sized beds and had running water. Even after the ship's bar had closed, stateroom parties would carry on almost until dawn, with liquor purchased on shopping trips in Canadian and American port cities flowing freely.

Everything about the *Noronic* spoke of elegance and class. She was an imposing sight, with her black hull and white upper decks, and her single stack painted red, white and black. Passengers walked on polished hardwood floors and thick carpeting. The high salon windows were hung with exquisite draperies. Her interior fittings were of finely carved and highly polished maple, ash, pine and birch. Among the *Noronic*'s amenities were a library, beauty salon, barber shop and a playroom for children. There was even a chapel for Sunday services. The officers of Canada Steamship Lines saw to it that their well-heeled guests should want for nothing.

However, queen that she was, the *Noronic* was a flawed monarch. There was her age to start with. The *Noronic* was built at Port Arthur in 1913, well before regulations were passed requiring Canadian passenger ships to have fireproof bulkheads. The *Noronic*'s bulkheads were of wood; wood that either had absorbed highly flammable oils and varnishes over years of polishing or was coated with many layers of equally flammable paint. She had no automatic fire alarm or sprinkler system. There were glass fire alarm boxes, but these were connected to the wheelhouse, where an officer would sound a general alarm if he thought the situation warranted it. There were fire extinguishers that were supposed to be thoroughly checked and tested on a regular basis, but they were not. Testing them meant "making a mess," and nobody wanted that. There were fire hoses, but these required pressure from the engine room to be of any use, and when the ship was in harbour the engine room generated just enough power to keep the lights burning and the hot water running to the staterooms.

Officers conducted regular lifeboat and fire drills for the crew, but they were always scheduled—never spontaneous. They became monotonous exercises in which the participants just went through the motions, and they never involved passengers. No muster lists—notices that told crewmembers and passengers where to go on the ship in the event of an emergency—were prepared. The only information passengers had regarding fire was a small card on a wall in each stateroom that said "FIRE: This steamer is equipped with modern fire prevention apparatus, in addition to which the steamer is patrolled day and night by experienced watchmen for the protection of the passengers." Moreover, the drills were for emergencies out on the water, not in harbour, which was a totally different situation.

Adding to the inevitability of a major disaster on the *Noronic* was a dulling complacency that had settled over the crew. The ship had never had a serious mishap in all her years of sailing. On her maiden voyage in 1914 the *Noronic* had shown herself to be top heavy, but that had been corrected. There had been a couple of small fires, quickly and easily extinguished. The *Noronic*'s captain, William Taylor, 65, of Sarnia, was one of the most experienced and well respected skippers on the lakes. He had to be, to be entrusted with the command of such a ship. It was his justifiably proud claim that he had never lost a passenger. It just did not occur to Captain Taylor that anything could happen to tarnish that fine record.

He probably didn't even give any thought to the time some gypsy stowaways had been found on his ship and made to pay their fare, resulting in one old woman putting a curse on the captain. If Captain Taylor remembered the incident at all, he undoubtedly put it aside as superstitious nonsense. Besides, it had been years ago and no "bad luck" had touched him. That was about to change.

On September 16, 1949, the *Noronic* sailed into Toronto harbour and tied up at Pier 9 at the foot of Yonge Street. This was to be but an overnight stop on the last voyage of the season, which would take her to Prescott on the Upper St. Lawrence. She had made stops at Detroit and Cleveland, so the great majority of her 524 passengers were Americans from Michigan and Ohio. Many of her all-Canadian crew of 171 were from Sarnia, the *Noronic*'s home port. As the queen of the lakes eased into her mooring for what was to be the very last time, most of the people on board were looking forward to an evening of dining, drinking or shopping in Toronto. As was its wont, fate would be quite contrary in its choices of who would live to see another day.

Docked on either side of the *Noronic* that day were two other cruise ships: the *Kingston* and the *Cayuga*. On board the *Cayuga* was a man named Nicholson who was a friend of Louisa Dustin, the senior payroll officer for Canada Steamship Lines. Miss Dustin was on a working holiday. She could have been home in Sarnia but had sailed with the *Noronic* to get some accounts up to date. When she had her paperwork finished, she intended to take a walk along the dock and visit Nicholson.

Also on board the *Cayuga* was musician Harry Pender. He had been playing with the *Cayuga*'s orchestra all summer but had received instructions to transfer over to the *Noronic* for the trip to Prescott. Pender lived in Toronto and wanted to spend a few hours with his wife, but decided that he had better take his instruments and luggage to the *Noronic* and get settled into his quarters there. In a few days he'd be back home for the season anyhow. Two of the *Cayuga*'s passengers were David James of Toronto and Catharine Card of Guelph. The two university students would have more than a pleasant cruise to remember before that night was over.

Among the many *Noronic* passengers who went ashore were an elderly Ohio couple named Wilder. They had been looking forward to a peaceful cruise and then were disappointed to find that many of their travelling companions were rowdy, noisy and often drunk. For them, a few hours in Toronto would be a welcome break from the party animals. There would later be considerable controversy over just how much drinking had been going on aboard the *Noronic*.

The majority of the *Noronic*'s crew went ashore that night. Of the few who remained aboard, only 15 were on duty; too few to adequately staff such a large ship. Tight purse strings was the main reason for this. Canada Steamship Lines preferred giving people time off when a ship was in harbour to paying them overtime. Remaining on duty were First Officer Gerald Wood, seven men in the engine room, four bellhops, two wheelsmen and one watchman.

Among those gone ashore that night were waitresses Florence Harris and Peggy Shaw, Lounge Manager Al Lingren, Purser William Nichol, Chief Linen Steward Chick Yates, and Captain Taylor himself. The captain was visiting a friend and allegedly was accompanied by Miss Josephine Kerr of Ohio. Josephine was travelling with her brother, businessman and politician Raynor Kerr, and his wife and three children. Whether or not she was actually with Captain Taylor that evening, Josephine was about to endure a night she would no doubt wish for the rest of her life that she could forget.

Some of the *Noronic*'s passengers chose not to head up Yonge Street for the bright lights of Toronto. They stayed on board for the dance that was being held that night, or just to play cards. Bertha Williams, at 86 the oldest person on board, intended to retire early. Mrs. Williams loved the *Noronic* and for several years had gone on two or three cruises every summer. She knew all of the crew "from bridge to stokehole," as she put it, by their first names. The good old *Noronic*, she said, helped keep her young.

There were some people who were actually heading *to* the *Noronic* while passengers and crew were fanning out through the city. One was the son of Toronto Fire Chief George Beatty. He had an invitation for himself and his girlfriend to attend the dance. Another was Sam Graham, a truck driver for Canada Steamship Lines. Graham was on his way to Toronto from Point Edward with a truckload of fruit and vegetables for the *Noronic*'s galley. He expected to make his delivery and then drive right back home to Sarnia. Little did he know that the fresh Niagara peaches in his cargo would be instrumental in saving two lives that night.

The evening progressed without any noteworthy incident. Bellhops hustled about. People danced, played cards or relaxed in their staterooms on A, C and D decks. Louisa Dustin finished her paperwork and went to the *Cayuga* to visit Nicholson. Sam Graham arrived with his truckload of produce and found there was no one to help him unload. He had taken a few baskets of peaches off and set them on the dock when he was made an offer that didn't come along very often. He could spend the night on the ship and his truck would be unloaded in the morning. Who wouldn't jump at the chance for a free night aboard a luxury cruise ship?

On the port side of C deck, near the stern, maids were finishing up with some cleaning. Their supplies for the staterooms in this part of the ship were kept in two linen closets that faced each other across the corridor, right by the men's and women's washrooms. From these closets they got towels, washcloths, bedding, soap and their cleaning equipment. When the maids had finished their work, one of them put the buckets and mops away, then closed and locked the closet doors. According to regulations, those closets should have been checked twice later that night; once by a porter and again by a Special Officer doing fire patrol. But there was no porter on duty that night and, by a careless error, no Special Officer was available.

It would never be determined just what started a smoldering fire in one of those C deck closets. Maybe it was a faulty electric wire. Perhaps a maid had absent-mindedly left a cigarette burning. Whatever the cause, the fire was allowed to slowly burn into the linens and towels undetected and undisturbed for hours. Just enough air got in through the cracks around the door to keep it alive.

The evening hours lengthened, and the passengers and crew began drifting back to the ship. The Wilders returned, still not happy with what they considered too much revelry on the *Noronic*. They went to their stateroom, hoping that for once they would get a good night's sleep. In the salon a few people were still playing cards. Harry Pender had brought his instruments on board but could not find anyone who could tell him where he was to be quartered. Then a strange feeling, such as he had never before experienced, overcame him. It told him that he had to get off the ship. Pender left his instrument in the band room and went home to spend the night with his wife. If the captain was indeed stalked by a gypsy curse, Harry Pender, it seems, had a guardian angel.

At 1:30 AM on September 17, there was a change of watch among the *Noronic*'s crew. Second Officer Fred Bowles took over from First Officer Wood. The wheelsmen, bellboys and others were replaced. There were still only 15 people on duty. Captain Taylor had not yet returned.

Special Officer W.A. Brown was asleep. He should have been on duty and would have done the fire patrol, which included checking the linen closets. He had expected to be awakened in time for his watch, but the other Special Officer had gone off duty hours earlier and no one thought to awaken Brown.

Shortly after going on watch, Second Officer Bowles joined the two wheelsmen, Jim Donaldson and George Pepper, at the gangway. This was another infraction. According to regulations at least one of those men should have been in the wheelhouse, which was supposed to be staffed at all times in case of an emergency.

Since neither Special Officer was available, Donaldson and Pepper were sent to conduct the fire patrol, a job for which they had not been trained. To get it done quickly, they took shortcuts and did not even pass the linen closets on the port side of C deck. Inside that smoke-choked little cubbyhole, a monster was waiting to be unleashed.

At 2:00 AM it was quiet aboard the *Noronic*. A half-dozen couples were still playing cards. A few of them were getting tired and suggested it was time to turn in. One woman, however, said she was hungry. Why not play another couple of hands and have some coffee and sandwiches? Some of her companions protested mildly, but others decided it wasn't such a bad idea. After all, no one had to get up early in the morning. "Might as well stick together until the end," one man sighed. They ordered their coffee and snacks, and dealt the cards again. The woman's untimely craving for a little something to eat would turn out to be very timely indeed. It would save their lives.

Special Officer Brown was still asleep. First Officer Wood was stretched out on his bunk, waiting for sleep to put an end to a busy day. In his cabin on D deck, Chief Steward William McLean lay wide awake. For some inexplicable reason he had a terrible feeling that something bad was going to happen, that there was danger of fire. He thought that the fire patrols had been properly carried out, but nonetheless he had given his bellboys instructions to be alert for any sign of fire.

One of the bellboys, Johnny Côté of Montreal, was busy cleaning up the salon on D deck. It was no easy job, looking after tourists, even the wealthy ones. And so many of them drunk! Another half hour, and Johnny would have the job done. But then, tomorrow night he would have to do it all over again.

Not far from where the *Noronic* was moored, Ross Leitch, George English and Cecil Mackie sat in a small boat Leitch operated as a water taxi between the mainland and the Toronto Islands. They were hoping they might get one or two more late fares before calling it a night. Nearby, David James and Catharine Card sat on a bench on Pier 9, talking and sharing a romantic moment in the moonlight. Alan Ferris, a Canada Steamship Lines watchman, followed his patrol route past the *Cayuga*, the *Noronic* and the *Kingston*. So peaceful and quiet was it that a watchman from an earlier era might have cried, "All's well!"

Except it wasn't.

Shortly after 2:00 AM Chick Yates returned to the ship. He decided to spend some time in the fresh night air before going to bed. Al Lingren was back, too, and he also preferred to stay on deck awhile, chatting quietly with a shipmate.

Florence Harris and Peggy Shaw returned from their pleasant evening in Toronto and boarded the ship. They were on their way to their quarters when Florence looked down and saw some baskets of peaches sitting on the dock, about 50 yards (45.7 m) from the ship. The fruit was obviously waiting to be loaded aboard the *Noronic*, so no one would mind if they pinched a couple of peaches. The two young women turned around and went back down to the pier. Meanwhile, fast asleep in their staterooms were the Wilders, Bertha Williams, and Raynor Kerr with his wife and eight-year-old son Peter. His daughters Kathleen, 11, and Barbara, 6, were asleep in Josephine's room, just on the other side of the wooden bulkhead.

At about 2:25 AM Captain Taylor stepped out of a cab at the foot of Pier 9. Allegedly, Josephine Kerr was with him. Some witnesses would say later that the captain was drunk. He would insist that he'd had only one small drink of scotch. He had a diabetic condition and said he could allow himself no more than that.

Captain Taylor escorted Josephine to her stateroom on C deck. She had forgotten her key, so the captain opened her door with his master key. He then went upstairs to his cabin just aft of the bridge, greeting a few passengers along the way. Before turning in for the night, Josephine went down the corridor to the women's washroom. She had to pass the linen closet in which the fire was smoldering, but she did not detect anything wrong.

It was not quite 2:30 when Don Church, a fire insurance specialist from Ohio, finished the nightcap he'd been having in the lounge and headed for his stateroom on C deck. He was in the starboard corridor when he caught the unmistakable smell of smoke and felt a burning sensation in his eyes. He followed the smell straight to the linen closet in the port corridor. He heard a rustling noise coming from inside, and thought that someone might be trapped within. Church tried to open the door, but it was locked. He ran for help.

Church found bellboy Garth O'Neill and told him of the problem. O'Neill should have immediately informed an officer. Instead, he went to look into the problem himself. He unlocked the door and carefully opened it as Church looked on. The bedding inside was smoldering, and flames leapt up as fresh air flooded the smoke-filled closet. O'Neill should have closed the door instantly and sent for an officer. Again, he did not. He left the door open, allowing the fire to grow, and fetched an extinguisher. He aimed it into the closet, but only a thin, useless stream came out.

A passenger named Gibson, disturbed by the noise in the corridor, watched from his doorway as O'Neill and Church hurried off and returned with a firehose. They opened the nozzle, but only a dribble of water came out. Now O'Neill ran to one of the fireboxes, broke the glass, and pulled the alarm. There was no one in the wheelhouse to hear it. It was now about six minutes since Church had first detected smoke. The fire was spreading out into the corridor, and from that moment the fate of the *Noronic* and many of her passengers was sealed.

Gibson awoke his wife, and the two of them hurried down to the gangway. Church, too, rushed to get his family off the ship. So far, no one had done anything to alert the other passengers.

The stately *Noronic* was a giant tinderbox. Fed by paint, varnish, carpeting and dry wood, the flames raced through her at an astonishing speed. One man would later say, "She went up like a paint factory." Another said, "It just went off like the head of a match."

Josephine Kerr was just getting into bed when she smelled smoke and heard shouts in the corridor. She opened her door and was horrified to see it full of smoke, with flames dancing along the floor and walls. She immediately awoke Kathleen and Barbara. When Josephine took the two little girls into the corridor, she was amazed to see how far the fire had spread in a matter of seconds.

She pounded on her brother's door and got no response. She hoped against hope that Raynor, his wife and little Peter had already escaped. But would they have left without her and the girls?

The little girls were now wide awake and terrified. Josephine could see that the corridor that led to the stairway and safety was a mass of flame, and the fire was coming right at them. They had no option but to go up. She grabbed the girls by their arms and dashed for the stairway leading up to B deck.

After he had pulled the alarm, Garth O'Neill ran down to E deck, where he met the wheelsman Donaldson and told him of the fire. Donaldson immediately raced to the officers' quarters. A few panic-stricken passengers were already trying to get off the ship, but most were still asleep in their staterooms.

Donaldson found Captain Taylor at the door of his cabin. The captain seemed to be having difficulty finding the right key. Some would say that was further evidence that he was drunk. Taylor would say that his key chain had broken earlier in the day, and he had put the keys back on it in a different order than they had previously been. Donaldson yelled that there was a fire on the ship, and then ran and pounded on First Officer Wood's door.

Wood opened up to smoke and advancing flames. He raced up to the wheelhouse and pulled the switch that set off the klaxon horns. Then he pulled on the whistle cord, intending to give the series of whistle blasts that was the emergency signal. But fortune had determined that nothing was going to go right on the doomed *Noronic*. The whistle jammed open, giving out a steady, haunting moan that drowned out the klaxons and utterly confused the passengers.

After telling Donaldson of the fire, O'Neill ran to the crews' quarters on D deck and awakened four sleeping bellboys. He grabbed some of his personal property, then left the ship through an open freight door, jumping across to the dock. It never occurred to him to awaken passengers.

Harold Sharrock and his wife were about to go to bed when Mrs. Sharrock said she smelled smoke. Harold opened the door and saw a woman with her hair and nightdress ablaze tumbling down a stairway. He tried to beat out the flames, and the woman's scalp came off in his hands. She was dead. Harold shouted to his wife, and the two of them got out.

In the lounge on C deck the card players were still waiting for their sandwiches when they learned of the fire. One woman wanted to go to her stateroom to get her belongings but was prevented by the others. They quickly ran to the gangway and escaped unhurt.

Two elderly women, Mrs. Max Peller and Mrs. Saul Kecti thought the racket they heard in the corridor was caused by carousing drunks. But when they opened their door they saw a scene of complete bedlam. People were screaming, fighting and running in both directions. The two women hurried toward a stairway and found their escape route blocked by flames. They turned and went in another direction, and were repeatedly jostled and shoved by younger people who were running around in wide-eyed panic. "We didn't know where the exits were, and we had no idea what we should do," Mrs. Peller said later. "We didn't know where to go... and there was no one there to tell us."

The women eventually made it to the port side of the ship and there found an unexpected escape route. The crew of the *Kingston*, which was moored alongside the *Noronic*, had run a gangway across to the burning ship so people could get across. Mrs. Peller and Mrs. Kecti were the last to use the improvised bridge. The *Kingston* had to throw off her lines and back out into open water because flaming debris was falling on her and her own paint was staring to blister from the intense heat. The *Cayuga*, too, had to distance herself from the *Noronic*, but not before Louisa Dustin got off and hurried back to her own ship. Apparently, she felt she had to save her payroll accounts.

Mrs. Paul Oakes and her good friend Anna Boukley, both of Detroit, were dressed only in their nightgowns when they heard a pounding on their door. Mrs. Oakes opened it and was almost overwhelmed by smoke and heat. People were stampeding like cattle. She spotted a steward in his white jacket and grabbed the man's sleeve. "Come on, Anna!" she shouted. Certain that her friend was right behind her in a corridor so thick with smoke that visibility was almost nil, she allowed the steward to guide her to safety. Only then did she realize that Anna was *not* behind her. She would never see her friend again.

Sam Graham, the truck driver who had thought himself fortunate to spend a night aboard the elegant *Noronic*, was awakened by noises outside his door. When he looked out and saw flames, he bolted for a stairway and ran down to the gangway. Along the way he ran into some passengers who were obviously unaware of the danger. He shouted, "FIRE!", but they only laughed at him. When Sam made it to the dock, he knew he'd have to move his truck so it wouldn't be in the way of the firemen who would surely be there any moment. He reached down for the keys in his pocket and suddenly understood why those passengers had laughed. They must have thought he was a drunken prankster, because he wasn't wearing any pants.

Florence Harris and Peggy Shaw had helped themselves to a few peaches from the baskets on the dock and were on their way back up the gangway, when flame and searing hot air suddenly blasted out at them. Before their very eyes, the ship seemed to go up like a Roman candle. They ran back down the gangway, suffering only singed hair and slightly scorched faces.

Scant minutes after Andrew Ferris had walked past the *Noronic* and seen nothing amiss, a security officer named Dan Harper was startled to see fire through the portholes of the ship, and flames erupting from B and C decks. He ran into the Canada Steamship Lines building and phoned the fire department and the police department. Then a passenger who had escaped the inferno on the *Noronic* burst in and told him to call for ambulances. "It's terrible!" he gasped. "There are people dead and burned in there. Dozens, maybe hundreds of them!"

The alarm was recorded by the Toronto Fire Department at 2:34. The first firetrucks reached Pier 9 at 2:41. But the six minutes wasted by the bellboy in trying to put out the fire himself proved fatal. It took only 15 hellish minutes for flames to engulf the *Noronic* from top to bottom and bow to stern.

Fire Chief George Beatty was on the scene, directing operations with all the professionalism at his command. Inside, he was frantic with worry that his son, who had been invited to the dance, might still be aboard. Only later did he learn that the boy had left the ship long before the fire had broken out.

Purser William Nichol was on his way back to the *Noronic* in a taxi when he heard the wail of sirens. Something told him that it was his ship the emergency vehicles were rushing to. When he reached the pier he jumped out of the cab and tried to dash on board. Dan Harper and some other men held him back.

Passengers who found their route to the gangway blocked by fire retreated to the upper decks. There was simply nowhere else to go. From lofty A deck it was a 70 foot (21.3 m) drop to the pier on one side and the water on the other. Those on the pier side could not get across to the other, and not all of those on the water side could swim. But anything was better than being roasted alive. Men, women and children leapt out from the rails and plummeted down.

David Jones and Catharine Card, who only minutes before had been spooning in the moonlight, now found themselves in the midst of a scene of horror as they rushed about trying to help people who had been forced to jump to the pier. They were screaming with pain from bloody lacerations and broken bones. One woman died after hitting the concrete head first.

Ross Leitch, George English and Cecil Mackie were astonished when they saw the *Noronic* in flames. As soon as they saw people plunging into the water, they went into action with their water taxi. They hauled people out of the water, took them ashore, then went back for more. They pulled over 50 people out of the water that night. Thanks to their heroic work, only one person drowned.

Firemen now had their hoses trained on the inferno, but the heat was so intense that the water evaporated before it reached the fire. Other firemen ran ladders up so they could get to the crowds of shrieking people on the upper decks. Those people, maddened with fear, made the situation all the more dangerous by trying to pile onto the ladders all at once. One ladder broke, spilling everybody into the water. Fortunately, the firemen were able to pull everyone out.

When Al Lingren realized that the ship was on fire, his first thought was for the passengers. But before he could do anything for anyone else, he found himself surrounded by flames. Almost like a living beast that was stalking him, the fire blocked one exit, and then closed in on him from behind. Lingren threw his arms up in front of himself, and made a mad dash through hell. He emerged on an open deck and jumped over the side into the harbour. He was badly burned, but alive.

Josephine Kerr and her frightened nieces emerged on B deck. All around was sheer pandemonium. People were running back and forth looking for a way out, and there was none to be found. Some were burned and others were bleeding. She saw people jump over the side, and knew that was the only escape. Barbara and Kathleen were good swimmers, so Josephine ran with them to the bow. There she hesitated. It was 60 feet (18.2) down to the water, and she was afraid that would be too much of a fall for the children. Fortunately, in all that panic-fuelled chaos there were some people who kept their heads. A man picked up Barbara and told her to put her arms around his neck and hold on tight. Then he went over the side. Another passenger put Kathleen up on the rail, and before she had time to think about it, gave her a push and launched her into space. Josephine quickly followed. But she had picked a bad spot at which to jump. She hit the anchor cable on the way down, scraping herself badly, before splashing into Toronto harbour. Josephine, Barbara and Kathleen all survived. Raynor Kerr, his wife and son did not.

The unidentified man who took the leap with Barbara was not the only hero of that terrible night. When Harold Sharrock and his wife reached the safety of the pier, Harold went back to get a woman he'd seen bleeding on the deck. He found the woman and carried her down the gangway, but she died in an ambulance.

Two of the first Toronto policemen on the scene were Detective Cyril Cole and Constable Robert Anderson. There was nothing they could do about the fire, so they plunged into the cold water and helped the lads in the water taxi with the rescue work. Many of the people in the harbour were burned or injured and would surely have drowned had it not been for the two officers.

A bellboy who was identified only as Eddy did not run straight for safety as some of his co-workers had done. He hurried to A deck to awaken other bellboys, then he and two others tried to rouse as many passengers as they could. Eddy battered down a door with an axe to get a hysterical woman out of her stateroom. Then he and his partners made a ladder out of knotted bedsheets and lowered it over the side so some waitresses and passengers could climb down. Only when they were certain that their particular part of the ship had been evacuated did Eddy and the other two youths make their own escape.

When Second Officer Bowles heard the fire alarm, he ran along a corridor, pounding and kicking at doors and shouting, "FIRE!" He got as many people as he could out of their staterooms, and then helped them get down to the dock by means of cables and ropes. He went back and pounded on more cabin doors. Getting no response, he slid down a hawser to the dock.

After First Officer Wood sounded the alarm, he found that his way aft was blocked by flames. He pounded on the windows of the few cabins he could reach, then hurried down a ladder to B deck. That deck, too, was in flames. People there were jostling about, bewildered and scared. Wood yelled at them to follow him, and led them down to C deck, where he found another 30 or 40, paralyzed with fear. With the help of Boatswain R.D. Morrison and a sailor from the engine room, Wood hustled the passengers over the side and down a rope to the dock. Then he tried again to go aft and rouse more people who might still be in their bunks. But the thick, choking smoke was as impenetrable as a solid wall, and the barrier of flame and heat impossible to breach.

Chief Steward William McLean was awakened by the fire alarm. He stumbled through the smoke and flames to C deck, where he banged on doors. When he had collected as many living souls as he could find, McLean led them safely off the ship.

Chief Engineer F.B. Bonnell was off-duty and asleep when one of his men awakened him with the chilling news that the ship was on fire. He went straight down to the engine room. Whatever was needed up above—lights for people to see their way out, pressure for the fire hoses—the power would have to come from there. Bonnell and his courageous men stayed at their posts, choking on smoke and sweating in the volcanic heat, until the last possible moment. When they finally had to evacuate the engine room, Bonnell was the last man out.

After wheelsman Donaldson alerted the captain and first officer, he ran along the port side of A deck, banging on doors and windows. Then, at the wheelsmen's quarters he spread the alarm to his colleagues. He hurried out to an open deck where he helped lower a lifeboat with three crewmen and three women in it. Like everything else that jinxed night, the lowering of the boat was an exercise in futility. Ropes became twisted and had to be chopped with an axe. The lifeboat fell, dumping the occupants in the water. It was the only lifeboat to be launched from the dying *Noronic*. Unable to do anything else, Donaldson slid down a rope and swung across the water to safety.

Special Officer Brown, whose awakening might have averted the disaster altogether, was at last aroused in the midst of the emergency. He ran up to C deck and rescued two women who were trapped in a stateroom (one of them died later). He smashed cabin windows and used a fire hose to battle the flames until the water pressure died. Then he went in search of the captain.

A watchman named Guest was going about his duties on E deck when he was startled by the sight of a panicked crowd trying to get off the ship through a freight door. He ran up to D deck and encountered thick, choking smoke. He found a woman and a small child, and whisked them to safety. He went back to the hell that was D deck and saw a woman who had fainted. Guest carried her down to the pier, then started back to look for others. But by this time even the gangway was in flames. No living soul would set foot on the *Noronic* again, until the monster had burned itself out.

No person's conduct would be more scrutinized than that of Captain William Taylor. He had been fumbling with his keys when he was first told of the fire. He then went to C deck, where he saw the smoke and flames. He hurried out to the starboard deck and shouted down to people on the dock to call the fire department (which Dan Harper had already done). Captain Taylor then grabbed a fire hose and tried to fight the blaze himself. But it was like battling hell with a water pistol.

Two crew members took over with the hose, and Captain Taylor walked to the bow and then back to the stern. He saw passengers escaping anyway they could, but he had not yet knocked on a single cabin door. He returned to the two men who had the fire hose, took it from them and used the nozzle to break some cabin windows. There was very little water pressure, but the captain moved the nozzle up and down as though spraying the rooms with a substantial stream.

Captain Taylor and the two crewmen were joined by Special Officer Brown. The four men went as a group to see to it that cabins were vacated, and alerted three or four people. It did not occur to the captain to divide his men up and send them to different parts of the ship.

The captain then left this group and went back to the bow, where he found First Officer Wood helping passengers go over the side. He asked Wood if everybody was out, and the officer said no. Captain Taylor went back along the port side, trying different fire hoses and finding them all useless. Finally, two sailors told him that he had better get off the ship. Special Officer Brown, meanwhile, escaped down a ladder at the stern. He thought that the ship had been successfully evacuated.

It was a dazed and befuddled skipper who walked down the gangway to the pier. With the flames from his beloved ship now shooting 100 feet (30 m) into the sky, Captain Taylor suddenly broke away from the throng of people on the dock and went back aboard the *Noronic* through a freight door. He fought his way through the heat and flames to the now-deserted engine room, then made it up to C deck. There he found a man named Dallas C. Condon. He also found himself and the passenger surrounded by fire.

The two men might have died right there, but a pair of firemen saw them and came to the rescue with a light ladder. However, as Taylor and Condon inched down the ladder, their combined weight caused it to snap, and they fell into the water. When the two were pulled out by firemen, the captain tried to go back aboard the *Noronic* once more, but was restrained by a policeman and a ship's officer. He had a badly injured hand and was talking incoherently. Was he in shock, or was he drunk? The question would never be satisfactorily answered. It was a sad end to what had been a sterling career.

First Officer Wood and Boatswain Morrison were the last living souls to leave the *Noronic*. They descended a fire department aerial ladder to a pier that was almost as chaotic as the last 15 minutes in the life of the *Noronic* had been. Scores of rubber-neckers and the morbidly curious had swarmed down to the waterfront, getting in the way of firemen who were pouring thousands of gallons of water a minute onto the burning ship, and causing problems for the police officers who were trying to keep them back. People were crying and screaming from the pain of burns and other injuries, or because loved ones had not escaped the conflagration. People numbed by shock and despair were milling through the crowd, looking for missing friends and family members. A steady parade of stretcher bearers carried the injured to ambulances. Almost every ambulance in Toronto was at the foot of Yonge Street that night, as well as those from communities within a 20 mile (32.1 m) radius of the city, and still they were not enough. Taxi drivers voluntarily whisked people off to hospitals in their cabs.

Toronto responded admirably to the crisis. Hospitals called in every off-duty staff member they could reach. The city's two best hotels, the Royal York and the King Edward, opened their doors to refugees from the *Noronic*. Toronto's biggest department stores, Eaton's and Simpson's, donated clothing for people who had escaped wearing nothing but their nightclothes or underwear. There was no end of praise for the truly heroic work of the Toronto Fire Department and Police Department.

But in the wake of one of the worst disasters in Toronto history, other people and institutions would be called into service. Funeral homes from all over the city would send their hearses to carry away the dead. Many of the charred remains would be taken to a temporary morgue set up in the Horticultural Building on the grounds of the Canadian National Exhibition. A building that was famous for its displays of aromatic flowers would now know the stench of death.

By 7:40 AM firemen were finally able to go aboard the *Noronic*—or what was left of her. The once-proud queen was listing to port, and had settled stern-down on the bottom of the harbour. Within the superstructure of twisted steel, not a scrap of wood remained. Every pane of glass had been melted. But it was the human remains that sickened even the most veteran firemen. Charred bodies lay singly and in jumbled piles. Some were missing arms and legs. Many had evidently died in their beds. Here and there were corpses locked in a final embrace.

The death toll of the *Noronic* was 118, including those who died in hospitals and the one drowning victim. Dead were the Wilders, Bertha Williams and Louisa Dustin. Not a single crew member had died, which gave rise to the accusation that the crew of the *Noronic* had saved their own skins and left the passengers to their fate. The burns that some of the crew had suffered while helping passengers were proof that the accusation was not entirely true. Canada Steamship Lines arranged for a special train to take the American survivors home. It would later be charged that the company wanted to get them out of town in a hurry so that they wouldn't be available as witnesses at the enquiry.

A five-week federal Court of Investigation headed by Mr. Chief Justice Kellock began on September 28. There was much debate over the question of heavy drinking on the *Noronic*. The court finally determined that alcohol had not been a factor in the disaster. In the end, the court held Canada Steamship Lines and Captain Taylor accountable for the destruction of the ship and the heavy loss of life. They were guilty of neglect on many points, the court ruled. Canada Steamship Lines had to pay over $2 million in damages, and Captain Taylor's certificate was suspended for a year. Taylor, a thoroughly broken man, chose to retire instead.

The dead were buried in Mount Pleasant Cemetery and a monument erected to their memory. The fire-ravaged hulk that had been the *Noronic* was towed to Hamilton and reduced to scrap. Only her whistle was saved, and placed in Toronto's Marine Museum. It remains as a mute relic of the Queen of the Inland Seas, and a reminder of the terrible night she died.

The Winnipeg Flood, 1950

LAKE WINNIPEG AND THE RED RIVER and its tributaries are the remains of a huge, prehistoric body of water scientists have named Lake Agassize. This product of the Ice Age was relatively shallow but covered more territory than all of the current Great Lakes combined. There are times, it seems, when the Red River decides to spread out and reclaim that lake's ancient glory, and reclaim large portions of Minnesota, North Dakota and Manitoba. From the time of its first recorded flood in 1826, when it wreaked havoc with settlers already ravaged by cold, starvation and the attacks of fur traders, until the great flood of 1950, the Red spilled over its banks 11 times. For decades it defied all human attempts to keep it in its place. Said one American engineer, "If I had all the money in the world, I couldn't stop flooding on the Red River." A Canadian colleague said that it might be possible to protect Winnipeg from flooding, but, "I doubt if it will ever be possible to protect the farms and small towns farther south."

The reason for such pessimism was that the Red does not flood like other rivers. The Red River flows like the glaciers that carved out its bed; slowly, sluggishly, creeping 730 miles (1174.5 km) from its source in Minnesota to Lake Winnipeg, across prairie that barely deserves the name "valley." (The distance from the source to the mouth, as the crow flies, is only 555 miles [893 km].) The riverbed's average slope is a mere 6 inches (15 cm) to the mile, and in some long stretches is even less. The Red carries tons of sediment, making it the kind of river settlers called "too thin to plow and too thick to drink." Indeed, the name of the lake it drains into comes from the Native word "ouinipeg," which means "dirty water." (The river gets its own name from the Cree word *miscousipi*; "red water.") When the Red floods, it does not become a raging torrent. It just slowly rises, and rises, and rises, and overwhelms everything near it with sheer, ponderous volume.

There were attempts to tame the Red River by damming its tributaries, but there was nowhere for the excess water to go. Dikes were built to keep the great river in its lazy, meandering course. The Red would just bloat and shrug, and the dikes would tumble down. During the 1950 flood, a man was piling sandbags on a dike at Winnipeg's Fort Garry riverfront. The dike had a 25-foot (7.6 m) base, but as the man laboured, he saw a "gentle finger of water" poke its way from the sandbag barrier, and trickle toward the streets beyond. Despairing that all his efforts had been for nothing, the man dropped the sandbag he'd been hefting, shook a fist at the sky, and cried, "How can you lick a river like that when the dirty, damned thing won't stand up and fight?"

The flood of 1950, which remarkably enough was not the biggest in Red River history but would cause the maximum amount of damage, had its origins—as do most of the Red's big floods—in the rains of the preceding autumn. One fall shower after another saturated the soft clay soil of the Red River country, and then the winter freeze held the water in readiness for spring. Heavy snowfalls, followed by torrential spring rains made the entire Red River drainage system a disaster just waiting to happen.

When the early-thawing, more southerly tributaries of the Red River—the Cheyenne, the Pipestem and the Wild River—burst their banks, communities along the northern stretches of the big river should have taken heed. Some towns did start piling up sandbag dikes, but the overall prediction from the federal government down to municipal councils was that the river would not flood. On April 3, as river towns in North Dakota and Minnesota were being evacuated, the Canadian government's district engineer in Winnipeg, D.B. Gow, stated, "We expect nothing this year to approach the 1948 flood. We will have high water, but we always have high water."

The waters surged into the ice-choked Red, the thaw crept north, and within two weeks, 600 square miles (1554 km^2) of prairie south of Winnipeg was covered with several feet of cold, brown water. This turgid lake was slithering toward Winnipeg at a patient but unstoppable 6 miles (9.6 m) a day.

Farms and ranches were swallowed up, the houses and out-buildings carried away by the muddy tide. Livestock that could not be evacuated or fed were shot en masse. Some of the more fortunate animals found refuge on hillocks, which were the only dry land for miles around. Helicopters air-dropped hay to keep them alive.

Desperate townships were pleading for federal aid, but Manitoba Premier Douglas Campbell refused any help from Ottawa or other provinces. Manitoba, he said, could handle the situation on her own. Yet even as the Premier spoke, the waters were conspiring to prove him wrong.

Meltwater from the south pushed its unhurried way north, mixing with the runoff of the late northern thaw, then crowding into the space already filled to capacity by the headwaters. As one journalist put it at the time, "When the river is abnormally high, it just doesn't move fast enough to get out of its own way."

One by one the little towns south of Winnipeg were engulfed: Ste. Agathe, St. Adolphe, St. Norbert, Morris and Emerson. People awoke to find that the river had crept into their houses like a thief in the night and was lapping at the sides of their beds. Some had to retreat to the second storeys of their homes to escape the rising waters. There they were rescued by RCMP officers in canoes. As they were taken to safety they saw their homes and belongings carried away by the current.

Some people tried to save precious items. One woman left behind all of her jewellery but took along a prized curling trophy. A preacher wouldn't part with his family Bible, and an elderly man wouldn't leave without his canary in its cage. A few would not leave their homes at all. A St. Norbert mink farmer was holed up in his attic along with some goats, roosters, and $20,000 worth of minks still wearing their valuable fur coats. "I have everything here that I own," he told the officers. "It is all under water, and the river makes it look like a ship. If my ship goes down, gentlemen, I am going down with it." Fortunately, the man survived in his strange little ark.

Evacuees in the Morris and Emerson areas were housed and fed in railway sleeper cars and bunk cars. An Emerson railroad man named Jim Boyd patrolled 35 miles of breakwater along the flooded railway in a little boat he called the *Empress of Emerson*. His navigational aids were the names on the tops of submerged grain elevators. Boyd's resourcefulness earned him the nickname "Barnacle Bill."

In both towns the telephone girls remained at their switchboards until the last possible moment, trying to keep the lines open. They sat on sandbags to stay above the murky water, wore hip-waders, and lived for days on canned beans. They remained at their posts until the sandbag dikes that were the only feeble defence against the deluge were washed away like children's slush dams in a gutter. Shirley Coates, a Morris switchboard operator, said later, "We were the last women in town to evacuate."

Finally, the last people in all of Morris were two RCMP officers who were left in charge of the inspector's office. One Mountie would sit on a chair fitted with stilts, and the other would report for duty in a canoe that he paddled right into the office.

By the end of April the flooding Red had oozed its sloppy, mucky empire over hundreds of square miles and had caused millions of dollars in damage. Twenty thousand Americans had been evacuated from their homes, and the number of Canadian evacuees was rising—and the full power of the behemoth had not yet reached the city of Winnipeg. The one consolation was that there had not yet been any loss of human life.

Winnipeg now looked like a fortified city digging in to repel an enemy attack. Sandbag ramparts were thrown up against the encroaching "lake." Thirty miles (48.2 km) of dikes rose along the banks of the Red where it loops its way like an anaconda through the heart of the city. Over 100,000 volunteers filled sandbags, tied them and piled them. One recalled later, "Our hands were shredded and bleeding. Our feet, unaccustomed to rubber boots, were blistered. Our backs ached, and it rained. But we toughened up."

By the first of May the Red River in Winnipeg was rising at the rate of a foot (0.3 m) a day and was sloshing over the tops of the dikes. Volunteers worked desperately to keep the walls rising higher, and then higher again. Not since the flood of 1861 had the waters of the Red risen to such a level, and still it crept up and up!

Then came "Black Friday," May 5. Nature unleashed a full-scale assault on the city. Rain, sleet and snow came down from the sky, and a 50 mile (80 km) per hour gale lashed the lazily rolling monster of a river into a boiling fury. Whipped by the wind, reinforced by the deluge from the sky, the Red punched through the sandbag barriers and rolled into defenceless neighbourhoods. Four of Winnipeg's 11 bridges crumbled like toothpick structures. The walls had been breached, and the enemy was in the streets.

One third of Winnipeg was swamped. Hospitals and schools were evacuated. A wall of water rolled across streets and yards and found its way into basements, living rooms and kitchens. Hundreds of families were forced out into the cold, many escaping with only the clothes on their backs. Sewers backed up, adding the threat of disease to what was already a disaster of monumental proportions.

Finally, on May 6 Premier Campbell declared a state of emergency. In Ottawa, and in cities across the country, aid for beleaguered Winnipeg began to mobilize. The city of Ottawa sent a chlorinator to purify water, and the University of Montreal donated typhoid vaccine. Trains loaded with flood-fighting equipment and other supplies were rolling toward the prairie capital. Navy divers and frogmen were dispatched from Halifax. The RCAF and Trans Canada Airlines airlifted over 1,200,000 sandbags to Winnipeg, some from as far away as San Francisco. Over 5,000 Canadian army, navy and air force personnel joined the battle. It was the largest peacetime operation in the history of Canada's armed forces. In command was Brigadier Ronald E.A. Morton. The fight to save Winnipeg was called "Operation Red Ramp."

One of Morton's top priorities was to protect the city's power stations. If they were knocked out, Winnipeg would be plunged into catastrophic darkness. Soldiers piled the sandbags high around those strategic installations and beefed up the defences with yet more sandbags. There were sporadic blackouts here and there in the city, but generally the lights stayed on.

Morton ran the operation just as he would a campaign in a war. He made frequent trips in an RCAF helicopter to get a first-hand look at trouble spots and to keep up with the overall situation. His officers saw to the stockpiling of food. Public places such as movie theatres and taverns were closed. Radio stations went on full-time flood duty. Emergency centres were set up to provide sandwiches and hot drinks for volunteers and evacuees. The Red Cross converted the city auditorium into a dormitory.

The river continued to press its attack. Still the waters rose. Manhole covers popped off the storm sewers under the pressure of water and gas. Foul, untreated sewage mixed with the muddy waters of the Red. Morton's heavy armour, bulldozers, scooped up earth from lawns, gardens and golf courses, and dumped it in the path of the spreading water.

For 20 days and nights after the floodwaters reached Winnipeg, the struggle tested human strength and mental endurance to the limits. Throughout the stricken sections of the city there were acts of heroism, scenes of pathos and even incidents of grim humour. In Fort Garry a man gave army engineers permission to dynamite his house after it was torn from its foundation and had become a hazard. "Guess I'm wiped out," he said stoically. "Guess I'll just have to live in my brother's trailer." In another part of town a woman lamented that she could not bury the body of her recently deceased sister. On Jubilee Avenue, an army officer told a group of sandbaggers, "Men, do you know that as much water has evap- orated during the last 24 hours as has run downstream?" The next day it began to rain. One of the sandbaggers quipped, "Well, here comes that damn evaporation."

Water was surging through Winnipeg at the rate of 100,000 cubic feet a second. On May 11, over 40,000 people—mostly women and children—were evacuated. Able-bodied men and older boys stayed to fight the river. They would be called "Flood Bachelors" for the days they had to spend without the company of mothers, wives or girlfriends. General Morton was not yet ready to implement "Operation Blackboy"; the complete evacuation of the city of Winnipeg. As it was, the evacuation carried out that day was the largest to date in Canadian history.

In North Kildonan a man used a block and tackle to hoist his car into the high-and-dry safety of a tree. At Portage and Main, while a group of muck-spattered dike workers looked on, a young lady daintily dipped the toe of her brand new, shiny rainboot into the water rushing down the gutter to wash off a spot of mud. In the Royal Alexander Hotel, safe on high ground, a guest complained that the Turkish bath was not operating.

A religious commentator in Toronto named Jane Scott announced that God had sent the flood as punishment for sins and urged the people of Winnipeg to "pray, lest ye enter into temptation, for Satan and his hosts are just like the Red River." Upon hearing of this, one Winnipeg man wrote to the press that sin had nothing to do with it, and that all of the praying in the world would be no substitute for sandbagging.

The Grey Nuns of St. Boniface evidently believed that a combination of both was needed. The 13 elderly women pinned the hems of their habits up to keep them out of the mud and whispered prayers while they filled sandbags. Their archbishop, the Reverend George Cabana, joined them in their labour, and was unknowingly filling the bags with too much sand. A private soldier who had to haul the dead weight to the dike, and who did not realize to whom he was speaking, growled at him, "Look, you big lug, either shovel four to the bag, or I'll plug you in the dike!" The archbishop quietly said, "Okay, Bud."

The sand stations at which the bags were filled were called "the salt mines." The volunteers who worked at them developed "sandbag shoulders" and "flood fatigue." They sang (to the tune of "Music, Music, Music"):

Chuck another sandbag on
On the dike that's wide and long
All we need is volunteers
And sandbags, sandbags, sandbags!

Winnipeg writer Scott Young later described the selfless efforts of the volunteers:

I never hope to see anything again like that fight for the
Norwood dike. Three human beings, one on a shovel, one
on a bag, and one with twine, can fill and tie five sandbags a minute at a pace they can keep up for hour after
hour. You get into an impassioned state of mind. You work
groggily until 3 AM and you're up at 7 AM, back for
more. Sleep gets to mean nothing. Yet there was no overall direction, nor foreman, no time-clock but the river.

Everyone from high-school students to elderly nuns was pitching in, but there were those who preferred not to get their hands dirty. Winnipeg author Laura Goodman Salverson told of some "snobbish neighbours" who stayed in the living room playing cards while others were breaking their backs at the sand stations and the dikes. She said, "In typical western revenge, the volunteer workers would stand outside the picture window of the snobs, fold their arms and just glare into the parlour malevolently. We called it the 'prairie evil-eye hex.'"

On May 18 the Red reached a crest of 30.3 feet (9.3 m) above normal. For a week the fate of Winnipeg lay in those sandbag walls that held millions of gallons of murky brown water 6 feet (1.8 m) and more above street level. If the water rose another foot or two, "Operation Blackboy" would be launched. The alternative, should the water go down, would be "Operation Rainbow," the massive cleanup in the aftermath of the worst flood ever experienced by a city that had known many of them. Then, on May 25, the river level began to drop. Winnipeg had withstood the seige but at an enormous cost.

Sadly, the river had claimed a life. On May 6, Lawson Ogg had gone into the basement of his Kingston Crescent home to fix a broken pump. At the same time the Fort Garry dike gave way. Ogg drowned in the water that rushed into his house.

There were other casualties, however. One man had both his hands amputated after burning them on a live hydro line that was hanging close to the water. The tension that had held Winnipeggers and other Manitobans for weeks gave way to nervous breakdowns and various forms of physical and emotional collapse, especially among those faced with the slime-coated ruins that had been their homes. The flood left in its muddy wake over 5,000 destroyed houses, factories and businesses. Total damage was over $100,000,000—five times that sum in 2005 dollars. Out of a population of 330,000 as many as 107,000 had been evacuated. Insurance appraisers had almost 9,000 claims to sort through.

Blame fell heavily on Premier Douglas Campbell for what was perceived to be his indecisiveness, and what one critic called "bungling, dallying and procrastination." Winnipeggers derisively called the muck left by the flood "Campbell's Soup."

But the flood had not carried away Winnipeg's pioneer spirit. The city dug itself out and rebuilt what the flood had destroyed. Campbell's successor, Premier Duff Roblin, oversaw the construction of the Winnipeg Floodway, a 29.2 mile (47 km) channel designed to prevent the 1950 disaster from happening again. "Duff's Ditch," as it has been nicknamed, has in fact saved the city from inundation several times since it opened in 1969. Nonetheless, the Red River remains slow, unpredictable and patient.

Hurricane Hazel, Toronto, 1954

H URRICANE HAZEL CAME INTO the world on October 6, 1954. Like her predecessors dating back to the beginning of time, she was spawned over the warm tropical waters of the Caribbean Sea. She began as a mild low-pressure area, then rapidly transformed into a monster that reached out 200 miles (321.8 km) from her 15 mile (24.1 km)–wide "eye" with winds that shrieked in a counter-clockwise rotation at 125 miles (201.1 km) per hour. As she spun across the warm sea, Hazel sucked up moisture that cooled in her massive crown of cumulus clouds, and then spewed back down in torrential rain. Like her siblings before and since, Hazel was destined to be short lived; a fortnight at best. But while it lives, a hurricane is the most awesome, powerful force on the face of the earth. Its sole purpose, if such a phenomenon of nature could be said to have one, is massive destruction.

Hazel pounced first on the island of Hispaniola, shared by Haiti and the Dominican Republic, where she savaged the croplands and killed as many as 1,000. Then she swept north along one of the "traditional" hurricane routes toward the North American continent. She filled her arsenal with more water, and carried on her winds debris from the battered island republics. Hurricane-wise residents of the southeast coast of the United States prepared for the onslaught they knew was coming.

Hundreds of miles to the north, in Toronto and other southern Ontario cities, most people did not give more than passing notice to news reports about Hurricane Hazel. Hurricanes didn't hit Ontario. Sometimes the climactic disturbances to the south resulted in strong winds and heavy rains, what residents of the Great Lakes-bound peninsula of Southern Ontario called "getting the tail end of the hurricane." But no hurricane had ever come slashing across Lake Erie or Lake Ontario.

Early in the morning of Friday, October 15, Hazel slammed into South Carolina. She rampaged north, travelling at 60 mph (96.5 km) through North Carolina, Virginia, West Virginia, Washington DC, Maryland, and into Pennsylvania, leaving devastation in her wake. But even as she thundered through the eastern states, Hazel's power was diminishing. Every obstacle in a hurricane's path—every car overturned, every tree uprooted, every roof ripped from a house—bleeds some of the hurricane's energy. Much of the water in even that vast airborne reservoir is spent by the time the storm reaches the Allegheny Mountains. American weather experts predicted that Hazel would deflect off those mountains and roll out into the Atlantic to die, as her predecessors had so often done. The city of Toronto expected no more than a heavy rain that night. Hurricanes didn't hit Ontario.

But Fred Turnbull, Chief Meteorologist for Toronto's Malton Airport, was worried. He had been keeping a close watch on Hazel's progress and told his colleagues that she was going to hit Toronto that night. Even with the force of her winds dwindling to 70 miles (112.6 km) per hour, Hazel could wreak havoc on an unprepared city. Moreover, the hurricane was on a collision course with a mass of cold Arctic air that would condense the warm moisture still locked up in her clouds and cause it to drop down into those gale-force winds. Fred Turnbull warned them, and they scoffed. No hurricane had ever hit Ontario.

Weather conditions in southern Ontario could not have been worse. It had been raining steadily for three weeks and the ground was sodden. Rivers and creeks were filled to capacity. There was simply nowhere in the natural drainage systems for any extra water to go. Indeed, ancient floodplains that had not been underwater in all of Toronto's recorded history now had neighbourhoods built on them; neighbourhoods like quiet Raymore Drive on the banks of the Humber River in the city's west end.

Skirting the Allegheny Mountains like some obsolete Maginot Line, Hurricane Hazel whipped up Lake Erie and Lake Ontario like a giant electric mixer would a couple of bowls full of egg whites, then assaulted the Ontario shoreline from Windsor to Kingston. She would deal out death and destruction in communities across southern Ontario—London, Orillia, Southampton—and even Hull, Quebec. But the brunt of Hazel's fury fell upon the west end of Toronto.

Hazel, as far as *official* records go, was now actually an extratropical cyclone, just a rung below hurricane status. But for those who suffered in Hazel's onslaught, that was just so much technical nit-picking. Also, according to *official* records, Hazel did not reach Toronto in full force until 11:00 that Friday night. But her heralds of wind and rain were sweeping past the shoreline and into the city hours before that. By early evening the Don River in the east and the Humber River in the west were already running dangerously high, and smaller streams like Etobicoke Creek and Mimico Creek did not at all resemble the peaceful little rivulets they usually were. And Lake Ontario, which had always proved itself an untameable beast when the winds were strong enough, was pounding the waterfront with unbridled rage. Woe to anyone who got carried into that unholy cauldron.

There had been no warning of a hurricane, and many Torontonians were unaware that their city was experiencing one for the first time in its history. Those who were still awake at 11:00 PM knew that the winds were extraordinarily high, and the rain coming down in unprecedented torrents. Many others slept right through it and did not realize until they turned on their radios the following morning what disaster had befallen the staid provincial capital that outsiders sometimes derisively called "Toronto the Good." These were the people lucky enough to be on higher, safe ground. For those lower down along the watercourses, it was a night of shrieking, high-water hell.

In just 12 hours, 44 inches (101 mm) of rain—some 300 million tons of water—fell on Toronto. A 200-year record! Almost all of it slid down saturated ground, seeking the ravines and gullies that carried it to the rivers and creeks, turning them into bridge-wrecking, dam-busting killers. Worst struck was the Humber Valley, where the water flooded to 30 feet (9.1 m) above its normal level and ploughed like a 40 mile (64.3 km) per hour liquid avalanche down to Lake Ontario.

At Thistletown, in the northwest, two people drowned. Seventeen babies in incubators had to be evacuated from a branch of the Hospital for Sick Children there when the heating generator was knocked out. In Long Branch, in the southwest, a neighbourhood of cottages was inundated and seven more people died. Fifty families fled their residences in Pleasant Valley trailer park, when what had so recently been little Etobicoke Creek swept their mobile homes away.

At Woodbridge, northwest of Toronto, a dam burst and waters surged through yet another trailer park. It smashed and twisted the flimsy homes and killed at least 20. Then the waters poured into the already roiling Humber, making it all the more deadly. The swollen streams carried cars, trees and houses, turning them into lethal battering rams that crashed into anything that obstructed their way. Forty Toronto bridges were wiped out or damaged beyond repair that night. Drivers who could not see through the blinding rain plunged their vehicles into the gaps left by the washouts. Some were rescued. Many, like Nora Wicks, 45, were not. She and her car were swallowed up after the Catfish Creek bridge was destroyed. The Islington Fire Station became a temporary morgue, as did Humber Heights School.

Warren Lanning of Oshawa, his ten-year-old son Bruce and an unnamed family friend found themselves trapped in their car at the Eckhard Bridge, with the water rising around them at a frightening speed. They got out and tried to make it to higher ground, with the boy perched on the shoulders of one of the men. There was a sudden surge, and the child was dragged from the adult's grip. The hysterical father tried to go after him, but it was hopeless. The boy's body was found days later in the mud, several miles downstream, little hands reaching out as though for help. Hazel took no pity on age nor innocence.

One child who almost became a victim of the deluge was four-month-old Nancy Thorpe. Her family had been forced onto the roof of their home by raging Etobicoke Creek. Fire Chief Albert Houston of the Long Branch Department, using a rope and a small boat, fought his way across the foaming stream that had been

Island Road and took the infant from the mother, Patricia. The Chief took the baby to another house where people had gathered on the roof, and she was taken into the arms of 16-year-old Sylvia Jones. Chief Houston tried to go back to the Thorpe house for the others, but the wild water carried them all away. Gone were Nancy's mother, her father Clifford, two-year-old brother Billy and maternal grandmother Mrs. Johnston.

Throughout that cold October night Sylvia kept the baby warm with her own shivering body while the waters raced past the house and threatened to carry all who were stranded on it to destruction. In the morning the survivors were taken from their miserable plight in the shovel of a bulldozer. Baby Nancy was whisked to St. Joseph's Hospital where she remained unidentified for several hours until her paternal grandparents arrived. Her picture appeared on the front pages of newspapers across the country as the "Hurricane Baby" and "Orphan of the Storm."

Nowhere did the powers of nature and fate come together with greater conniving cruelty than at an unassuming little street called Raymore Drive. What happened there seemed almost to have had the hand of some murderous devil at work. In a long night of tragedies, this would be the costliest of them all.

Raymore Drive was a short street in Weston, running between Scarlett Road and the Humber River, just south of Lawrence Avenue. About three-quarters of Raymore ran parallel to the river. It was a street of modest, comfortable bungalows that were in some cases home to three generations. Within 24 hours it would be remembered as the "Street That Never Was" and "Calamity Crescent."

It was raining heavily when 63-year-old Joe Ward walked across the wooden swing bridge over the Humber River on his way home from work. The bridge provided an easy shortcut to his house at 141 Raymore Drive. Joe couldn't know that he would be one of the last people to set foot on that familiar little bridge.

Joe and his wife Annie loved their little cottage on the banks of the Humber; the setting reminded them so much of their native England. They were two mortgage payments away from owning it outright, and Joe was just two years away from retirement. All seemed well with them as they eased into their sunset years. But on that stormy evening as Joe crossed the bridge he could not help but see that the Humber was running high—mighty high! And it looked ugly!

At 9:00 PM, as the couple watched TV, the lights suddenly went out. No cause for alarm; it was storming, after all. Annie went to bed. Joe dozed off in his easy chair, his feet propped up on a hassock.

Things would have been pretty much the same up and down Raymore Drive: in the home of Ted Jeffries and his wife Elizabeth, the Wards' next-door neighbours; in the home of Lambert Peasley, his wife Doris and their daughter Sylvia, just across the street; in the house at 36 Raymore shared by families named Edwards and Neil; in the Harwood household at 149 Raymore; and in the homes of families named Smith, Topless, Newing and LeBlanc. People lit candles when the power failed, or just went to bed.

However, some Raymore Drive residents grew concerned over the rapidity at which the Humber was rising. It was claimed later that they went up and down the street, warning neighbours that they had better get out and head for higher ground, but that another resident convinced people that they should stay put. If anyone knocked on Joe Ward's door, he didn't hear it.

Sometime that evening, the swing bridge Joe had crossed a few hours earlier began to strain under the incredible pressure of the water pressing against it. Finally, one end broke loose and the bridge swung out into the current. Had it broken away completely and washed down to the lake, a tragedy would have been averted. But strong wires held the bridge so that it swung just a few feet; enough to cause it to redirect the flow of the river straight at Raymore Drive. It was like aiming a water cannon.

Joe Ward awoke at midnight to find cold water flowing across his floor and rising fast. He opened his front door and was horrified to see swirling water where his yard had been. He thought he heard screams coming from the Jeffries' house. He closed the door and hurried to open his cellar door. Out swam his English terrier, Lassie. Joe picked up Lassie and hurried to the bedroom. As he shook Annie awake, the water was already above his knees. Annie pulled on a dress and grabbed a flashlight, but any chance of escape seemed lost as the house suddenly lurched and broke free of its foundation.

The couple climbed up to the rafters. Using a screwdriver and his bare hands, Joe hacked and tore a hole in the roof just large enough for he and Annie to crawl through. They had to leave Lassie behind.

Now they were trapped on the roof of a house that was roaring down Raymore Drive like a canoe shooting the rapids of a wilderness river. To make matters worse, the house was being torn apart under them. Then their house crashed into the home of another Raymore Drive resident, Jack Anderson (who had already escaped). Joe and Annie clasped hands, and with a promise to make it together or die together, they jumped from their roof to Anderson's.

They landed hard but were unhurt. The Wards looked back in time to see their house and everything they had in the world sucked down into the maelstrom. Perched atop Jack Anderson's ruined house, with the brown water rushing by only 2 feet (0.6 m) from them, Joe and Annie spent a night of shivering terror. At dawn they were rescued by a helicopter. Remarkably, Lassie also survived.

While Joe Ward was still dozing in his easy chair, down at 149 Raymore Ruth Harwood was typing out a letter by the light of an oil lamp. Her husband Walter and her mother Hope were asleep upstairs. At midnight she looked outside and saw the same alarming sight Ward was looking at a few houses away. She ran upstairs, yelling to her husband and mother, "Wake up! We're flooding!"

While Walter and Hope pulled on some clothes, Ruth made a frantic phone call to warn their friends the Jeffries. "Thanks, Ruth, for calling," Ted Jeffries said. They were the last words anyone would hear the 69-year-old gardener say. He and his wife both perished.

The Harwood house was filling up rapidly. Walter, Ruth and Hope retreated to the second floor and climbed onto a bed that by sheer good fortune had shown a tendency to wobble, and so was bolted to the floor. Their house shuddered when the Jeffries house crashed into it. Then with a loud crack the top floor of the building broke loose from the bottom and floated away on the wild torrent of Raymore Drive.

Water poured through the window as the three clung for their lives to the bolted bed. It sucked the shoes off their feet, collapsed the walls, and carried away the furnishings. Walter told the women, "I love you both. But this is the end, and we're going to die. Life, after all, is the only nightmare that is real."

But Ruth was more concerned with surviving than with being philosophical. "I'm not going to die!" she cried. Hope prayed, "O God, save us sinners."

They had nothing but the bed bolted to the bedroom floor. That unlikely raft washed onto the flat roof of a neighbour's house, and stayed there. The three crawled onto the roof and huddled there as the waters swirled by. Like the Wards, they shivered on their tiny, insecure island for hours.

In the morning Walter took off his pants and underwear, put his pants back on, then spread the underwear on the roof as protection for his bare feet. He began to dance and whoop and cry out, "We're alive, folks! We're alive!" A team of firemen heard him, and rescued the three.

Other Raymore Drive families were not so fortunate. In the Edwards-Neil household, nine out of ten people died: Ken and Joan Edwards and their two sons, Frank, 2, and John, 3 months, and their daughter Caroline, 3; Jean Neil and her daughters Adele, 1, Susan, 3, and Darlene, 4. Only the girls' father, John, survived. Lambert, Doris and Sylvia Peasley were dead. So were Mr. and Mrs. Al Topless; John and Grace Smith and their son John Jr.; Gerald Newing, his mother Katherine and his son Gerald Jr.; Alice LeBlanc and many others. Of the 83 Torontonians killed by Hurricane Hazel, 38 were from Raymore Drive.

In the aftermath of Hurricane Hazel, as the dying storm thrashed its way north to finally die over the Davis Strait, the people of Toronto heard many stories of heroism, unbelievable luck, disgraceful negligence, and even humour. A ten-year-old boy was rescued from a trailer where he had been left alone while his parents went to a movie. Gerry Lewis, an Englishman boarding at the Little Avenue home of Ella Louise Norman, looked out the window and dryly remarked to the landlady, "It is a bit of a shock to see houses floating over the top of the bridge." Then he went upstairs to bed. When Mrs. Norman awoke him in the morning and told him that they were in a disaster area, he calmly said, "My dear Mrs. Norman, I think you'd better go downstairs at once and put the kettle on for tea."

The Dutch family of Johannes de Peuter found themselves afloat in their farmhouse when Holland Marsh, north of Toronto, was flooded. Mr. de Peuter used an axe handle to keep the house from bumping into hydro poles. When the high winds rocked the house and threatened to capsize it, mother and father kept their 12 children moving from side to side to provide balance. The de Peuter house travelled five miles, then ran aground on a gravel service road beside Highway 400. All within survived.

At a swamped bridge over the swollen Don River, a salesman named Alex Nicholson tried to warn drivers not to attempt crossing. He heard cries for help and saw a man clinging to a clump of trees in the middle of the river. He attempted to go to the man's assistance and was himself swept away by the powerful current. He managed to climb onto an overturned car and was there for two and a half hours before the river began to push the car downstream. Nicholson jumped and grabbed hold of a tree. Numb from the cold, he was rescued by firemen three hours later.

Many people risked their lives to save others that night, and but for their bravery the body count would have been much higher. Constable Ronald Nuttley of the Long Branch Police Department rescued 20 people stranded in a rowboat and was himself very nearly drowned. Toronto Harbour Police Officer Ernie Norrey likewise put his life on the line to pluck a man from the middle of the raging Don River. Another Harbour policeman, Max Hurley, made repeated attempts to get to a man trapped in a tree in the Humber at the washed-out Old Mill bridge. He finally accomplished what 250 other rescue workers had been unable to do and got the man ashore.

In one sad incident, it was the rescuers who became the victims. Six members of the Kingsway-Lambton Volunteer Fire Department sped off in their six-ton fire engine in response to a call about some youths being trapped on a rooftop. The engine itself was soon awash, and then was rolled over by the seething waters. Five of the men—Clarence Collins, Frank Mercer, Roy Oliver, David Palmeteer and Angus Small—were drowned.

On the morning after Hurricane Hazel, much of Toronto—and other parts of southern Ontario—looked like a war zone. Wrecked houses and cars littered the landscape. Smashed-up streetcars lay scattered like a child's broken toys. Two Ontario trains had been derailed. City streets and vast areas of farmland were under water. The bodies of dead livestock were suspended in tree branches where the flood had deposited them. Three thousand people were homeless. Damage was estimated at $25 million (perhaps five times that amount in 2005 dollars). Worst of all, 100 Canadians had died; five more than Hazel had killed in her romp through the better-prepared United States at the peak of her strength.

The army and civilian engineers turned out in force to assess the damage and start cleaning up the mess. Boy Scouts and university students joined police in the search for bodies. The Red

Cross, Salvation Army and other agencies pitched in to help people start putting their lives back together. Relief funds poured into Toronto from across Canada and around the world. Torontonians rebuilt, but October 15, 1954, became a landmark date in the history of their city. The staid provincial capital that had been called Toronto the Good would never be the same.

Vancouver Bridge Disaster, 1958

JUNE 17, 1958; "BLACK TUESDAY," as it came to be called in Vancouver, began pleasantly enough. It was warm and sunny, with a gentle, westerly breeze blowing. The kind of day that, if one put aside Vancouver's high annual rainfall, made the West Coast city the envy of Canadians unfortunate enough to live east of the Rockies. But 19-year-old Gary Poirier had a bad feeling that day, one that the summery weather could not dispel. The night before, he had dreamed of his own death.

Poirier was an apprentice ironworker employed at the site of the latest construction project of British Columbia Premier W.A.C. Bennett and Highways Minister Phil Gagliardi, the Second Narrows Bridge over Burrard Inlet. As a young man learning the dangerous trade of working "high steel," Poirier knew that he was in training for a place in the ranks of the construction industry's elite. The "cats," the men who built bridges like this one now reaching to span 2 miles (3.2 km), 200 feet (60.9 m) above Burrard Inlet, had to have nerves like the steel with which they worked. The job called for a man who could walk along a six inch (15 cm) wide girder suspended many storeys high with the same ease with which lesser mortals strolled a city sidewalk. Gary Poirier could do that. But the night before he had dreamed that this very structure on which he was working had collapsed into the inlet, and that he had been cut in two by a snapping cable and killed. Now he couldn't shake the bad feeling.

For people who work at high-risk jobs, sudden death is always a possibility. One simply cannot dwell on it too much, lest it become a dangerous distraction. Since work had begun on this bridge in 1956, there had already been four fatalities. One steelworker had fallen 105 feet (32 m) into the inlet. Another man had been electrocuted when a crane touched a high-tension wire. Yet another had been crushed. A tug man working on the inlet had drowned when his boat overturned. There was even an old Native legend that claimed that this place was cursed by evil spirits.

Indian folklore notwithstanding, the city of Vancouver badly needed a new bridge across Burrard Inlet. The old Second Narrows Bridge, just yards away from where the new one was being built, simply couldn't handle the increasing volume of traffic between the expanding suburb of North Vancouver and Vancouver proper. This new $23 million span of concrete and steel would carry six lanes of traffic above the riptides of Burrard Inlet where, as Bennett and Gagliardi liked to remind people, Captain George Vancouver himself had sailed 160 years earlier. The work was being done by the Dominion Bridge Company, and the chief engineer was Colonel William George Swan, a man who had been designing bridges for 50 years and who was described as "the best consulting engineer in Canada." When the graceful marvel was completed, it would become the responsibility of the British Columbia Toll Authority. No one would have guessed that it would come to be known as "the bridge of sighs and tears."

At 3:35 PM a 35-ton diesel engine hauling two railway cars full of steel beams rolled onto the fifth anchor span of the bridge. This would be the last section to be completed before work began on the actual 1,100-foot (335.2 m) -long cantilever arch. As such, it was, for the moment, a bridge to nowhere; a great platform reaching out into the void above the angry waters of the inlet. It was supported by "falsework grillage," a temporary platform and steel legs holding up the fifth span. At the edge, a 155-ton crane awaited delivery of the tons of steel in the railway cars. Nearby, Gary Poirier and his friend George Schmidt were at work driving bolts. In all there were 79 men working on the bridge that afternoon, most of them bolters and painters.

Everything appeared normal; there was no sign that a calamity was about to occur. Gary had just told George about his nightmare. The painters' foreman, Juergen Wulf, was standing by the railway tracks, supervising his crew. Painter Zaci Szokol had run out of paint and was going for a refill. John Olynyk had been working on the outside of a hollow diagonal beam while his partner Al McPherson worked on the inside. Al had just stepped out to trade places with John to give him a break. Bill Wright was standing on a load of steel on the train. Byron Maine, Tommy Moore and Ray Gjelstad were all painting. Bill Moore and Sam Ruegg were working on the concrete pillar that connected and helped support the fourth and fifth spans.

Down on the water, Bill Lasko circled around in a 25-foot, (7.6 m) yellow barge. His job was to rescue anyone who fell off the bridge before the powerful currents could carry them away. From his home on nearby Edinburgh Avenue, a bridge buff named Jack Newman was watching the construction through his binoculars. He had been watching the advance of the span across open space for months, admiring the courage and skill of the men who worked the high steel. And then, at 3:40, before his eyes, the wonderful example of man's engineering genius trembled.

The temporary support buckled, and the end of the fifth anchor span dropped into Burrard Inlet with a shriek of tearing metal. The crane plummeted down into a great cauldron of foaming water. The diesel engine and the railway cars crashed down after it. The men working on that section had no warning, no chance. Some were hurled into the void and then plunged down to the inlet. Others, their safety belts attached to the bridge, were helplessly carried down by falling steel. A few quick-thinking workmen rode the girders down like cowboys, leaping off just as they hit the water.

One end of the fifth span was still attached to the concrete support, thereby making a giant ramp. The violence of the collapse yanked the pillar out of position, so that the end of the fourth span had nothing to hold it up. It, too, went crashing down with a monstrous roar. The men on that span had at least a split second warning, and some were able to run to safety.

All of the men who plunged into the water wore yellow lifejackets, but some were encumbered with heavy tool belts that carried them to the bottom like lead weights. On the ruined structure, which now resembled a giant letter M, men clung for dear life to twisted girders. Bill Moore and Sam Ruegg were stranded atop the great concrete pillar that now leaned at a 15 degree angle, with the fifth span sloping down one side and a sheer drop on the other.

"I heard the crash," Ruegg said. "I ducked and lay face down on the concrete pillar. A natural instinct, I guess. I was lucky."

George Schmidt was having a laugh over Gary Poirier's story of his bad dream, when the two heard a "double boom boom." Then they were falling like stones. The thought flashed through Poirier's mind that his nightmare had come true. Then he struck the icy water.

"When I came to the surface," he said later, "I found the impact had torn my yellow life jacket almost off. But I managed to hang onto the jacket and a two-by-four, and I drifted in the swift current. And when I was fished out by a rescue boat ten minutes later, all I could think of was, 'I sure am lucky. All I got is a possible fractured leg. I dreamed it all. Only in my dream I was killed. I'm mighty glad that part of my dream was wrong.'" As it turned out, Poirier suffered only a sprained knee.

George Schmidt, though he survived, was not quite as fortunate. After his terrible fall, Schmidt found himself amidst a tangle of twisted steel with several bodies for company. He looked down and saw that a girder, slicing down like a huge knife, had cut off one of his legs just above the knee. He calmly took off his safety belt and used it as a tourniquet. Then he lit a cigarette and waited for rescue. Two men came along and helped him into their rowboat. "Thanks, fellas," Schmidt said.

When Al McPherson took over his place outside the diagonal beam, John Olynyk slipped inside the hollow beam to carry on with the work McPherson had been doing. "I'd no sooner got inside the beam than I felt it plunging down," Olynyk told reporters. "It's an awful feeling when you're going down and you know you're trapped." But Olynyk survived the fall, while McPherson was crushed to death.

Still, when Olynyk landed he was in serious trouble. He was 8 feet (2.4 m) under water, trapped inside what could very soon be a steel coffin. Olynyk was a big man, 200 pounds (90.7 kg) and over 6 feet (1.8 m), so he didn't have much room to maneuvre. He started crawling up the tube, like a giant gopher going up a burrow. He reached an opening and poked his face through, but the hole was too small for his broad shoulders. To his horror, he saw that the tide was rising—fast! Olynyk yelled to some people in a nearby boat to get a cutting torch. Fifteen anxiety-ridden minutes later, John Fullager and five other welders were on the scene. They had been working in a nearby garage when they heard a great crash and saw a cloud of dust and spray. "We... just threw our equipment in a truck and raced down there," Fullager said later.

Fullager and his men worked desperately to cut Olynyk free while the waters rose. The big man was choking on blood and water and barely had his face above the surface when they finally pulled him out of the beam. Olynyk said the experience was "like living in hell." But he was luckier than six other men Fullager's crew pulled out of the wreckage—all dead.

Painting foreman Juergen Wulf heard "a sort of rumbling noise," and saw the crane and the fifth span go down. The fourth span, upon which he was standing, began to shake. He said later that it was like being on top of a smokestack when an earthquake starts. He ran for safety, but when he'd gone about 150 feet (45.7 m) he looked down and saw a man struggling in the water and yelling for help. Without a moment's hesitation, Wulf dropped a rope over the side and slid down 100 feet (30.4 m). He was still 30 feet (9.1 m) above the water, so he dropped the rest of the way and rescued the drowning man. His own hands were burned and bloody from the slide down the rope.

Laci Szokol never did get his paint can refilled. He heard snapping and clicking noises under his feet, so he ran. "I ran 30 feet along the catwalk like crazy," he said. But when he saw two men in trouble in the water, he stopped to throw them a rope.

Tony Romaniuk was one of those dragged to the bottom of the inlet by the beam to which he was safety-belted. "I told myself, 'Don't panic, Tony. Keep cool, Tony.' And I unfastened my harness, and my life jacket popped me up to the surface."

Don Gardiner was sure he was finished. "As I whistled through the air, I thought of my mother at home in Winnipeg," he said later. "I had a big belt of tools, and it pinned me under water, and held me there for more than a minute. I was sure I couldn't make it up. But then I fought, and I made it up."

Painter Byron Maine said it was like being on a shunting railway car. "It got worse, quivering and shaking, then rumbling! All at once, I knew it was going to go," he said. Maine ran like he had never run before, and got off the fourth span just before it collapsed. Two of his colleagues had an even more frightening brush with death.

"I was right in the middle of the section when I heard this terrific roaring," Tommy Moore told the press. "I looked around and saw the front end of the bridge disappearing. The section I was on began to shake like an earthquake, so I grabbed one of the steel cross-sections and hung on. When the section hit bottom I scrambled up again on the bridge approach."

Ray Gjelstad was inside one of the box girders in the fourth span when it went down. He was pitched 60 feet (18.2 m) down the inside of the giant tube before he managed to grab the steelwork. "I scrambled through a hole in the girder and climbed up the outside of the section back to the deck. I took a couple of bumps on the head and a few bruises, but otherwise I'm okay."

Colin Glendinning fell off the bridge backward, and later recalled thinking, "Oh God! I wish I had a parachute." He hit the water hard and went all the way to the bottom before rising back to the surface. He had a blackened lung and a broken leg, and one ear had been torn off. He was in the water for 40 minutes before help came. Floating right in front of him was the body of one of his friends.

Bill Wright, standing on the train, thought at first that the engine had gone through the bridge. "It was a roar, just one big roar. I was swinging through the air ... It went down, down, down, like a bat out of hell. I said to myself, 'This is it!'"

Wright plunged straight to the bottom of Burrard Inlet. Then his life jacket carried him back to the surface. He grabbed hold of two planks, and blacked out from pain just as a boat approached. He had two broken ribs, a fractured cheek bone, a dislocated right hip and a dislocated left shoulder. He would be crippled for the next 11 months.

Less fortunate was Joe Chrusch. Ironically, the night before Joe had said to his wife Margaret, "Listen, honey, if anything happens to me, you'll look after the kids?" After the collapse, Chrusch was one of the dead men pulled out of the water. The only consolation anyone could offer his widow was to assure her that he had been killed quickly and had not drowned.

Down on the water, Bill Lasko in his yellow rescue barge had a ringside view of the terrible spectacle. He was just 150 feet (45.7 m) from the end of the fifth span when suddenly he heard a loud crack, and then a roar like thunder. "All of a sudden she just come right down," he said later. Steel girders, oil drums, equipment, lunch boxes, men—all plunged down in a horrific shower. A huge wave almost swamped Lasko's boat. For the next six hours Lasko worked like a madman, racing around the debris-strewn inlet pulling out men both dead and alive. Soon there were almost 60 vessels—tugs, fishing boats, pleasure craft, police boats—probing the scene of the disaster. Most of the civilians in the boats genuinely wanted to help, but there were some who just wanted a closer look at the destruction and were hampering rescue work. "Ghouls!" officials called them. Police ordered them away.

An RCAF helicopter was sent to the scene, and divers went down to retrieve bodies. One of them, Leonard K. Mott, a professional who had been a stuntman for actor Peter Lorre in the film *Twenty Thousand Leagues under the Sea*, was sucked down by the powerful Burrard riptide and drowned.

In spite of official requests for people to stay away from the disaster area, a crowd gathered on the old bridge. They shouted down instructions to the men in the boats, directing them to yellow jackets in the water. The decks of the boats were soon covered with blood. There weren't enough ambulances to carry all of the injured to hospital quickly enough, so hearses were brought in to help with the task.

One steelworker who had survived the fall relatively unhurt was Lloyd McAtee. He quickly joined in with the rescue work. His friends said that he rescued "a whole bunch of guys." McAtee modestly admitted to helping "a couple." He told reporters that he hadn't been able to find his brother Mac. "He's down there somewhere," McAtee said, waving a hand toward the wreckage. A few minutes later he stepped aboard a tug and lifted a blanket off a twisted body on the deck. McAtee turned away and wept. He had found his brother.

When a woman phoned the offices of the *Vancouver Sun* and said that the bridge had collapsed, reporters thought at first that it was a prank. Someone had made a similar report a year earlier, causing a radio station considerable embarrassment when they flashed a news bulletin that turned out to be false. Now, even when the phone started ringing off the hook with reports that the bridge had gone down, the newsmen thought that it must be the *old* bridge. After all, modern engineering marvels didn't just fall down like a pile of children's building blocks.

When Bill Wright regained consciousness in hospital, he had a visitor, Highways Minister Phil Gagliardi himself. "You will be well taken care of, sir," the minister told him. Gagliardi had been in Victoria when reporters first told him of the disaster. His initial response had been to laugh, "You're joking!" He soon realized that it was no joke. He said that he would go to Vancouver the following day, but Premier Bennett came out of a Cabinet meeting and told him to go immediately. Gagliardi visited the bridge site and the hospital. "It's terrible," he told the press. "Steel and concrete don't matter, but men do." Then he went on to discuss how much the clean-up would cost and assured everyone that the tragedy would not cost the taxpayers a cent because the contractors were responsible. The political wrangling and name calling that erupted in the wake of the bridge disaster shook the British Columbia government for months. There was a lengthy strike by the steelworkers before construction on the bridge could be resumed, but the principal issue was wages, not safety at the worksite.

Eighteen men were killed when the bridge collapsed, making a total of nineteen deaths on that tragic day. Most of those who were injured eventually returned to work on the bridge. "I like high places," said Laci Szokol. "The view is nice." But there were a few who could not return to high steel, for either physical or psychological reasons.

It was determined that the bridge collapsed because of a pair of small mathematical errors made by two engineers. They had miscalculated in their design for the temporary support under the fifth span. It was not strong enough to bear the weight of the steel structure, the crane, and the diesel engine and its cars. Because the two engineers were among the dead, their names were never made public.

The new bridge finally opened on August 25, 1960. It was named the Ironworker's Memorial Second Narrows Crossing in honour of those who were killed and injured that fatal June day. A survivor of the disaster cut the ribbon. A clergyman cast 19 roses onto the turbulent waters of Burrard Inlet in homage to the 18 workers and the diver; men whose everyday work was a dance with death.

Bibliography

Books

Armstrong, Frederick H. *A City in the Making: Progress, People and Perils in Victorian Toronto*. Toronto: Dundurn Press, 1967.

Benedict, Michael (Ed.). *In the Face of Disaster*. Toronto: Viking Press, 2000.

Boyer, Dwight. *True Tales of the Great Lakes*. New York: Dodd, Mead & Co., 1971.

Brown, Cassi. *Death on the Ice*. Toronto: Doubleday Canada, 1972.

Craig, John. *The* Noronic *Is Burning*. Don Mills: General Publishing, 1976.

Glazebrook, G.P de T. *The Story of Toronto*. Toronto: University of Toronto Press, 1971.

Filey, Mike. *Toronto Sketches*. Toronto: Dundurn Press, 1992.

Finsten, Lucile and Varkaris, Jane. *Fire on Parliament Hill*. Erin, ON: Boston Mills Press, 1988.

Gifford, Jim. *Hurricane Hazel: Canada's Storm of the Century*. Toronto: Dundurn Press, 2004.

Henning, Robert J. *Ships Gone Missing: The Great Lakes Storm of 1913*. Chicago: Contemporary Books, 1992.

Jones, Frank. *Trail of Blood: A Canadian Murder Odyssey*. Toronto: McGraw-Hill Ryerson, 1981.

Kitz, Janet F. *Shattered City*. Halifax: Nimbus Publishing, 1989.

Looker, Janet. *Disaster Canada*. Toronto: Lynx Images, 2000.

Monnon, Mary Ann. *Miracles and Mysteries: The Halifax Explosion*. Hantsport, NS: Lancelot Press, 1977.

Petroski, Henry. *Engineers of Dreams: Great Bridge Builders and the Spanning of America*. New York: Alfred A. Knopf, 1995.

Pettigrew, Eileen. *The Silent Enemy: Canada and the Deadly Flu of 1918*. Saskatoon: Western Producer Prairie Books, 1983.

Rasky, Frank. *Great Canadian Disasters*. Toronto: Longman's, Green & Co., 1961.

Rawson, Nancy and Tatton, Richard. *The Great Toronto Fire*. Erin, ON: Boston Mills Press, 1984.

Robertson, John Ross. *Old Toronto*. Toronto: Macmillan Company of Canada, 1954.

Savours, Ann. *The Search for the Northwest Passage*. New York: St. Martin's Press, 1999.

Scadding, Henry. *Toronto of Old*. Toronto: Oxford University Press, 1966.

Walker, Frank N. *Sketches of Old Toronto*. Don Mills, ON: Longman's Canada, 1965.

West, Bruce. *Toronto*. Toronto: Doubleday Canada, 1967.

Newspapers

The Guelph Mercury
The Globe and Mail
Toronto Star

Acknowledgements

THE STORIES IN THIS BOOK ARE NOT, of course, the first accounts to be written about most of these Canadian disasters, nor are they likely to be the last. While in the case of a tragedy like that which befell the Franklin Expedition, many years can pass before the public learns as much of the truth as investigators can uncover. In most instances journalists are on the scene almost immediately to record what happens and what the people involved have to say. I have been fortunate in having at hand the scores of articles written by newspaper reporters who witnessed events with their own eyes and met victims and survivors face to face. Without their front-line work, writing a book like this one would not be possible. To those men and women I owe a debt of gratitude.

I am indebted, too, to the many authors who have covered these events in other books, sometimes devoting an entire volume to one particular event. These writers pick up the stories told by the reporters and then dig deep to uncover all of the hard facts as well as the many facets of the human element that, due to space restrictions, a newspaper column must omit. This requires much time and a lot of exhausting legwork. In my narratives I have attempted—where possible—to include anecdotal material that other writers did not use, and have tried to bring some fresh perspective to the stories. I therefore must acknowledge the fine work of all those authors who have gone before me.

I could not have gathered the research material necessary for this book without the assistance of the staff of the Guelph Public

Library, particularly the people responsible for Interlibrary Loans. Thanks to them I had access to many books that have long been out of print. Their work and patience are certainly appreciated.

Finally, I owe many thanks to John Robert Colombo for the vital part he played in bringing this project to my desk, and to the editors at Key Porter Books for entrusting me with it.